HISTORY
OF RUSSIA

Sergei Mikhailovich Soloviev

The
Academic International Press
Edition
of
Sergei M. Soloviev

History of Russia From Earliest Times

G. EDWARD ORCHARD
General Editor

Contributing Editors

HUGH F. GRAHAM

JOHN D. WINDHAUSEN

ALEXANDER V. MULLER

K.A. PAPMEHL

RICHARD HANTULA

WALTER J. GLEASON, JR.

WILLIAM H. HILL

G. EDWARD ORCHARD

LINDSEY A.J. HUGHES

NICKOLAS LUPININ

GEORGE E. MUNRO

DANIEL L. SCHLAFLY, JR.

ANTHONY L.H. RHINELANDER

PATRICK J. O'MEARA

PETER C. STUPPLES

T. ALLAN SMITH

MARTHA L. LAHANA

SERGEI M. SOLOVIEV

History of Russia

Volume 23

Tsar Alexis. A Reign Ends

Edited, Translated and With an
Introduction by

Martha L. Lahana

Academic International Press
1998

The Academic International Press Edition of S.M. Soloviev's
History of Russia From Earliest Times in fifty volumes.

Volume 23. *Tsar Alexis. A Reign Ends.*
Unabridged translation of the text of Chapters IV and V of Volume
12 of S.M. Soloviev's *Istoriia Rossii s drevneishikh vremen* as
found in Volume VI of this work published in Moscow, 1959–
1966, with added annotation by Martha L. Lahana.

ISBN: 0-87569-193-5

Composition by Diana Godwin

Printed in the United States of America

A list of Academic International Press publications is found at
the end of this volume.

ACADEMIC INTERNATIONAL PRESS
Box 1111 • Gulf Breeze FL 32562-1111 • USA

CONTENTS

Discord over Question of Peace with the Turks—Poles Demand Armed Aid from Moscow—Hetman Pats's Advice and Promise—First Polish Resident Swiderski in Moscow—First Russian Resident Tiapkin in Warsaw—Negotiations on Making Tsarevich Fedor King of Poland—Tiapkin's Predicament and Complaints—The Royal Election—Rumors about the New King's Disposition toward Moscow—Więsławski's Embassy to Moscow—Congress of Plenipotentiaries at Andrusovo—More Difficulties for Tiapkin—Tiapkin Begs to Be Recalled—The Resident's Journey to the King at Lvov—Conversations of the Elder Tiapkin with Polish Lords—Conversations of the King with the Russian Resident—Conduct of the Poles at the Enemy's Departure.

Austria and Sweden—Denmark—Reflections on a Baltic Fleet—Holland and England—France and Spain—Italy—Menzies in Rome.

Greece—Georgia—Persia—The Company of Persian Armenians—Construction of Ships for Caspian Sea—More on the Armenian Trading Company.

WEIGHTS AND MEASURES

Linear and Surface Measures

Arshin: 16 vershoks, 28 in (diuims) 72.12 cm
Chetvert (quarter): 1/4 arshin, 1/2 desiatina, 1.35
  acre (sometimes 1.5 desiatinas or ca 4.1 acres)
Desiatina: 2,400 square sazhens, 2.7 acres, 1.025
  hectares
Diuim: 1 inch, 2.54 cm
Fut: 12 diuims, 1 foot, 30.48 cm
Obza (areal): c. 10 chetverts, 13–15 acres

Osmina: 1/4 desiatina, 600 sq. sazhens, .256
  hectare
Sazhen: 3 arshins, 7 feet, 2.133 m
Vershok: 1.75 in, 4.445 cm, 1/16 arshin
Verst: 500 sazhens, 1,166 yards and 2 feet, .663
  miles, 1.0668 km
Voloka (plowland): 19 desiatinas, 20 hectares, 49
  acres

Liquid Measures

Bochka (barrel): 40 vedros, 121 gallons, 492 liters
Chetvert (quarter): 1.4 bochkas, 32.5 gallons
Kufa: 30 stofy

Stof: Kruzhka (cup), 1/10 vedro, c. 1.3 quarts, 1.23
  liters
Vedro (pail): 3.25 gallons, 12.3 liters, 10 stofy

Weights

Berkovets: 361 lbs, 10 puds
Bezmen: c. 1 kg., 2.2 lbs
Chetverik (grain measure dating from 16th century):
  1/8 chetvert, 15.8 lbs
Chetvert (grain measure): 1/4 rad, 3.5 puds, 126.39
  lbs, c. 8 bushels
Funt: 96 zolotniks, .903 lbs, 14.4 ozs, 408.24 kg
Grivenka: 205 grams
Kad: 4 chetverts, 14 puds, 505.56 lbs
Kamen (stone): 32 funt

Korob (basket): 7 puds, 252 lbs
Osmina (eighth): 2 osmina to a chetvert (dry
  measure)
Polbezmen: c. 500 g, 1 lb
Polosmina (sixteenth): 1/2 osmina
Pud: 40 funts, 36.113 lbs (US), 40 lbs (Russian),
  16.38 kg
Rad: 14 puds, 505.58 lb
Zolotnik: 1/96 lbs, 4.26 grams

Money

Altyn: 6 Muscovite dengas, 3 copecks
Chervonets (chervonny): gold coin of first half of
  18th century worth c. 3 rubles
Chetvertak: silver coin equal to 25 copecks or 1/4
  ruble (18–19th centuries)
Copeck: two Muscovite dengas
Denga: 1/2 copeck
Grivna: 20 Muscovite dengas, 100 grivnas equals 1
  ruble, 10 copecks
Grosh: 10 peniaz
Grosh litovsky (Lithuanian grosh): 5 silver copecks
Kopa grosh: 60 groshas, one Muscovite poltina, 1/2
  ruble
Moskovka: 1/2 copeck
Muscovite Denga: 200 equals 1 ruble
Novgorod Denga: 100 equals 1 ruble

Novgorodka: 1 copeck
Peniaz: 10 equals one grosh (Lithuania)
Poltina (poltinnik): 50 copecks, 100 dengas, 1
  ruble
Poltora: 1 1/2 rubles
Polupoltina (-nik): 25 copecks, 50 dengas
Ruble: 100 copecks, 200 dengas
Shiroky grosh (large silver coin): 20 Muscovite
  copecks.

Foreign Denominations
Chervonnyi: c. 3 rubles
Ducat: c. 3 rubles
Efimok: c. 1 ruble, 1 chervonets or chervonnyi
Levok: Dutch silver lion dollar
Thaler (Joachimsthaler): c. 1 ruble, 1 chervonets
  or chervonnyi

Note: Weights and measures often changed values over time and sometimes held more than one
value at the same time. For details consult Sergei G. Pushkarev, *Dictionary of Russian Historical
Terms from the Eleventh Century to 1917* (Yale, 1970).

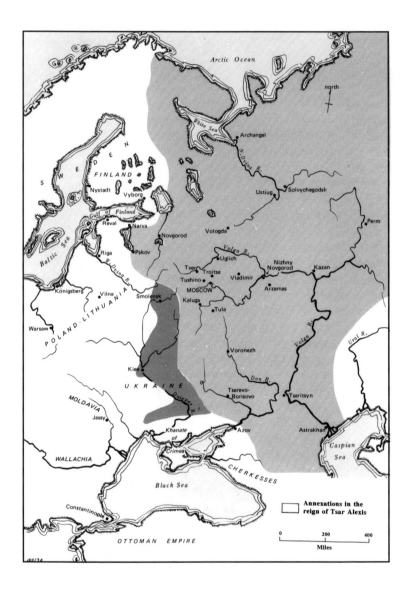

Muscovy at mid-Seventeenth Century

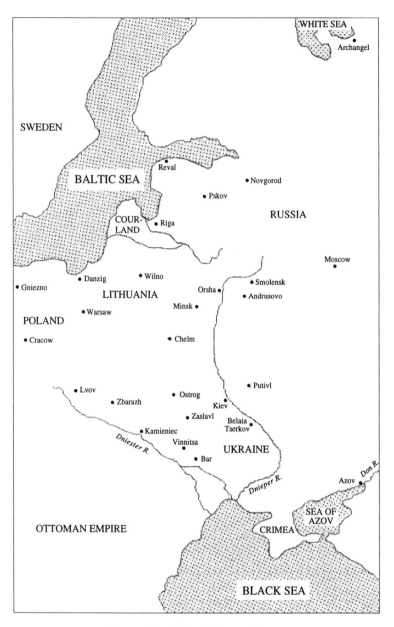

Western Russia and Eastern Europe

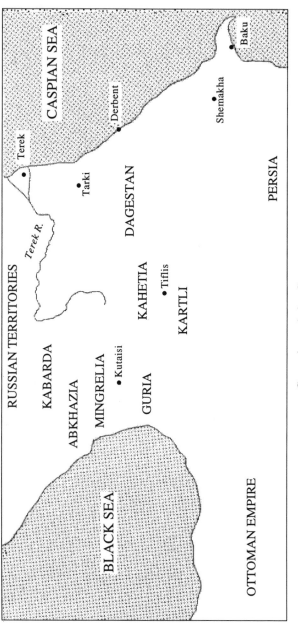

Georgia and the Caucasus

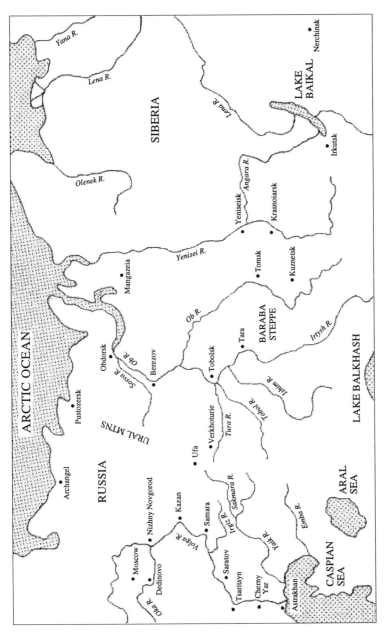

Western Siberia

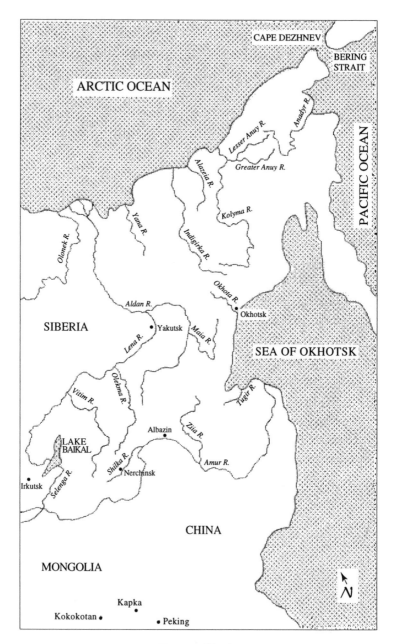

CAPE DEZHNEV

BERING STRAIT

ARCTIC OCEAN

PACIFIC OCEAN

Lesser Anuy R.

Anadyr R.

Alazeia R.

Greater Anuy R.

Yana R.

Kolyma R.

Olonek R.

Indigirka R.

Okhota R.

Aldan R.

Okhotsk

SIBERIA

•Yakutsk

Maia R.

Lena R.

SEA OF OKHOTSK

Vitim R.

Olёkma R.

Tugir R.

Albazin
•

Ziia R.

LAKE
BAIKAL

Shilka R.

Amur R.

Irkutsk
•

Selenga R.

Nerchinsk
•

CHINA

MONGOLIA

Kapka
•

Kokokotan •

• Peking

N

Eastern Siberia

PREFACE

The present work covers Chapters 4 and 5 of Volume XII of Sergei M. Soloviev's *History of Russia from the Earliest Times*, first published in 1862 (*Istoriia Rossii s drevneishikh vremen*, 29 vols., St. Petersburg, 1851-1879). The text was translated from the fifteen-volume edition published in Moscow in 1959-1966, in which the original Volume XII appears as the second half of Book VI.

Most Russian terms have been translated, except for those frequently found in English. Tsar, boyar, and certain other titles and expressions appear in all but the smallest English dictionaries, and so are retained in the present text. Less common words such as *okolnichy* or *murza* are presented in translation, with the original word included in the endnotes the first time the term appears. *Voevoda* is included in many dictionaries under the spelling "voivode" but in Muscovy its meanings were so varied— military commander, military governor, mayor, provincial governor, or viceroy—that it usually has been translated to the most appropriate English counterpart. On rare occasions it has been left in the Russian to retain the tone of the original, as when Soloviev quotes a reference to the voevoda (the lord mayor) of London.

Names of historical figures familiar to most English-language readers are given in their customary anglicized form, such as Peter the Great and Tsar Alexis. Other Russian names have been transliterated. Non-Russian names are given in the form most likely to be familiar to the reader or most likely to facilitate further study, or are transliterated from Soloviev's usage. Place names and geographical locations are presented in English (Moscow rather than Moskva) except for a few instances where the original has been translated directly to preserve the flavor of the text ("the German lands" rather than Germany).

Transliteration follows a modified Library of Congress system, omitting all ligatures and diacritical marks. In addition, the Russian letters commonly transcribed as "ia" and "iu" have been maintained within words and at the end, but altered to "ya" and "yu" at the beginning (for example, Yaroslav rather than Iaroslav, but Buriat rather than Buryat). The terminal forms "-ii" and "-yi" have been replaced with "-y," and "-oi" with "-oy," and the "-iia" ending of many feminine names has been simplified to "-ia." The soft sign normally indicated by an apostrophe has been omitted in most cases and signified by "i" in others (for example, "Soloviev"). Plurals have been anglicized (efimoks rather than efimki).

The goal of this translation project is to render Soloviev's magnificent treatment of Russian history into readable English prose, suitable for the widest possible range of readers. To achieve such a goal, it has been necessary to deviate considerably from a literal treatment. Some of the author's rhetorical devices have been interpreted fairly freely in an effort to preserve the intent and tone of the original while rendering it comprehensible and graceful to the modern reader. Occasionally information has been inserted, either in the text (in which case it appears in square brackets) or as a footnote. An exception to this rule is the addition of such phrases as "the tsar said" or "the envoy continued," which have been added freely to clarify some of the longer quotes. All material in parentheses is Soloviev's own. The original bibliographic notes to this volume have been omitted since they consist almost entirely of archival references and as such are valueless to the general reader.

The two chapters of the original text have been redivided into five, and many of the long sentences and paragraphs have been broken into more manageable lengths. The author's topic headings, which appear at the beginning of each chapter, have been transformed into subheadings and inserted into the text at the appropriate points. In a few instances where Soloviev provided a topical heading for nearly every paragraph, these have been combined or omitted, and where he let one heading (for example, "Siberia") cover dozens of pages and several aspects of the subject, additional subheadings have been added. These are minor changes, adopted for the sake of clarity and comprehensibility. With the exception of the endnotes and a few headings, none of Soloviev's material has been deleted, and as far as is consistent with English syntax, its order of presentation has been retained.

Martha Luby Lahana

INTRODUCTION

Sergei Mikhailovich Soloviev (1820-1879) had a profound influence on Russian historical thought. He attempted to produce a survey of his country's entire history, a survey which not only would explain events but also would illuminate the trends, principles, and characteristics which underlay Russia's past and connected its phases in a process of organic growth. He succeeded, although his project was cut short. The *History of Russia from Earliest Times* proceeds no further than 1774 and even then the last volume was published posthumously in the year of the author's death. Despite its premature conclusion the series provides a unified study of Russian history and development to that point, combining a penetratingly insightful narrative with extensive quotations from primary sources, many of the latter still not available in any other published form.

The present volume contains the concluding chapters of Soloviev's examination of the reign of Tsar Alexis Mikhailovich. Opening late in the year 1672, the book explores Moscow's relations with Western powers between that time and the tsar's death in 1676. It goes on to discuss relations with the lands east of Russia during the third quarter of the seventeenth century, including both settled civilizations like Persia, Greece, and China, and the nomadic expanses of Siberia. The last portion summarizes the personality of the ruler, his family and advisors, and the significance of his reign within the broader sweep of Russian history. The present volume displays an "old-fashioned" emphasis on war, diplomacy, and heads of state, as opposed to today's interest in social or cultural developments in the population at large. To some extent this is unavoidable since Soloviev, for all his brilliance and originality, could build only upon the resources and theories available in his lifetime. Although he sensed many limitations in the historical science of his age and attempted to remedy them, he had neither the materials nor the background in such present-day related studies as anthropology or psychology, for example, to prepare a late-twentieth-century manuscript in the middle of the nineteenth century. This does not at all mean that his work is obsolete or irrelevant today. Even in the present volume the author's broad vision and incomparable use of archival materials allows the flavor of other times and other places, and of individual personalities, to emerge from the factual accounts of diplomatic missions, succession crises, or colonial expansion.

It is also true that the present volume's stress on diplomacy and dynasty is partly an artifact of the division of the original material into manageable segments for publication. Indeed, the chapter that follows the present portion explores the social and spiritual development of the Russian people and the special conditions of the middle and later seventeenth century, covering markets and commerce, urban unrest, relations between social groups and classes, changes in military organization and the church, literature and intellectual life, and so on. This chapter is already available as Volume 24 of the present series, *The Character of Old Russia*, edited and translated by Alexander V. Muller (Academic International Press, 1987). The sometimes awkward divisions are not the fault of later editors but of Soloviev's own organization; even his original volumes often began in the middle of some course of events. The one drawback to his majestic creation is that its parts were never intended to stand alone.

The *History of Russia* is not only enduring, but geographically balanced. Soloviev avoids the narrow perspective of many modern Western readers, who approach Russian history through its comparisons and relationships with Western Europe and thus see only a small part of the world of seventeenth-century Muscovy. The space he devotes to places like the Crimea, Imeretia, Zaporozhia, or the Nogay territories serves as a reminder that these areas often held more immediate importance to pre-imperial Russia than did the more familiar (to us) powers such as Austria, France, England, or Italy. In addition, the section on Russia's expansion into the untamed tribal regions of Siberia illuminates not only the economic and political aspects of this colonization, as well as some of its danger and adventure, but also the author's view that this process was one of the epic contests of human history.

Soloviev's original text contained, by modern standards, very little bibliographic data. The material in the present volume includes only one narrative footnote and no citations at all. Only a few sentences at the end reveal the author's sources. These consisted chiefly of documents from the Moscow Archive of the Ministry of Foreign Affairs, the Archive of the Ministry of Justice, and the State Archives, all of which are now held in the Russian State Archive of Ancient Acts, abbreviated as RGADA (known during the Soviet period as the Central State Archive of Ancient Acts, or TsGADA). Some, but by no mean all, of this material was printed in various document collections published between the late eighteenth and early twentieth centuries. Soloviev reports using one of these collections, *Dopolneniia k Aktam Istoricheskim, sobrannye i izdannye Arkheografi-cheskoiu Kommissieu* (Supplements to the Historical Acts Collected and Edited by the Archeographical Commission), 12 vols. (St. Petersburg, 1846-1872), for information on the construction of the ship *Orel* and for his sections on Siberia and China. He also cites an eighteenth-century monograph on Siberian history, I.E. Fisher's *Sibirskaia istoriia s samogo otkrytiia Sibiri do zavoevaniia sei zemli rossiiskim oruzhiem* (Siberian History from the First Discovery of Siberia until the Conquest of This Land by Russian Arms) (St. Petersburg, 1774), and an article in the journal *Severnyi Arkhiv* (Northern Archive) entitled "Kharaktery velmozh i znatnykh liudei v tsarstvovanie Alekseia Mikhailovicha (Character of the Grandees and Leading Figures of the Reign of Alexis Mikhailovich)," from which he draws much of the last part of the present volume.

Those who read Russian and wish to pursue the topics covered in this volume may refer to the edition of 1959-1966, which not only gives the archival locations of Soloviev's sources, but also bibliographical informa-tion on many of the published Russian- and Polish-language collections and a few recommendations for supplementary reading. Those who do not read Russian will find that English-language sources on the history of late-seventeenth-century Muscovy remain somewhat scattered. The annota-tions in this volume offer suggestions on accessible materials on the specific topics under discussion, and, as with any scholarly topic, the best clues to further reading lie in the bibliographies and reference notes of just such related works.

To summarize, for brief definitions and explanations the two best sources are the *Modern Encyclopedia of Russian and Soviet History* (abbreviated as MERSH), edited by Joseph L. Wieczynski et al. (Aca-demic International Press, 1976-), and the *Great Soviet Encyclopedia,* 31 vols. plus index (New York, 1973-1983). General overviews of Russian history and society include V.O. Kliuchevsky, *A Course in Russian His-tory. The 17th Century,* translated by Natalie Duddington (Chicago, 1968) and, as noted above, Vol. 24 of the present series, *The Character of Old Russia.* S.F. Platonov, *Moscow and the West,* edited and translated by Joseph L. Wieczynski (Academic International Press, 1977) is useful for its treatment of international relations, especially in terms of cultural and intellectual developments. Many other studies offer valuable insights and information, though they may deal primarily with military developments, with a particular ethnic or social group, or with a slightly different time span. Examples include Richard Hellie, *Enserfment and Military Change in Muscovy* (Chicago, 1971); Robert O. Crummey, *Aristocrats and Servitors. The Boyar Elite in Russia, 1613-1689* (Princeton, 1983); or Michael Khodarkovsky, *Where Two Worlds Met. The Russian State and the Kalmyk Nomads, 1600-1771* (Ithaca, 1992).

Biographies are another good source, providing vast information on their subjects' society as well as a more personal or individual perspective. There are two English-language studies on Tsar Alexis, one by Philip Longworth, *Alexis, Tsar of All the Russias* (New York, 1984), and Joseph T. Fuhrmann's less detailed *Tsar Alexis. His Reign and His Russia* (Academic International Press, 1981). Other biographies covering the approximate time period include Lindsey Hughes, *Russia and the West. The Life of a Seventeenth-Century Westernizer, Prince Vasily Vasil'evich Golitsyn (1613-1774)* (Newtonville, Mass., 1984), and her *Sophia, Regent of Russia, 1657-1704* (Yale, 1990).

There does not seem to be a satisfactory English-language history of Georgia or the Caucasus for the later seventeenth century, but Muscovy's relations with Siberia and China enjoy better coverage. James Forsyth, *A History of the Peoples of Siberia* (Cambridge, 1992) is recent and highly readable, but does not discuss all the tribes and regions mentioned in the present volume. M.G. Levin and L.P. Potapov, *The Peoples of Siberia,* translated by Stephen Dunn (Chicago, 1964), is a wider compendium of Siberian peoples from the earliest times to the mid-twentieth century. *Russia's Conquest of Siberia, 1558-1700,* Volume 1 of *To Siberia and Russian America,* translated and edited by Basil Dmytryshyn, E.A.P. Crownhart-Vaughan and Thomas Vaughan, 3 vols. (Portland, Oregon, 1985), is a collection of translated seventeenth-century documents providing lively eye-witness accounts of Russia's movement into Siberia. For Moscow's early dealings with China, V.S. Miasnikov, *The Ch'ing Empire and the Russian State in the 17th Century,* translated by Vic Schneierson (Moscow, 1985), is probably the most useful. John F. Baddeley, *Russia, Mongolia, China. Being some Record of the Relations between Them from the Beginning of the XVIIth Century to the Death of the Tsar Alexei Mikhailovich...,* 2 vols. (London, 1919, reprint ed. New York, 1960-1969) is dated and clumsy, but still valuable for its scope and its translations of original documents.

The accounts of some Western observers exist in English, though most can be found only in the largest libraries. *The Travels of Olearius in*

Seventeenth-Century Russia, translated and edited by Samuel H. Baron (Stanford, 1967), is an excellent and readily available source. *The Present State of Russia, in a Letter to a Friend in London* by Dr. Samuel Collins (London, 1671), offers an interesting view of life and the leading personalities in Moscow in the 1660s as observed by the tsar's personal physician. It is a rare book, but is preserved on microfilm, and authorized photoduplicates exist. *Passages from the Diary of General Patrick Gordon* ([London], 1859, reprinted. *Russia through European Eyes,* N° 3, edited by A.G. Cross, New York, 1968) is massively abridged, but interesting and much easier to find. Finally, since this segment of Soloviev's *History* deals primarily with international relations, studies of the individual powers with which Russia had dealings can provide useful background and insight.

Many authors have dismissed Alexis as a weak and malleable tsar who merely marked time between two more important reigns. His father (Michael Fedorovich) rebuilt the country after its Time of Troubles, and his son (Peter the Great) enacted the vast reforms so often referred to as a "watershed" in the country's history, reforms which affected matters as diverse as justice, men's and women's fashions, the socio-political hierarchy, economics, diplomacy, education, the calendar, and the alphabet. Soloviev did not deny the importance of Michael or Peter, or the qualitative differences between Alexis's Muscovy and the empire that followed it. He simply held a different focus.

Soloviev disapproved of excessive division or periodization in history, seeking instead to find continuing interconnections and processes of development. From his perspective Alexis was an important bridge between the older Muscovite Russia and its imperial successor of the eighteenth century. Even some of the tsar's personal attributes hinted at the changes that would come. The events and character of his reign grew from patterns begun in the past, and in turn laid the foundations upon which the country's future transformation could occur.

Soloviev thus traces how Tsar Alexis's busy and eventful reign prepared the way for the massive changes and reforms of the ruler's heirs, first the short-lived Fedor and then the tireless Peter the Great. In the chapters preceding this volume the author examined the character of the young tsar and that of his advisors, the unrest that plagued the first years of his reign and the state's response to it, Russia's annexation of the Ukraine, and the country's successes (and failures) in the Thirteen Years War against

Poland and Sweden. He explored subsequent developments in the Ukraine, and Russia's relations with that area and with Poland and the southern cossacks. He investigated the financial repercussions of the Thirteen Years War, the deterioration of relations between the tsar and patriarch and the church council that followed, and the rise and fall of the rebel leader Stenka Razin.

Then, just as Russia succeeded in achieving peace with its enemies to the north, and in pacifying its local rebellions and unrest, the Turks and their allies began encroaching on the southern borders of Poland. New fighting broke out along the Don and the Dnieper, and new alliances came under consideration. The retirement of A.L. Ordin-Nashchokin as Moscow's head of international affairs, a man who believed wholeheartedly in maintaining friendly relations with Poland and in acquiring Baltic ports, whether or not these goals were of immediate practicality, opened the way for a more flexible and opportunistic successor, A.S. Matveev, who attempted to use the current situation to acquire more southern territory for Russia and to enhance the tsar's standing in his diplomatic relations with Western nations. As the present volume opens, the Ukraine is split between pro-Muscovite and pro-Turkish supporters. The Turks have captured the city of Kamenets-Podolsky, causing Poland to beg the tsar for military aid lest more of its cities fall to the infidel invaders. The Russian army is poised along the banks of the Dnieper, and diplomats hasten between Moscow and the neighboring capitals.

HISTORY OF RUSSIA

Volume 23

Tsar Alexis
A Reign Ends

I

RELATIONS WITH POLAND AFTER
THE TURKISH INVASION

The Russian army went to war on the Dnieper and the Don to fulfill the agreement concluded with Poland.[1] Still the Polish government demanded more active aid, including union of Russian troops with its own forces for a joint foray against the Turks, but the Ukrainian hetman Samoilovich[2] resolutely opposed this union, and Poland could not force the Muscovite government to act against the wishes of the hetman and the Ukrainian Cossacks.

DISCORD OVER QUESTION OF PEACE WITH THE TURKS

According to the report of the courier Protopopov,[3] the king held a general assembly of senators and Sejm [Diet] deputies in January of 1673. In this council, called the Rada, the Polish senators advised against fighting the sultan that spring.[4] They recommended giving tribute instead, since the season in question already was approaching but the army was not ready for action. They felt that it would be better to gather their forces and take to the field the following year.

The Lithuanian senators[5] disagreed. "If we do not march against the enemy this spring, but give him tribute," they argued, "after taking the tribute, he will fall upon the Muscovite Ukraine according to his age-old infidel plan. This would break the treaty from the king's side. It would be better to use the tribute money to pay the army and take to the field against the enemy. If you Poles really want to become Muslim subjects, say so, but the Lithuanian principality has never lived under the infidel yoke and will not do so now. If we do not see you giving true service and trying to defend your country, the Lithuanian principality will separate from the crown of Poland and will free itself from Muslim captivity by the grace of his majesty the tsar, for it is better to live under his autocratic hand than under the Muslim yoke."

Hetman Mikhail Khanenko[6] bowed in submission to his majesty the tsar. "The Lithuanian hetman Michael Pats,"[7] he said, "told me not to leave his side, for many senators in the kingdom of Poland have revealed themselves as traitors eager to sell their homeland. From this sale the kingdom of Poland will come to an end. Unless we see the Poles making a sincere effort to defend their homeland, we will ask the great sovereign to accept us as subjects." The Lithuanians already had assigned two ambassadors to the tsar, the Vitebsk governor Antoni Chrapowicki and Trotsk governor Marcjan Ogiński.

POLES DEMAND ARMED AID FROM MOSCOW

In Moscow the royal envoy Jeronim Kamar[8] held a secret conversation with the lord-in-waiting Matveev and the crown secretaries.[9] He said that the sultan had attacked Poland unexpectedly, forcing the king into a burdensome treaty, but despite all the burden of the treaty the king and the Polish Commonwealth could not violate it, for they were not protected by a union with their neighboring powers. Thus the king now depended more than ever on his majesty the tsar and begged his advice as to whether he should make peace. If not, he demanded military aid, at least forty thousand troops with good commanders and plenty of artillery, "because we must not wait for the enemy to come to us, but seek him in his own territories." The king, leading his own and the Lithuanian and friendly cossack armies and the general levy,[10] will have to join his units with the Russian and Austrian armies in Wallachia. The Russians are coming there by way of the Ukraine, and the Austrians by way of Hungary. Thus the great sovereign tsar should deign to announce the number of his troops, the number of cannon, and the names of the commanders, that this army can be at the Wallachian border by the first of May.

Matveev answered that all conditions of the last aid treaty were fulfilled religiously. By the tsar's order the Kalmyks and Cherkess were waging war on the khan.[11] Supplies and fortified transport boats had been sent to Zaporozhia,[12] and the conciliar noble Ivan S. Bolshoy-Khitrovo[13] was sent to the Don with many distinguished officers to attack the Turks in concert with the Don and Zaporozhian Cossacks, by sea and land routes. When he learned of the fall of Kamieniec[14] the great sovereign sent out his couriers to all the neighboring Christian sovereigns, calling them to unite against the Turks in aid of the king. Since he had not received their answer and had not concluded treaties with them or otherwise reinforced his position with their oaths of support, his majesty the tsar could not aid the king beyond what already was being given at great loss to the tsar's treasury.

"We marvel," Matveev continued, "that you ask advice about whether to preserve your treaty with the sultan while a treaty exists between tsar and king. Neither of these sovereigns can conclude peace independent of the other with either the sultan or the khan! If your lord was forced into such an agreement then as quickly as possible, before the conclusion of the treaty, he should have informed his majesty the tsar. Yet before your arrival we received no word of this treaty, nor did you bring us its text. We know that this treaty with the sultan resolves, among other things, that the Ukraine belongs to the cossacks according to its ancient boundaries. The interpolation of such treaty articles is not acceptable, because our great sovereign rules the Ukraine on this side of the Dnieper. Now you ask whether you should keep this treaty or not. Is this really the act of a brother and a friend? His majesty the tsar cannot send out his armies until he receives an answer from the other sovereigns. He cannot do so because the king and the Polish Commonwealth have been in serious discord with Mikolaj Prażmowski, the first senator of the Polish crown and archbishop of Gniezno, as well as with Hetman Sobieski and the other senators and nobles, and to this time it has not been quieted."[15]

In the spring of 1673 an undersecretary named Prokofy Bogdanovich Voznitsyn came to Moscow[16] to explain that his majesty the tsar had written to all the neighboring sovereigns inviting them to support Poland. "Report to the tsar in the name of the king," the Lithuanian vice-chancellor Michael Radziwiłł[17] told Voznitsyn, "that his royal majesty, all of Poland, and we, its senators, are good friends to his majesty the tsar. His majesty the tsar must not believe the traitorous hetman Pats,[18] who causes our sovereign to fall out with us. Pats, from envy at seeing the warlike sovereign inconvenienced by this deception, pretends loyalty to his majesty the tsar, promising to become his subject and inciting hostility toward the king and the crown of Poland. Pats not only wants enmity between your sovereign and ours, but also has given his support to the foe of the Polish crown and of all Christendom. This came about because Doroshenko,[19] having learned that Pats had retreated from the king at Bar with several squadrons, told the khan that all the Lithuanian forces had retreated and because of this information the khan even now is advancing toward our borders.

"The khan," continued Radziwiłł, "claims that our sovereign made peace with the sultan, giving up to him the Ukraine and Podolia, and thus opened way into Muscovy. The king responds that the khan, if he wishes, may negotiate with him in the field but that he, the king, trusts in the good will of his majesty the tsar and never will open the way into Muscovy. The testimony of traitors has made your great sovereign wary of joining his

Artamon Sergeevich Matveev

army with ours against the enemy of the holy cross. The tsar's agents send men to our army and our nation to collect news. These spies hear a great many injudicious rumors from unknown sources and carry them to Muscovy. The great sovereign should believe neither Lithuania nor these reports, but by the grace of God and his deathless honor must have mercy on all Christendom, especially on the innocent souls of our people, and come to the aid of his majesty the king, uniting his army with the Polish armies. The whole world calls him to this, for he stands not only as brother but also as father to his majesty the king. In gratitude for such favor we would no longer keep mentioning our cities which are now in the hands of his majesty the tsar."

In his turn Hetman Pats told Voznitsyn "Make known our plea to Privy Boyar Artamon Sergeevich Matveev.[20] Tell him that his majesty the tsar must come most quickly to aid us from the rear against our common enemy, because final destruction marches on our country. I shall march to the king with all my forces, for nothing else now is possible, and later I shall issue also a universal[21] calling for a general levy. Alone, without the aid of your army, we cannot hold such a powerful enemy. If the great sovereign does not order his army to attack the infidel from the rear we must conclude peace with the Turks unconditionally, which would not be without danger for your country either."

When summer came the courier undersecretary Maksim Burtsov, who was in Poland during the summer, brought news. The king was not safe in Warsaw, he said. The senators as before had become agitated and lost their respect for his majesty, rebuking him and calling him unmilitary. Hetman Sobieski,[22] scorning the royal writs and dispatches which summoned him to Warsaw, did not go. Those aligned against the king awaited the hetman's arrival with joy, while the king's supporters would prefer not to see Sobieski anywhere in this world.

The bishop of Wallachia and the Moldavian ambassador came to visit Burtsov. "We were sent to the king with a plea that he hasten his campaign," they said, "for our countries are united and have eight thousand troops at the ready. If only the Polish armies would march, we would join with all Christians and deal with the Turks, but they place obstacles in our way here. The Poles refuse us any answer on the grounds of Hetman Sobieski's absence, for they place all reliance on him. Such delay may be disastrous for us, because we were sent in secret. Should the Turks learn of our mission we and all our servants will be in peril of death, nor will they show mercy to our lords who sent us. It looks to us as if the lord senators not only do not intend to free us from the Muslim yoke, but themselves want to become willing subjects of the Turk. If we shared a border with the countries of his majesty the tsar and were sent to him, we have no doubt that our duties could be discharged quickly and our purposes would not differ from those of the tsar." Saying this, the bishop and ambassador wept.

HETMAN PATS'S ADVICE AND PROMISE

In Wilno Hetman Michael Pats spoke differently to Burtsov than he had to Voznitsyn. "Should his majesty the tsar deign to undertake this campaign against the Turks, he himself should remain in Moscow so as not to raise unnecessary concerns for his safety. Should he decide to carry his war to those Turks near the Kievan borders, he must send a boyar to drive them back. He should not order his army to cross the Dniester lest such impetuosity relieve Poland at the cost of bringing down great troubles upon himself. The tsar's armies should not unite with the king's armies by Belaia Tserkov and other places, lest the crafty Polish forces take it into their heads to do as they did at Chudnovo.[23] The tsar's armies must not attack the Turks without provocation from their side, but first should observe what the king's forces do, whether they stand firm to defend their homeland from the Turks. His majesty the tsar must use great caution in dealing with Doroshenko, who also bows to the king, for we consider him a friend of Sobieski. I am ready to go to war against Turkey, only the Lithuanian army will not unite with the king's. If the inconstancy and negligence of the king's men continues even a little longer, I will present myself and all Lithuania as subjects to his majesty the tsar."

FIRST POLISH RESIDENT SWIDERSKI IN MOSCOW

In August the privy noble Pawel Swiderski arrived in Moscow from Poland with the unprecedented status of diplomatic resident. "I have been sent as resident," announced Swiderski, "to provide more convenient communication with his majesty the king. This is especially important now, for this year the king will go on campaign. Through me his majesty the tsar may know all the movements of the king and his army, and in turn his majesty the king may know of all the tsar's designs. Further, in the Andrusovo treaty Ordin-Nashchokin suggested establishing a residency, for which a courier route was founded,[24] and Tiapkin already has been made resident to King Jan Kazimierz."[25]

Swiderski demanded that he have free access to his majesty the tsar, to all boyars, lords-in-waiting, governors, commanders and councillors, that he be allowed free conversation with the residents and ambassadors from neighboring countries, and that he be given oats, hay, and firewood, though his food should go on a bill to the king and Commonwealth. The Russians agreed that he could have access to the tsar as soon as his authorization papers were sent to him from the king, and also that he might meet with the boyars, lords-in-waiting and council members and also with foreign ambassadors and residents, once his authorization was made known in the Chancellery for Foreign Affairs.

FIRST RUSSIAN RESIDENT TIAPKIN IN WARSAW

The tsar's table attendant Colonel Vasily Mikhailovich Tiapkin was sent to Warsaw as Russia's resident. Among the nobles with him were his son Ivan, whose rank was that of palace attendant, a translator, a clerk, a monk with a portable altar and full church service, and six musketeers. On the road in Smolensk on November 24 Tiapkin learned of the death of the Polish king Michael.[26] He informed Moscow of this news and received instructions to continue on to his original destination. In Orsha he was stopped by order of the lords of the council. Because of the king's death, no foreign ambassadors were allowed to enter Warsaw. Tiapkin, heeding only the order of his own sovereign, set off in his wagons without even an escort.

On January 30, 1674 Tiapkin arrived in Warsaw. After several days he was given a text in Polish discussing the election of Tsarevich Fedor Alekseevich[27] to the Polish throne. "Both glorious peoples differ little in language, customs, and belief," it said. "They live in one land, not separated by the sea or by any impassable borders. For the most part they have common neighbors. They would be able to stand as a solid wall of Christianity against the Muslim forces, were they to conclude a permanent union. This union might be achieved if the tsar's eldest son became king of Poland and grand prince of Lithuania. Because the eldest son is specified his majesty the tsar, being still in the flower of his years, might long rule his lands and raise his younger son to succeed him, while the manners and customs of our fatherland, especially at present, require a sovereign who is already adult.

"There are many advantages to such a union," continued the paper. "An alliance with the house of Austria, with which his majesty the tsar has long been friendly, could be enhanced by marrying the tsarevich to the widowed Polish queen, who is an archduchess of Austria.[28] This three-way union would lead to the good fortune and enrichment of all three countries' subjects through free and safe trade. Other benefits to the union include the fear it would inspire in all neighbors, especially Turkey, an open path to expansion of all three countries without mutual affront and hatred, and rapid mutual aid.

"There would be the possibility of a Polish and Lithuanian inheritance for descendants of the tsarevich, for although in Poland the ruler is elected, still there is no precedence for passing over the king's sons. On the contrary, at times they have been brought out of monasteries and dispensation obtained from the Pope to elevate them to the throne.[29] The freeing of the Greek and Slavonic peoples from Muslim captivity is yet another desirable possibility, should our peoples unite. Should the tsar not agree to this union, the Poles may choose a ruler from house of France. Such a sovereign would be no friend to the German emperor, nor to the tsar, because the French king is united with the Turkish sultan, and also with the king of Sweden."[30]

On February 6, 1674 Tiapkin set out for the archbishop-primate in the six-horse carriage sent for him. With him in the carriage, at his left hand, sat an escort and a translator.[31] The palace attendant Ivan Tiapkin carried the tsar's letters, riding before the carriage on horseback, with two clerks. Twenty mounted Polish nobles preceded the letter-bearer, while behind the carriage walked the Moscow musketeers, armed with halberds,[32] and the ambassadorial staff. The resident was honored with three formal receptions. The first took place at the carriage, by the staircase of the archbishop's palace, the second in the vestibule, and the third at the doors of the audience chamber. At each meeting the guest was told "His grace the most illustrious archbishop awaits you, the envoy of his majesty the tsar, with love."

The archbishop himself, accompanied by five senators, met Tiapkin in the middle of the hall. "To you, the primate and first prince, and to all you lord senators and to the whole Polish Commonwealth," began the envoy, "the great sovereign promises his grace and favor for all time, and has instructed me to call upon you and ask after your health." The archbishop and senators stood without their hats[33] and heard the ambassador with all courtesy. The envoy brought the great sovereign's letter to the archbishop on taffeta. The cleric accepted the letter, asked after the health of the great sovereign, and made a speech, giving names and titles fully as they were set out in the letter. After Tiapkin assured them that his majesty the tsar was in good health, the primate asked "The great sovereign's boyars and all his council, are they in good health?" "The boyars and all the council members prosper and are well," replied the envoy.

There followed questions about the envoy's own health and his journey. When Tiapkin answered that "by the grace of God and the generosity of the great sovereign we traveled the road in all health and safety," the archbishop and senators took their seats, commanding the envoy to sit in the middle of the chamber facing the prelate. After sitting for a while, the envoy stood and announced that he was sent to serve as resident, as Swiderski was sent to Moscow. He presented a document to the Lithuanian chancellor Krzysztof Pats, authorizing him to stay in Warsaw under the same conditions as Swiderski in Moscow. "The great sovereign has granted your resident free admittance to his presence, to his privy councillors, and to the foreign residents. He gives him weekly fodder for his horses and a monthly firewood allowance, the first at five chetverts[34] of locally grown oats and five cartloads of threshed hay per week, and twenty cartloads of firewood per month. Besides this, he has given a cash stipend of seventy rubles per week for three weeks from his arrival."

NEGOTIATIONS ON MAKING TSAREVICH FEDOR KING OF POLAND

At the same time an envoy of the Lithuanian hetman Pats, Augustin Konstantinovich, was in Moscow. He presented Matveev with stipulations for electing Tsarevich Fedor to the throne of Poland. The tsar's son might become king if he (1) accepted Catholicism, (2) married the widow of the deceased King Michael, (3) returned all Polish territories conquered by Russia and (4) established a military alliance against the Turks and provided financial aid to Poland.

The privy boyar Prince Yury Alekseevich Dolgoruky[35] answered the envoy. "The great sovereign," he said, "does not choose for his son to receive the crown of Poland and the grand principality of Lithuania, but consents to become sovereign himself, in his own royal person, in the Orthodox Christian faith of the Eastern church. The condition that he become Catholic creates difficulties for both sides. During his coronation your king promises not to persecute anyone for their religion, and if he breaks this oath, by this act he releases his subjects from their duties of citizenship. Yet if a king of the Greek dispensation becomes a Catholic, there will be dissension between the Eastern Orthodox and Western Catholic churches, about which nothing can be done."

"Between the Greek and Roman faiths," answered the envoy, "there is little difference. It is just that our Polish kingdom has always had a Catholic king, just as in other neighboring countries the rulers also hold the Catholic faith, and can agree about it."

"Clerics will have to gather to make decisions about faith, which will take a great deal of time," said Dolgoruky. "The great sovereign wants to rule the Polish and Lithuanian people in the Greek faith, though he confirms all rights and liberties of the Commonwealth. The fact that earlier Polish kings were Catholic and that other neighboring sovereigns are Catholic is irrelevant. Those of the great sovereign's subjects who follow the Roman, Lutheran, Calvinist, Kalmyk or other religions serve truly, and are not oppressed for their beliefs. The great sovereign rewards them for loyal service."

"In Poland and Lithuania there never has been a sovereign of the Greek faith," repeated the envoy. "They were of various faiths," the Russians answered him. "You yourself said that there is little difference between the Greek and Roman religions, and therefore you can have a sovereign of the Greek faith. It is also possible because in the last treaty with the sultan you pledged to give him tribute. Therefore you made him sovereign over you without requiring him to become Catholic. Regarding your condition that the tsarevich marry the queen, there is nothing to be said, because the tsar himself wishes to be king. On the return of the conquered territories, we will negotiate a treaty when the Polish and Lithuanian ambassadors come to his majesty the tsar. Concerning financial aid, many thousands of millions already have been spent on the sovereign's armies which aid the crown of Poland. His majesty the tsar does this now only from a Christian spirit, but when he becomes ruler of Poland and Lithuania his conscience will compel him to defend his citizens both with his own and with foreign troops. The sovereign will order that all royal revenues gathered by the Commonwealth be used to hire armies, and will supplement these sums from his own treasury."

Konstantinovich was dismissed with following statement. "The great sovereign will not forsake the holy faith of the Greek dispensation, neither for the crown of Poland and the grand principality of Lithuania nor even for the whole world. The tsar wishes to be your sovereign himself, and does not choose to send his son for the honor. Therefore there is no one for the queen to marry, and commissioners of both sides may arrange how she is to live.

"When his majesty the tsar is sovereign of all three countries, no borders will divide them. Your rights and freedoms will not be disturbed, but during the coronation the senators and all the Polish Commonwealth must swear true service and obedience. The great sovereign never will interfere in your customs and estates, nor will he order anyone else to do so.

"When the tsar becomes your sovereign, Poland and Lithuania will be defended from all enemies by their own armed forces, not requiring any tax revenues from royal or Lithuanian sources. The tsar's forces will supplement the Polish and Lithuanian armies against any enemy, in an amount equivalent to the Polish and Lithuanian expenditures, for it does not please the tsar to gather into his treasury any exactions and taxes that the king gathered into his treasury from his own resources, and he will order any such exactions and taxes disbursed to the armed forces. You mentioned the donation of millions to the Polish Commonwealth, whereas the great sovereign rules his own Russian realm and maintains it by his own vigilant intellect, without seeking other countries by purchase. Thus the Polish Commonwealth should give up this practice.

"Should the Commonwealth wish to have a wise and pious sovereign, skilled in military affairs, with a realm populous and burgeoning with all qualities congenial in Europe, let it turn to our own great tsar. Let it send its ambassadors with a petition, and the sovereign will dispatch his own plenipotentiary ambassadors to negotiate for the election."

A copy of the Russian conditions was sent to Tiapkin in Warsaw with instructions that he meet with Hetman Pats and tell him to demonstrate his zeal for the great sovereign by leading his brother lords and the Polish Commonwealth to elect the great sovereign as their ruler, exactly as set forth in these articles.

TIAPKIN'S PREDICAMENT AND COMPLAINTS

These instructions were written to Tiapkin on March 4. In the meantime the resident found himself in a difficult position, for he had not received any documents from Moscow. On February 25 he had addressed a plea to Matveev. "Gracious lord my father and benefactor Artamon Sergeevich! I send my customary most humble and obedient greetings to you, my gracious lord, and ardently and constantly do I pray that the Lord God Most High grant you many years of good health, and that you, my lord, long enjoy a fortunate and orderly dominion, lord, forever.

"By your great fatherly kindness to me, my lord, you will be pleased to know that I have taken up my post in the service of the great sovereign here in Warsaw. I live as well as the Almighty wills, with the help of God and the tsar's grant and you, my lord, who have graciously been as my sovereign father and all the world to me. Yet never can I be free of care because for many posts I have had no word from you, neither have I heard anything of your lordship's health, which I heartily, lovingly desire. Glad would I be at any hour to hear and rejoice in it, as your humble slave and one who desires God's mercy for you, my lord. Because as time and decay consume all things, only the memory of a good deed will not grow old through the ages. Thus once having experienced your paternal benevolence, my lord, I must hold it in my heart, even unto my last breath.

"In particular I tearfully ask mercy of you, my lord, regarding my orphanhood. Why have I been consigned to oblivion? For never, over the course of many posts, has anything come for me. To this date I have received no official response to my reports and briefs from Minsk, from Wilno and from Warsaw. I have not received one single note about anything. Meanwhile, lord, the senators incessantly ask me for news, especially about the armies of our great tsar. I learn little from them, and I myself remain without news. This shames me greatly before the other residents, since letters come to all of them by every post, while already I have lived in Warsaw for four weeks by this date and have heard nothing about anything. I beg, gracious lord, my father and benefactor, do not be angry at my rude letter and request, but order, lord, that I be sent news, however little, by each post. They intensely desire to have ambassadors present at the election, and speak of it to me, that I may write so to you, lord. In particular, lord, the Lithuanian referendary Pawel Brzostowski[36] ordered me to write specially to you, so that you may be pleased to hold him in friendship and to exchange cordial letters. My lord, he strongly desires your friendly favor and frequent correspondence."

After complaining that he received no news from Moscow, Tiapkin went on to criticize the Poles. He said that they did not give him any opportunity to send letters to Moscow, and that it was difficult to get accurate news from them. "The Warsaw postmaster[37] sent two posts without telling me," the resident complained to Matveev. "He told us that he sent the post on Wednesdays, so I prepared letters, and sent them early on Wednesday to the postmaster, yet he had sent the post already on Monday! All this they do for their little gifts, of which many are needed every year in order to give to everyone. I do not believe that their resident gave many gifts to our people, but here everyone performs his services for some trifle or other. He brings a vain little bit of news and looks sharply to see that they reward him. Such corrupt and lying people are hard to find even among pagans. I gave fine gifts to the postmasters, not only of Warsaw, but of Minsk and Wilno as well, just to stop them holding back our letters, and what I buy from others I also have to verify. God knows how I can live among such corrupt and greedy people."

Tiapkin complained that he received little money for firewood and fodder, which was much more expensive in Warsaw than in Moscow, costing four rubles per week. In Moscow Tiapkin's counterpart Swiderski met twice a week with Matveev, on Sundays and Wednesdays, but the Lithuanian chancellor Pats set aside only one meeting a week for Tiapkin, on Sundays after dinner. Tiapkin asked Pats for permission to send the translator and clerks to the chancellery for news, and also asked that the chancellery send him their writs and notices to read over, but Pats answered that they had no chancellery and there were no writs or notices, and that if it were necessary to inform the resident of something, that would be done when he visited the chancellor on Sunday. In the event of extreme necessity the chancellor would send for him specially. "Therefore, lord, Swiderski's men should not be allowed in our Chancellery for Foreign Affairs," wrote Tiapkin to Matveev. "I get not the slightest touch of benevolence from the chancellor, nothing but arrogance. Only the archbishop is a very cordial man, courteous and humble. The Lithuanian hetman Pats and the Lithuanian marshal Połubiński[38] also have shown kindness to me, and have sent me food, vegetables, and drink."

Even with this, Tiapkin's reproaches did not stop. "Here in Warsaw we live one step above poverty. We are given neither charity nor esteem. We receive less than half of what my lord Swiderski gets. Perhaps when there is a king our situation will improve, but now they don't need us, yet dare not refuse to have their resident living in Moscow because they fear that the trans-Dnieper side of the Ukraine will fall under the scepter of the great sovereign. The chancellor told me that Prince Grigory Grigorievich Romodanovsky[39] must observe great caution regarding Hetman Samoilovich, and Doroshenko wrote to him, saying 'We will fight one another so that both our armies remain safe. My protector is the Turkish sultan and your defender is the tsar, and if our armies remain whole we will enjoy great honor and favor from our sovereigns. It would be better if his majesty the tsar ordered all his armies to act together with ours.'"

THE ROYAL ELECTION

When the articles concerning the selection of the king arrived from Moscow, Tiapkin carried them to Hetman Pats. "Since I desire the favor of his majesty the tsar," he responded, "I worked together with the Lithuanian senators, Governor Ogiński of Trotsk, Marshal Połubiński, Referendary Brzostowski, and Castellan Kotowicz of Wilno. We worked diligently to see that Tsarevich Fedor Alekseevich become king, and we won over the Lithuanian chancellor Krzysztof Pats to this goal. Were his majesty the tsar to agree to have his son become Catholic according to our ancient law, we would elect the tsarevich, forsaking all other rulers, yet the articles brought by Konstantinovich from the boyars proclaim that his majesty the tsar himself wishes to be king. We cannot do this, for we cannot leave the queen without a consort. What is more important, the articles state that the great sovereign refuses to become Catholic, even to gain the whole world. We cannot say this to the Polish lords. Nor indeed has there been any opportunity to speak, because the dietines in Lithuania and Poland have all adjourned, and there is nobody to whom to propose this matter. Without a proposal by the gentry at the dietines, the matter cannot be broached."[40]

In April the elections began. Ambassadors of the Pope and the Holy Roman empire pleaded their case for the duke of Lorraine.[41] On April 28 the deputies from Volhynia announced in the Council of Knights[42] that no longer would they pay taxes into the royal treasury because the Muscovite governors had sent notices around all the Volhynian lands and Podolia forbidding them to send their taxes to the royal treasury. Meanwhile the tsar's armies were approaching Polesie, Zaslavl and Ostrog. They suspected a possible agreement between the tsar and sultan to attack the Polish state together. Many Polish nobles became disturbed. "For all these years we could not wrest Kiev from the tsar by treaty," they said, "and now that will become even harder when the tsar takes all the Ukraine." The Polish nobles blamed Lithuania.

Here the ambassador of the Holy Roman empire broke into their speech. "Does the Ukraine," he asked the Poles, "now remain in your hands?" Hearing that the Ukraine and Doroshenko had gone over to the sultan, he said "Why are you angry? You will be better off when a Christian sovereign who is your ally rules this land!" Governor Ogiński of Trotsk also spoke in defense of the tsar. "It is hard to please you Polish lords! In earlier years, when the tsar gave no aid at all against the Tatars, you were angry that he did not fulfill the treaty. Now, when tsar begins to help and frees the whole Ukraine from subjection to the sultan, you are angry and say he has taken it away from you."

RUMORS ABOUT THE NEW KING'S DISPOSITION TOWARD MOSCOW

On May 8 the great Polish hetman Jan Sobieski was proclaimed king. On May 11, at request of the Trotsk governor Ogiński, Tiapkin sent him the interpreter Lavretsky, to whom the governor said the following. "We wrote to his majesty the tsar, and asked that he grant us his son Tsarevich Fedor Alekseevich as king. We are amazed that his majesty the tsar did not care to fulfill our desire. Now by his own efforts, by bribes and secret dealings with the Lithuanian vice-chancellor Radziwiłł and all the Sapiehas,[43] to whom he has distributed many hundreds of thousands of gold pieces, Hetman Jan Sobieski has become king. Hetman Michael Pats and the chancellor and many other Lithuanian nobles and I all protested this. We stood firmly against his election from the eighth to the eleventh of May, but now we must accede to his kingship whether we want to or not, although secretly, of course, we will work to bring upon him whatever form of death for which we find good means.

"We have no love for Sobieski," explained Ogiński, "because he is a great foe of the Muscovite state and because we fear that even now he is making peace with the sultan. He wants to set the Turk at war with the Holy Roman empire, in order to divert him from France, and he himself is sure to go against Muscovy with a detachment of Turkish and Crimean troops. If he reveals any intention to break off peace with his majesty the tsar, we Lithuanians will refuse to permit it. Let it be known to his majesty the tsar that if the royal forces take up arms we will go to Lithuania and work with all our might to convince the Lithuanian gentry of the dietines not to give any taxes for the war with Muscovy, nor as much as one single soldier, from any district or province.

"I believe that all Lithuania will secede completely from Poland and bow in submission to his majesty the tsar," Ogiński continued, "when we perceive that the time is right. At present we unwillingly permit Jan Sobieski to be king because he won over many Polish and Lithuanian nobles with gifts, and intimidated others by bringing the Polish army up to Warsaw, but we no longer want to have him as king."

Ogiński wept and kissed the cross. "Lithuania," he concluded, "does not by any means want to fight with the tsar. Let the great sovereign order his army to go warily in the Ukraine, if it happens to join up with the Polish

Jan III Sobieski

armies. For now the tsar should display favor to the king, not severity. He must keep watch over future statements by the king and the king's men, and if some action is announced the tsar's army needs to stand ready on the Lithuanian border. This will spread great fear in Lithuania, and Lithuania will excuse itself from its commitments and not give aid to the Poles. In all these and in other matters the sovereign should order secret correspondence and dealings with Hetman Michael Pats and with me, not trusting any others."

The Lithuanian vice chancellor Prince Michael Radziwiłł spoke otherwise to Tiapkin. "His majesty the tsar should find the present king desirable for many reasons," he said. "For example, when the Polish hetmans gave up Boyar Vasily Borisovich Sheremetev to the Crimea[44] he strongly opposed this unjust action, and said they were not acting in accordance with Christian custom. Now that he has received the crown he desires even more strongly to live in friendship and love with his majesty the tsar. Write to your sovereign so that he may enjoy true friendship with our king, and not believe any adverse rumors so that now, as in previous years, he may order his military forces to fall upon the Crimea and Azov and thereby draw off the Tatars from assisting the Turkish army. Write also to urge that he send his forces against the Turks and join with the Polish and Lithuanian armies and stand as one with us."

Hearing that the king had postponed his coronation and was preparing to set off on campaign, Tiapkin returned to the Lithuanian chancellor with the request that he, in his post of resident, be allowed to wait upon the king in camp. "It is our ancient custom," answered the chancellor, "that ambassadors and residents do not travel at all out of Warsaw, let alone go on campaign with the king." Reporting this answer to Matveev, Tiapkin wrote "So far they have not distributed my three-day food allowance. Alas, we have eaten up all our supplies, and we have used all of the sovereign's cash and stores. Now only God knows how we are going to live. If his majesty the king does not take us with him, I know not what use my residency will be."

The Muscovite resident had to wait a long time for his food allowance, for there was no money in the king's treasury. The Poles sent to borrow funds in Danzig, carrying the royal diamonds to pawn. Without money they could not set out on campaign. In the forthcoming fearsome war with Turkey there was only one source of help, namely Moscow. From the beginning great concern was felt in Warsaw about how seriously Moscow viewed the election of Sobieski, and now they worried that the congratulatory letter from the tsar to the new king was long in coming. At last the letter arrived, and on July 11 Tiapkin delivered it to the king. The royal vice chancellor Andrzej Olszowski, bishop of Chełm,[45] swore to the resident in secret conversation that the king desired true brotherly friendship with the tsar and a union of forces against the Turks and Tatars.

"If this union occurs," said the bishop, "the combined forces of our peoples are certain to drive the Turks back to the Danube. We already know how to deal with the Turks in combat, only in earlier battles there were no Tatars, who are always serious for our people. As soon as the Christian peoples living along the Danube, the Wallachians, Serbs, Moldavians and Slavs, hear that the tsar's armies have united with the Polish forces, they will join with them immediately, especially the troops of his majesty the tsar. They will devise various means, secret and open, when God grants that his majesty the tsar and the king's men meet in brotherly friendship and unity. Then swiftly they will offer themselves to both great sovereigns because they are fellow Christians, not only with the Muscovite people but also with those of us who are Roman Catholics. Although there is a distinction in faith among us, the disagreements arose from the pride of the Popes and the Greek patriarchs. If the combined army of both peoples liberates the trans-Danubian countries from the Turks, by this very act they will forge the foundation for eternal peace."

A novice in these matters, Tiapkin was very confused by the different opinions about King Jan and his intentions. "What amazing voices there are among the people here! Some are very grateful to his majesty, believing him so wise and so skilled in military affairs as they have not had among them for two hundred years. Others consider him wily and sly, and inclined toward the pagans. Some maintain that he goes on campaign in defense of the Commonwealth, and that he genuinely wishes to unite his armies with those of his majesty the tsar, to stand together against the infidel. Others say that he goes on campaign to achieve closer ties with the Turks and Crimeans, in order to give them all of the Ukraine, and to get back Kamieniec and the other conquered regions, and then together with the Turks and Tatars to march against Muscovy. Only God knows which to believe. The soldiers, who have served for a long time without receiving their salaries, come forth and say clearly 'If our military forces could be informed reliably that his majesty the tsar regards us with favor and promises to pay our arrears immediately, not only Lithuanians but also all the king's forces would come forward and serve the sovereign against any enemy.' The prefect of Sakhnov, who had been in Moscow, undertook to persuade the army to go over to the tsar's side."

On August 12 the king left Warsaw for the army. Except for court officials none of the senators went with him, but all dispersed to their estates. Only the crown treasurer Morsztyn,[46] an enemy of Russian interests, remained in Warsaw. "There is no watch on my house," wrote Tiapkin, "though theft and murder are incessant. I am afraid of being robbed or beaten. I have nothing to do. I have eaten up all my supplies, and I am in debt."

Still greater unpleasantness awaited the Muscovite resident when Warsaw learned of the Turkish successes in the Ukraine, and of the retreat of Romodanovsky and Samoilovich to the east side of the Dnieper.[47] "Great malice is felt toward us by these frivolous devils, who are infected with French envy and given over to corruption and greed," wrote Tiapkin. When he sent a clerk to Morsztyn to ask if there were no news from the Ukraine, the treasurer dictated this answer. "We have no news of any kind, except that your Muscovites ran away ignominiously, without being chased by anyone and without having seen the Turkish forces. They destroyed all their cannon and drowned more than ten thousand men, and it would have been better had they vanished completely!"

"Living in Warsaw," Tiapkin continued to complain, "I buy all kinds of intelligence at a high price. Even those who were friendly have begun to fail me. They want rewards, and say unashamedly that they themselves must pay dearly for intelligence, and risk even their health if they draw suspicion. Avram Sokolski, prefect of Sakhnov, is very benevolent and very devout in his faith. He is eager to serve his majesty the tsar in any way possible. 'I would be happy,' he says, 'to ride all the way to the border to gather information,' and could not be more enthusiastic! Then he asks for a reward. This man of Sakhnov is very able and trustworthy, but about a large payment sent through this same Avram to Metropolitan Antony of Vinnitsa,[48] from whom we hear not a word of friendship, he writes nothing to me.

WIESŁAWSKI'S EMBASSY TO MOSCOW

In this difficult time the Polish state had only one goal in its relations with Russia, namely to prevail upon the tsar to give more active help in the Turkish war, especially by uniting his army with the king's forces. Not content with merely declaring this desire to the Russian resident, in September the Poles sent an envoy to Moscow, Samuil Więsławski, whom the Russians already knew.[49] As was the custom, the arriving diplomat greeted the great sovereign with a magnificent speech. First, in the name of the Polish and Lithuanian peoples, he offered good wishes for the New Year (which the Russians celebrated on September 1).[50] He then went on to express various hopes regarding the tsar, namely that in victories, long life and elegance Alexis might be the equal of Casimir III and Sigismund I,[51] that he might be revered among Christian sovereigns as a peacemaker, and that he might rival Heraclius in good fortune and Justinian in length of days.[52] Finally, Więsławski suggested that Alexis might revive the memory of Charlemagne. As Charlemagne had done in the West, so now in the East might the tsar, together with the Polish king, prop up the failing imperial crown.

The envoy also reiterated the old request for a union of armies. Matveev replied that the Turks had destroyed the tsar's forces at Ladyzhin, when the Polish and Lithuanian forces failed to engage the enemy from the rear.[53] This action, or lack of action, aroused doubts on the part of his majesty the tsar. Had the king moved all his forces against the enemy attacking the Ukraine the Muscovite forces then in the Ukraine certainly would have united with the Polish troops, but the king did not choose to do so, as a result of which the Turks ravaged the Ukraine. This devastation made it impossible for the tsar's forces to advance across the Dnieper, although they always stood ready.

"Now that the Turkish army has attacked Poland," Matveev continued, "the king desires a union of forces, but when the enemy was in the Ukraine the Poles did not fight him. The tsar's forces, although exhausted, nonetheless stand ready in the Ukraine, but the Polish forces are not there. How then can there be a union of forces? When the king sent you here he surely knew that the Turks were marching to the Ukraine, but he did not set out after them." "The king was reassured by the khan," said Więsławski, "who sent word to him not to move the Polish forces." "Before this we only suspected it, but now it comes out straight that the king obeys the khan," retorted Matveev. "Clearly, the enemy forces attacked the Ukraine with the king's approval!"

Więsławski. If by now the enemy has left the Ukraine, let the tsar's forces at least cross to the other side of the Dnieper.

Matveev. Until spring our forces will remain on this side. In the spring, whatever the enemy's purpose may be, both great sovereigns will discuss their plans with each other. As regards a general peace with the Turks, his majesty the tsar is agreed on peace, so long as it is advantageous to both great sovereigns.

In the document sent with Więsławski to the king the tsar wrote that a union of armies was not possible during autumn and the coming winter. "Your royal highness desires a union of armies at this time because of the great Muslim force descending upon your country, but it is difficult to imagine that you would call for this unification of forces had not the Muslims turned towards your country. Nonetheless we have not ordered our own forces to disperse to their homes, despite their exhaustion. Rather we have ordered them to repel the enemy, and we have sent them many reinforcements. We are ready to aid you, should your royal highness deign to join with the ranks of the Polish Commonwealth and the grand principality of Lithuania to form a free Sejm, and together determine how to rebuff the enemy in a united way. We will aid you if this joint resolution is strong and constant, and not such as is now made from the side of your royal highness, that only those who feel like it need go against the enemy."

CONGRESS OF PLENIPOTENTIARIES AT ANDRUSOVO

Two Odoevsky princes, Boyar Nikolay Ivanovich and Table Attendant Yury Mikhailovich,[54] were given full diplomatic authority and sent to the new Andrusovo sessions with their party. Their orders were to refuse the commissioners regarding unification of military forces and to refrain from entering into any treaties. The Polish commissioners Marcjan Ogiński, governor of Trotsk, and Antoni Chrapowicki, governor of Vitebsk,[55] together with their party, threatened that if there were no union of forces the Poles had no alternative save to conclude peace with the Turks. They could not agree to establish eternal peace, inasmuch as the commissioners refused to cede forever to Moscow the cities granted by the terms of the earlier armistice. Without a treaty on unification of forces they did not want to speak of extending the duration of the armistice. "If," said the commissioners, "unification of forces does not occur and Kiev is not given up,[56] we will seek it by force. We now have a warlike sovereign who will seek not only Kiev but also other cities, and who can defend himself from the enemy even without the tsar's help!"

This incident inspired Tsar Alexis to write to Sobieski. "The high ambassadors have gathered to foster brotherly love between their sovereigns, not to threaten. It is unseemly to wave the sword at one who himself, by the aid of God, holds a sword in his hand. This action is the evident result of the past war. Your commissioners have no business talking about Kiev, which has been withheld because of the many dishonors you have heaped upon us, and our uncountable disappointments in the way you have written our name and title even in printed books. In documents sent from your chancellery my name was written Michael Alekseevich! Kiev also has been withheld because of the numberless losses we have incurred in aiding your royal highness against the sultan and the Crimean khan. You gave up the Ukraine, in which Kiev is located, to the sultan. How could Kiev be given back to you after that?"

The Andrusovo negotiations stretched from mid-September to the end of December and resolved nothing. In the meantime Sobieski's letters did not cease to beg the tsar for immediate aid, informing him of Polish successes and indicating that now would be the best time to attack the enemy in concert and liberate the countries along the Danube.

MORE DIFFICULTIES FOR TIAPKIN

On December 8 the clerk Timofeev arrived in Warsaw with a letter from the tsar. He was under strict orders to give the letter to the king in the presence of the resident Tiapkin. Tiapkin went to Chancellor Pats, informed him of the tsar's command, and demanded that he and Timofeev be allowed to set out for the royal camp immediately. "The safe-conduct mentions only the clerk," Pats responded. "Your name is not there. The clerk may have his pass without delay, but you cannot go with him. By Polish custom all residents are obliged to live in the capital." "The tsar sent this special order for me to travel with the clerk," objected Tiapkin.

"His majesty the tsar is free to send his command about whatever he pleases," answered Pats, "but I am surprised that nothing is mentioned in the safe-conduct about you! I cannot let you go because not long ago the king sent instructions. If his majesty the tsar leaves Moscow with his armies for Putivl, as he has announced to the king, and if the Polish resident accompanies that campaign, Tiapkin too may join our royal retinue. If his majesty the tsar and the Polish resident remain in Moscow, Tiapkin must remain in Warsaw."

They decided that the chancellor would write to the king and Timofeev would await the answer in Warsaw. During this interval he succeeded in falling out with the resident. One of his traveling companions, a bailiff from the Chancellery for Foreign Affairs named Repiev, started visiting taverns with two cavalrymen from Smolensk and getting drunk. Then in the night they attacked Polish citizens with sabers and knives, tore off their clothing, and took their money. The watch caught the ruffians red-handed, with drawn sabers and stolen goods, and took them directly to Tiapkin because they claimed to be members of the Russian resident's household.

The next day the Lithuanian chancellor and the governor of Warsaw sent reprimands to Tiapkin, demanding that the guilty be punished. Tiapkin sent them to Timofeev, to have him deal with them, but the clerk took the bailiff's side, and one of the cavalrymen cursed Tiapkin, calling him perfidious. Tiapkin sent a complaint about him to the sovereign.

On February 15, 1675 Timofeev set out to the king by himself. Tiapkin was not allowed to go, and the Poles alarmed him with talk of the king making peace with the Turks, who then would advance upon Muscovy. A confidant of the king named Wieniawski swore solemnly that his majesty was traveling to Lvov not to attend the Sejm and to hold his coronation, but rather to conclude peace with the Turks, the Tatars and Doroshenko. This was because the Muslims promised to return all his conquered territories if the king let the Turkish and Tatar armies pass across his domains into Muscovy. Muslims of Kazan, Astrakhan, Siberia, and even those living in Moscow itself tearfully begged the sultan, as their God and tsar, to deliver them from Christian slavery, and promised that as soon as they saw the Turkish and Tatar forces approach they would rise against Muscovy immediately and unanimously. "If his majesty the tsar," concluded Wieniawski with the customary refrain, "gives aid to the king's armies when spring comes, we will make no treaties with the Turks."

TIAPKIN BEGS TO BE RECALLED

Timofeev was not allowed to depart before he promised to give the royal treasurer thirty rubles' worth of sables. Tiapkin wrote to Matveev on the subject. "Such is our life here," he complained, "in the very resolutions between governments it is difficult to manage things without resorting to gifts and bribery!"

As in the past Tiapkin complained that it was difficult for him to obtain accurate news because "they scatter many complex schemes about, each according to his whim, because of their usual giddy and fickle conceits. They constantly lament and reproach that no aid is forthcoming from his majesty the tsar, though they do not see that they have quarrelled among themselves and drifted apart. The Lithuanian army is camped in the grain fields some five hundred versts from Braslavl. I think that it will not be in time to aid the king tomorrow."[57]

Actually Sobieski's old enemy the Lithuanian hetman Michael Pats withdrew his forces from the royal armies. The hetman's elder brother, the Lithuanian frontier commander Bonifacy Pats, explained this defection to Tiapkin by saying that the king intended to make peace with the Turks and to attack either Moscow or the emperor with them, but that Pats and all Lithuania would not permit this. Pats further complained that the king ruled despotically, telling his conciliar nobles merely "Your job is to stand before me, to hear me and to carry out my orders."

"The Polish senators," continued Pats, "have been accustomed to a sovereign who asked their advice about everything, heeded them, felt that he needed them, and wooed them with petitions, but this one does not do so. The election of the tsarevich might be accomplished easily now, before Sobieski is crowned."

Tiapkin did not cease to alarm the tsar with rumors of a great danger facing Muscovy. The French king was using all means at his disposal to make peace between Poland and Turkey and to move them against Moscow in the spring, and Sweden already was allied with France. "Therefore it is imperative," wrote the resident, "to keep a sharp ear along the Swedish border and other frontiers, as we do in the Ukraine, and to maintain a state of military preparedness, lest we become a victim of that French concept. Let us weave bast shoes, not just sew boots, in which they could extend their foot into the Muscovite state, and vanish like smoke."[58]

The resident also reported that the Lithuanian chancellor assured him on oath of the falsity of all these rumors. The chancellor repeated the same old line, that the Polish forces could not move because the Muscovite armies did not join with them. They were waging war separately, on different sides, he said, and this disunity made it possible for the enemy to gain the upper hand with ease, fighting the defending armies one at a time. "The Turks could drive the Poles from the field without the Russian forces knowing of it. Then they could attack the Muscovite forces while the Poles remained in ignorance. It is impossible for one army to be more than ten miles from the other. Should Russia send no aid, the Polish Commonwealth has no choice but to permit the king to make peace with the Turks under any conditions he pleases, except a union against Muscovy."

In his reports to Matveev about the Poles' reproaches Tiapkin did not cease to complain about his own position in Warsaw and to ask for recall. "Be merciful to me, O lord my gracious father! If it remains impossible for you to take me from here or to replace me, order that I be sent a cash allowance instead of sables, and for the gifts I must distribute send cash also.[59] I could have bought the sables necessary for distribution here no more dearly than in Muscovy, and Vasily Timofeev brought me the very worst ones that were rotting, and kept the better ones for himself. At least order the least little village signed over to the great sovereign to supply me with the sovereign's salary, so that I might not wander here borrowing from people, and might not be in disgrace among the foreigners.

"In particular take pity, lord," begged Tiapkin, "and for God's sake order me to another country, wherever you wish me sent, I am ready to go anywhere. Again and again, gracious lord my father, have mercy! Truly, lord, the residents of all foreign sovereigns here are rich and important men. They style themselves councillors of their kings and are sent full salaries. I also have a family. My little son and I form the duo at the core. There are also two clerks, a priest and six musketeers, four servants without whom it is difficult to manage, and six horses. For all these mentioned, for all foodstuffs and for firewood, besides repairs and new clothing and the soldiers' supplies, it comes out daily to three rubles a head. The colonels in Moscow who are paid in kind receive a great allowance of foodstuffs every month, not only for themselves but also for their horses, but although I am in a foreign land, especially among such lying and evil people, I can hope for nothing beyond the sovereign's mercy and your fatherly charity. Soon I will have to release all my dependents, dispose of my horses, and remain in the smallest possible household, if I do not receive your paternal charity."

In April the resident reported a groundswell of feeling against Sobieski, a broadly based party which opposed his coronation. The main provinces to turn against him were Cracow, Greater Poland, Mazuria, Lvov and all the Rus regions, Lithuania and Samogitia.[60] In all these districts they held great love for Queen Eleanor, and wanted Tsarevich Fedor to marry her and be their sovereign. If this could not be, they were agreed to have the Swedish king for their sovereign, again with the condition of marriage to Eleanor. The emperor was making great efforts to this end for three reasons. First, he found it desirable to have family ties with the Swedish king. Second, he would like to see a near relative on the neighboring throne. Third, and most important, he wanted to detach Sweden from its alliance with France. It was said that this situation was driving King Jan into despair, and this great sorrow was weakening his health.[61]

"There is no constancy among them, however," added Tiapkin, "because as free men they have willful and unlocked mouths. They say whatever they want, one this way, another otherwise, and none of them can be believed. One thing is sure, that when Sobieski appears in Poland the voices of his opponents will heat up with wine at the banquets, and instead of words of rejection they will shout 'Vivat! Vivat!' Others will be appeased with money and honors. There is little constancy in the people here. It cannot be discovered which of them is straight or crooked. They are all clever, all wise. They are all in a whirl with malicious impulses, not only in their minds but in their very souls. They would rather gratify their insatiable greed than increase the general good and truth."

Yet in spite of his opinions of the Poles Tiapkin clearly agreed that the Polish government's desire must be satisfied. Vigorous aid must be given and the tsar's armies united with those of the king. This was, in the resident's opinion, the best means to break up the Franco-Swedish faction, which lay like a gaping chasm before Muscovy. The Polish resident Swiderski reported to the king from Moscow that the tsar's armies stood ready on all the western borders, starting at Great Novgorod, although he did not know which way they would move. "Yet I," wrote Tiapkin to Matveev, "remain forgotten and mute, because rarely does correspondence from the tsar's court arrive for me. When it does arrive it contains no military or other news which is needed here. Because of this I suffer great reproaches from the chancellor and others. Whatever they ask about, I don't know. If I continue to be left so forsaken and uninformed, I trust your greater wisdom to know what good can come of a life so devoid of purpose as mine is here."

Tiapkin continued to grumble about his extremely straitened circumstances. At beginning of June he wrote to Matveev that he was forced to pawn his ceremonial caftan.[62] To be free of Warsaw the resident resorted to guile, writing that a trusted person had told him of a large treasure (several millions) hidden by the Shuisky princes in Smolensk. If he were recalled to Moscow, Tiapkin promised he could give a reliable report about the treasure, but he could not safely write about it. Finally, despairing of a full recall from Poland, Tiapkin asked to be given a regiment and sent to aid the king. At least there in the army he could see everything for himself and would not have to purchase information as he did in Warsaw.

THE RESIDENT'S JOURNEY TO THE KING AT LVOV

At last Moscow sent permission for the resident to promise the Poles immediate aid, in consequence of which Tiapkin was summoned to the king in Lvov. In July he set off at a gallop, but not to joy. The king and the nobles were anxious for rumors about movement of the tsar's armies to abate. There was no respite from reprimands for the unfortunate resident. Yet another unpleasantness arose. The priest who attended Tiapkin in Warsaw had been sent back to Moscow, where slandered the resident to Matveev. "I honestly urged him to go to Moscow," wrote Tiapkin, "because no longer could I bear the shame he drew upon me from Catholic clerics and others. He was known in Warsaw in all the taverns, as a rebel, a brawler, a hater of all good men, a drunkard, a sorcerer, a complete heathen! A quart of vodka was nothing to him, no matter what the hour, and he went through beer at the rate of a barrel a day. Have mercy, do not believe his hostile speech. Take pity, and order me brought home, even just for a while, and hold him until that time."

On August 7 the resident was summoned to the royal presence to receive Sobieski's documents to the tsar. Before handing over the papers the king ordered the Lithuanian vice chancellor to tell Tiapkin "In this letter his royal highness includes new requests for aid, which has long been promised, but has not been given. His royal highness is amazed and insulted by this, and commands that you, as resident, write these my words to the privy boyar Matveev."

Tiapkin's son, who then and there was presented to Sobieski, carried the royal correspondence to Moscow. Before leaving, young Tiapkin thanked the king for "his royal favor, for bread and salt, and for his education, which he would put to use in his own country." This speech was made in Latin, "considerably mixed with Polish, as customarily was used in local schools." The father boasted that his little son "made his oration so clearly and graphically that he did not trip over a single word." The king thanked the orator with a gift of one hundred gold ducats and fifteen arshins of red velvet.

CONVERSATIONS OF THE ELDER TIAPKIN WITH POLISH LORDS

On August 12 a letter arrived from the tsar announcing that Prince Romodanovsky and Hetman Samoilovich had received their orders to move toward the Dnieper, and that all the Polish and Lithuanian armies should march there to join them. "This is impossible at present," said the nobles. "It would mean leaving Polish territory, Lvov and other cities, exposed to the enemy. Our foe is fighting only twelve miles from Lvov, near Zlochev and Zbarazh. Let the tsar's forces cross the Dnieper and unite with those units of the Polish forces which await them there. Then together let them attack Doroshenko, because he has very few cossacks and Tatars with him, and after that the very greatest forces of his majesty the tsar should also take up their arms. Last year you Russians stipulated that in winter it was difficult to wage war across the Dnieper, and thus the tsar's armies would be there in the spring. Now not only spring but also summer have come and gone. When are we to expect your armies? In the fall and winter things are difficult because of severe cold and bad weather, in spring there is no food, and in summer it's too hot!"

In August Romodanovsky and Samoilovich wrote to the king's hetman saying that the tsar's forces had reached the Dnieper and that several detachments had crossed the river and joined their Polish counterparts. The king was extremely happy and sent one of his nobles to Tiapkin with the news. In the meantime the enemy destroyed a city not far from Lvov, threatening the royal baggage train. The king left the train, taking with him the Russian resident, who wrote to Matveev that the Polish armies were very well ordered and keen to fight, save for great disagreement among the officers. Knowledgeable and honorable men told Tiapkin straight out "The king and the hetmans have gone into the field, and although each of them would be happy to fall upon some enemy, the next one would act as though he had not heard of it. May God himself take mercy on Christian people and give us aid and unity."

"Why are your Poles and Lithuanians angry," replied Tiapkin, "that our armies have not united with you until now, when you cannot agree among yourselves? The armies of a foreign sovereign, seeing yours ranged in such scheming factions against one another, and hearing how you denigrate your monarch, could hardly believe you and unite with you."

To this there was a single answer. "Your sermon has been heard, lord resident!" The Lithuanian hetman Pats took it into his head to ridicule Tiapkin, and told him in a plenary session "See, lord table attendant, how we and the king constantly return to the field with a small handful of men and repulse the foe. Yet your Muscovite regiments, which are said to number 1,150 men and more, merely watch from the Kievan hills to see what befalls us. If even one Tatar comes running up to Kiev they all hide in the ramparts and dare not show themselves, but afterwards in committee they will vindicate themselves, bragging that they marched in aid to the Poles."

The resident adroitly laughed this off. "Lord hetman," he said to Pats, "do not wonder that the armies of his majesty the tsar have not hastened to aid you. Perhaps their slowness is not without reason. The boyars and military commanders have heard about the extraordinarily rapid assembly of the Polish and Lithuanian armies. Not very long ago your excellency the hetman rode to the aid of his royal highness not from the Kievan hills but from the Wilno valleys. Your honor very quickly defended your fatherland and rushed to its aid, but not until the Turks had taken twenty-four cities!"

Pats lost his temper. "No russky[63] has ever spoken to me so sharply!" the hetman repeated over and over. He demanded that Tiapkin immediately repay his debt of a thousand Polish gold pieces, but the resident persuaded him, through the intermediacy of the Jesuits, to wait another month.

CONVERSATIONS OF THE KING WITH THE RUSSIAN RESIDENT

Tiapkin could not sufficiently praise his treatment by the king. "He has instructed me always to be in his quarters, whenever there is need. He converses with me very graciously, and when the name of the great sovereign is mentioned he always removes his hat and speaks of the tsar affectionately and with all courtesy."

The resident, however, soon left the king and returned to Lvov. Here he made friends with Józef Szumlanski, bishop of Lvov,[64] and entered into correspondence with Anthony Winnicki, bishop of Peremyshl.[65] Anthony sent Tiapkin his own secretary, who privately asked advice about how the great sovereign might grant the metropolitan see of Kiev to the bishop because the previous incumbent Joseph Neliubovich Tukalsky[66] had died and he, Anthony, held the privilege of the metropolitanate from two Polish kings. "As the lord bishop truly serves his majesty the tsar and remembers his sovereign favor," answered Tiapkin, "so he may receive reward according to his merit."

In a letter to Anthony the resident explained in more detail, and conveyed his surprise that the bishop only now thought of the benevolence of the great sovereign. It was not even known whether he had offered a single prayer or one bloodless sacrifice for the tsar, and only now did he speak of his desire to serve.

CONDUCT OF THE POLES AT THE ENEMY'S DEPARTURE

The royal campaign came to nothing. The enemy tranquilly left the royal borders, burdened with plunder. "The Poles," wrote Tiapkin, "saw off the Turks as honored guests, giving them numberless gifts taken from Orthodox souls. They escorted them beyond the Dniester, almost to the Danube. When they saw that the Turks and Tatars were leaving Wallachia, they displayed great valor against the holy churches and monasteries, and began to raze them to their foundations and burn them. They plundered the church utensils like brigands, and beat to death several bishops and many abbots and priests. They billeted men and horses in the churches and, what is worse, passed the night there with captive women. Now they drive Wallachian slaves around their estates, in herds like dumb animals.

"The Orthodox Christians in Lvov sigh bitterly and weep over this, fearing that the seduction of Latin[67] ways at last may gain the upper hand over them also. I hear from pious clergymen and laity that the higher clerics here only wear the outward mantle of the holy Eastern faith. Inwardly they threaten the holy church, like wolves, and accommodate the Roman church more than they defend the church of God."

II

RELATIONS OF TSAR ALEXIS WITH WESTERN EUROPE

AUSTRIA AND SWEDEN

In his reports Tiapkin could not sufficiently praise his friendly relationship with the Austrian resident Zierowski. "He wants to hold himself as an equal with me, and to agree amicably with me in all things. Only I cannot be compared with him, because he is very rich and renowned. He travels in a gilded six-horse carriage, while I have two nags, barely alive, and nothing to feed them."

We have seen how the Austrian ambassadors played the role of mediators in concluding peace between Russia and Poland, and in the question of electing Tsar Alexis as successor to Jan Kazimierz.[1] Afterwards the unfavorable turn of affairs, as well as a strong desire to end the war that was exhausting his country so completely, forced the tsar to turn once more to the mediation of Emperor Leopold.[2] This stratagem was like the efforts of a drowning man to save himself by grasping a straw, and arose from a very inadequate knowledge of contemporary European courts and their relationships. The Polish government, more experienced, declined the Austrian mediation. The Viennese court attributed this to the intrigues of the French-born Polish queen,[3] who wanted to see her nephew the French prince on the Polish throne. They further explained that Jan

Kazimierz's alliance with the Crimean khan, and through the khan with the Turkish sultan, placed Poland in inimical relations with Austria. This made things no easier for Moscow, which did not cease to urge cooperation to end this costly war. As if in mockery, in late 1661 the Austrian ambassador Augustin von Mayerberg announced that the Turkish army had invaded the imperial domains, and asked that the great sovereign deign to proclaim his thoughts about how to effect military support against the Muslim foe of all Christians. The conciliar secretary Almaz Ivanov[4] responded "You know that the Polish king, the enemy of our country, is united with the Muslims, so it follows that his imperial highness must endeavor to draw the Polish king from his Muslim alliance and to arrive again at his previous state of brotherly friendship and love with his majesty the tsar. When both these sovereigns are at peace, it will be safe to think of acting against the common Christian adversary.

"His imperial highness may reconcile our great sovereign with the Polish king both by worldly and by sacred means," Ivanov continued, "the worldly means of war, and the sacred means of his own sworn word. He may do this because they share a common papal faith. For many years the Pope has endeavored to bring all Christian sovereigns into concord, so that they might not be friends and allies with the Muslims. You know that at present the Polish king is the foe of his majesty the tsar, and all our armies stand ready against the Poles. Therefore, since we have not made peace with the Polish king, we require deliberation before we begin a war with another great enemy."

The Andrusovo treaty and the subsequent attack on Poland by the Turks changed matters. In 1672 the Russian envoy Major Paul Menzies[5] rode to Vienna with word of the Turkish capture of Kamieniec and the arming of Russia. He also brought a question. Would the emperor aid Poland, and if so, how? The emperor answered that he was moving a large and well-trained army to the Polish border. The election of Sobieski and the disquieting news coming from Poland about the new king's intentions forced Tsar Alexis to send a new embassy to Vienna in 1674. The envoys, Table Attendant Peter Ivanovich Potemkin and Secretary Yakov Cherntsov,[6] warned the Austrian emperor's advisors of danger.

"In the kingdom of Poland," they said, "Jan Sobieski, a former hetman, was elected king, though in the Lithuanian principality the senators and the whole Commonwealth opposed this election and yielded only to great gifts and to fear, because Sobieski brought soldiers with him. He besieged

Cracow and Warsaw with his infantry, and became king not so much by election as by force of arms. Some have said secretly that Sobieski is a great enemy of both the tsar and his imperial highness, and soon may be reconciled with the Turkish sultan. The French ambassador already has set out to the sultan's court from Warsaw to establish this peace. Once peace is achieved the sultan will attack the Holy Roman empire so that the emperor will not be free to fight the French king, while the Polish king will join with part of the Turkish and Crimean forces to march against Muscovy. Through its present king the Polish state will experience its ultimate eradication, because he has few supporters and makes peace with the Turks because his personal possessions are all on the Turkish border."

"When your envoy Menzies was here," the advisors answered, "the emperor truly intended to send an army to the Silesian border to aid Poland, but the French king attacked the Dutch, and his imperial highness, at the request of the Dutch, sent many of his troops to aid them against the French. If our troops conquer the French king, the emperor will go to Poland's aid. His imperial highness believes that the hostile intentions of the new Polish king are revealed by his deeds rather than his words, but many senators do not want even to hear that the sultan might go to war against the emperor. If the senators and all the people in Poland hear that our sovereign feels strong brotherly friendship and love for yours, they will not dare to attack either us or you, for they will be wary of finding themselves caught between two such great sovereigns."

The war with Turkey revived Russia's diplomatic relations with other European states also. Until 1673 there were continual squabbles with its nearest neighbor Sweden regarding non-observance of treaty terms, particularly those concerning trade. In 1670 a foreign colonel in Russian service, Nicholas von Staden, visited Riga, where the Swedish generals Wrangel and Totte commissioned him to propose a defensive union to the tsar's privy councillors.[7] Alexis responded that he was ready to help with money and supplies if Sweden were invaded, but that he would neither send his soldiers nor use any of the king's because when soldiers were on campaign many fights broke out among them. The generals told Staden that [the cossack rebel] Stenka Razin[8] was sending out notices under the signature and seal of the former patriarch Nikon[9] urging the peasants of Karelia and Izhora[10] to revolt. The tsar sent Staden back to Sweden, charging him to send to Moscow both the documents and those who carried them.

Staden also was instructed to tell Wrangel and his comrades "The king wants an alliance with his majesty the tsar, but his subjects print lies in broadsheets and thereby cause quarrels between our two states. For example, on November 19 a pamphlet published in Riga related that the former Muscovite patriarch had gathered a large number of soldiers to go to war against the tsar, because the tsar dishonored him, dismissing him from his patriarchal rank without any cause although he was a wise patriarch and a learned man, and in all ways better than the tsar himself. His only fault lay in permitting Lutherans, Calvinists and Catholics to attend Russian churches. The tsar seeks an opportunity to make peace with Stenka Razin, who himself has no objection to peace on the following terms: that the sovereign (1) make him tsar of Kazan and Astrakhan, (2) give him twenty barrels of gold for his army, (3) deliver to him eight privy councillors whom, for their sins, Stenka plans to execute, and (4) restore Nikon to the office of patriarch." The sovereign ordered Staden to demand that those who printed such news be punished severely.

In late 1673 the Swedish ambassador Count Gustav Oxenstierna[11] arrived in Moscow with his suite, but a great difficulty interrupted the preparations for their reception. The Russians required that the ambassadors uncover their heads while in the palace, just as the Russian ambassadors in Stockholm must go hatless before the king. Oxenstierna could not agree to this new requirement without royal approval, and had to send a special courier to Stockholm. Permission arrived, but the exchanges took a great deal of time, and the real negotiations commenced no earlier than April of 1674. These negotiations were conducted by the boyar princes Yury Alekseevich and Mikhail Yurievich Dolgoruky,[12] and the lord-in-waiting Artamon Sergeevich Matveev.

Oxenstierna began. "Our sovereign Karl XI[13] has reached full maturity and wishes a firm alliance with his majesty the tsar. Seeing this alliance, foreign sovereigns will fear us. Such union is necessary also because the Turkish sultan, the enemy of all Christians, has gone to war against the kingdom of Poland, captured many cities, and seized the best and most secure fortress of Kamieniec in Podolia, and the borders of his majesty the tsar are no great distance from these lands. When the sultan hears that an alliance has been concluded between our two sovereigns he will become wary, and will put aside his intentions, for the king will always help against this foe."

Oxenstierna ended with the unvarying complaint that conditions of the Kardis treaty were not fulfilled, since not all prisoners had been released.[14] An argument began over what to discuss first, the union or the unfulfilled treaty terms. The boyars insisted that they begin with the union. The ambassadors objected that they could not conclude new treaties without having settled the earlier ones. "Then why did the king not send his plenipotentiaries to Courland?" asked the boyars. "All disputed matters could have been settled there." "It was not fitting to speak of the unfulfilled terms of the Kardis treaty in Courland, in the presence of Polish ambassadors," answered the Swedes. "You began first of all with talk of the alliance," repeated the boyars, "and only later mentioned the unfulfilled treaty terms. You should conduct these negotiations in the same order!"

The Swedes conceded, and proposed a union against the Turks. They announced that their king promised to send five thousand infantry troops to aid the Poles, unless Sweden went to war with another state, in which case he would send three thousand. These troops would march wherever the Poles deemed necessary, and would help them to a successful conclusion of the war. The Swedish king proffered this aid to the kingdom of Poland in Christian fellowship, not in expectation of any reward.

The boyars replied that five thousand men were very few, and that the great sovereign desired the Swedish king and all his forces to set out against the Turk in concert with his majesty the tsar. Five thousand men did not suffice to conclude an alliance unless these five thousand men were all skilled engineers, not common soldiers. Then none could stand against such great forces.

"The Poles themselves," protested the ambassadors, "asked no more of us." "What the Poles asked of you is not our affair," replied the boyars, "but now let the king agree to stand together with his majesty the tsar against the sultan, with all our forces united, lest the Turk take Poland. For if the Turk, from which God save us,[15] takes possession of the Polish state, this will be serious for the Swedish state also."

The ambassadors explained that they were not authorized to negotiate such an alliance. To settle the matter his majesty the tsar might send his ambassadors to the king. "Then why have you come?" asked the boyars. "We need such a union," they continued, "so that our forces can number some two hundred thousand men from both sides. Ours will wait across the Dnieper and along the Don, and yours by Kamieniec in Podolia or in some other place." "Did not the paper sent with von Staden," asked the Swedes, "say straight out that his majesty the tsar does not desire auxiliary troops?" "That was long ago," answered the boyars, "before the Turk advanced on the Polish king and took Kamieniec." The ambassadors flatly declared that such an alliance against the Turk was not at all advantageous for Sweden, only for Muscovy. The Turkish borders marched along with Russia's, and not at all with Sweden's. Why then should Sweden bind itself to keep helping Russia without hope of receiving any reciprocal aid?

Thus the ambassadors proposed to conclude the union in general terms, against all enemies of both sovereigns, without mentioning the Turk by name. In vain did the boyars explain that the remoteness of the borders was irrelevant, that the danger from Turkey was very substantial for Sweden as well. In vain they pointed to historical evidence, relating how the Greeks, threatened by the Turks, asked aid of neighboring powers but did not receive it on grounds that the dangers were far away. When the Greek empire fell for lack of help, the neighboring powers also fell one by one under the Ottoman yoke.

The ambassadors remained adamant and the boyars gave in. It was resolved that if his majesty the tsar sought aid from his royal highness against an enemy from this side of the sea, he might expect to get it, while if his royal highness must ask aid of his majesty the tsar against an enemy from this side of the sea, from the Livonian side, he too might ask with confidence. The aid in question was understood to mean troops as well as cash and military supplies.

The sovereign ordered that all Swedish prisoners, whether or not baptized into the Orthodox faith, be brought to Moscow and questioned in the presence of Boyar Ivan Bogdanovich Miloslavsky[16] and the king's representatives. If any of them accepted the Greek faith but said that they were forced to do so against their will, they were to be released to Sweden.[17] Those who accepted the Greek faith voluntarily, and those who did not convert but still wished to remain in Russia, should stay. The same procedure was enacted in Novgorod and Pskov with Swedish prisoners and in Sweden with Russians.

The question of trade duties was set aside because without royal approval the ambassadors could not commit to the boyars' proposal for the collection of duties according to regulations already in place in both countries. The ambassadors also set aside for royal consideration a proposal to punish turncoats with death on the side to which they defected, and also to give up earlier deserters without detention.

DENMARK

We have noted the active relations of the tsar with the Danish king Frederik III in 1656 and 1657, in connection with the Swedish war.[18] Although the successful conclusion of this conflict eliminated Moscow's main interest in relations with Denmark, Russia did not want to end them altogether. Thus in 1660 the crown agent Yakov Kokoshkin[19] visited Copenhagen with a letter in which the tsar expressed his desire for firm brotherly friendship, love and amicable neighborly relations with the king, even more so than previously, without fail, forever.

Kokoshkin was received very courteously, and heard an important piece of news. On October 14 a royal interpreter came to him. "Soon after the peace with Sweden," he said, "the archbishop of Copenhagen visited the king, accompanied by the bishop and members of the higher clergy, and with them representatives of the townsmen of Copenhagen. They said to the monarch that previous Danish kings, and his father King Christian,[20] and himself, did not conclude state or any other business according to their own pleasure, without the approval of councillors. These privy advisers ruled the realm, but many were traitors and caused great harm to Denmark. Now they, the clergy and townsmen, proposed that the king rule his country personally, see to all matters and carry out his own will, not waiting for the advice of his councillors. He must act according to his own pleasure, as it may seem meet to him, so that never again would the country suffer by the treason of councillors, and the king should convoke an assembly to discuss this as soon as possible.

"In accordance with their words," the interpreter continued, "the king sent his writ around to all cities of the realm, instructing them to send to Copenhagen two or three men from each city, chosen from the ranks of respected citizens. When the representatives arrived in Copenhagen the king ordered a council convened and informed it that in future he would rule the Danish realm personally, see to all affairs and fulfill his personal will without the advice and consent of councillors. The advisors and privy officials objected and took an obstinate stance, whereupon the clergy and representatives of the towns spoke to them forcibly, at length, and persuaded them to agree. Today the assembly ended. It advised that henceforth the present king and his descendants were to decide all affairs of state and other matters in Denmark, not waiting for advice and verdicts from councillors, according to his will, as it pleased the king. The councillors, clergy, nobles, military officers, and representatives from the cities stood before the king to take their oath that this matter would be immutable forever."

On October 17, 1660 the king sent a carriage for Kokoshkin. The Russian envoy was brought to the square beside the palace to observe the formal oath to the autocrat. "On the square," reported the envoy, "a wooden structure was built, like the Lobnoe mesto[21] in Moscow, with an elevated platform upon it. Both the structure and the platform were covered in red cloth, and eight armchairs covered in red velvet were set on the platform. Nearby soldiers stood on guard. At the sixth hour of the day the king came out of the palace, with his nobility, councillors, and privy councillors walking before him. These attendants carried a banner of red taffeta, the royal sword, a silver orb, and the crown. The king walked under a covering or canopy of crimson velvet with the queen, the two princes, and the four princesses. After the king came the clergy and the town representatives. The king and his family sat in the armchairs, and the archbishop, bishop, and councillors brought him the crown. The king stood up, removed his hat, took the crown, and gave it to the privy councillors, who placed it on a chair. Then the chancellor read the articles to which everyone swore, and after taking the oath they came up to the hand of the king and the queen."

Kokoshkin brought to Moscow a letter in which Frederik advised the tsar that he had become a patrimonial king.[22] "We hope," he wrote, "that such increase in the honor of our royal house will be pleasing to you, as our loving brother, special friend and neighbor."

Two Russian nobles, Grigory and Bogdan Nashchokin,[23] were sent to Denmark at the beginning of 1662 to congratulate the king on his heightened eminence. The Muscovite diplomats did not wish to lag behind the Ukrainians and Poles in oratory, and Grigory Nashchokin made the following elaborate speech to the king. "Our majestic sovereign, his majesty the tsar, has heard of the present great gift poured out to your royal highness by divine grace, and of the splendid great good fortune of your royal highness. Therefore he sends up praise to the Tsar God, lord of all, rejoicing at such good fortune for your royal highness as though the gain were his sovereign greatness's own. As a sign of his constant and long-standing regard he has deigned to send us as high ambassadors to your royal highness, to inform you that he, our great sovereign, prospers in his vast domains by the maintenance of the celebrated Triune God, creator of all things, and zealously, in genuine admiration, he greets your royal highness through us.

"May you live long, your royal highness! May there be good fortune in your hereditary autocratic kingdom, and may the Divine Almighty with His magnificent right hand watch over your royal highness in long life and prosperous health. May He preserve your authority in unchanging unity, your dignity in fitting well-being, and your kingdom in honor and in the befitting service of your people. Lo, you will be like a precious diamond in the beauty and strength of your nobility. You shall not be taken by even one of your foes, but shining in the clear brilliance of your regal accomplishments you will overcome the splendor of those who oppose you, and will please those who wish you well.

"To these you will radiate the illumination of desirable descendants. Yea, the descendants of your kingly greatness will be scintillations of that same diamond. They will hold dominion over your state, they will not diminish. Nay, their firmness shall overshadow that received through the remoteness of time and strengthened by a multitude of ancestors and kindred. With the passage of time the high honors of friendship and fraternal love will flower between our great sovereign and your royal highness. It will abide eternally like the strongest diamond, not defaced by any of the weak-minded. Yea, and the surrounding countries, noting the image of this constant friendship, will embrace among themselves the tranquility born of good instead of the discord of evil-doers. Even so has Almighty God, the source not of wordless confusion but of peace and good love, bestower of all blessings, eternally renowned from the mouths of the wise, been accustomed ever to crown those who love truth and those who are constant in amity, as is fitting."

Bogdan Nashchokin offered a similar speech from the tsar's sons Alexis and Fedor, "two noble and priceless royal scintillations, emanations of a precious and priceless diamond." The ambassadors then announced that among the gifts from the tsar to the king were five thousand puds of hemp.[24] The king instructed them to be told that hemp was very welcome at this time, and he sent a ship to Archangel for it immediately.

In 1665 Peter Marselis[25] traveled to Denmark with a request that King Frederik undertake to sway the Polish king toward peace with Russia. Frederik answered that he would send word to Jan Kazimierz of his intentions. Of course the intervention of the Danish king could not help matters in any way. We have seen [in the preceding chapter] what did help. Upon conclusion of the Andrusovo treaty in Moscow they considered it necessary to notify even the Danish king about it.

REFLECTIONS ON A BALTIC FLEET

Denmark was not renowned for its wealth, industry, or commerce, and thus Russia did not apply there for the loan of money, nor for master craftsmen.

We have observed the impoverishment of the Muscovite state at the time of the Polish war when financial resources were exhausted and the government cast anxious glances everywhere, wondering where it could borrow money or how it could increase revenues.

Moscow knew how rich the Western maritime powers were. It knew that they were rich from seafaring and trade, that their merchants sailed to distant wealthy countries from which they imported costly goods. As early as 1662 the thought emerged as to whether Russia might not acquire its own ships and send them to these rich countries for valuable merchandise. It did not have harbors on the Baltic Sea, but might it not go seafaring from others' harbors?

The Muscovite realm enjoyed friendly relations with the duke of Courland,[26] for whom it had done some services. During the war with Poland it left his territories undisturbed, and interceded with the Swedish king on his behalf. The tsar's envoy Ivan Afanasievich Zheliabuzhsky,[27] during his tour in England and other countries, summoned the Courland chancellor Fölkersahm in Riga and said to him "Your prince, mindful of the great sovereign's favor, may render his service and obligation to the tsar. He may inform the great sovereign where his ships go for powdered spices and vegetables, over which boundaries and across whose realms. He may tell him when they sail and when the ships return home. He may relate how much a ship costs, including its rigging and all its gear, and the costs of a venture in terms of the men's salaries and supplies. The prince may do this for the favor of the great sovereign, so that the sovereign's ships may sail to those places for those purposes. He may order that ships for those purposes be prepared for the great sovereign, with everything in readiness, and however much those ships cost him, he will be repaid from the tsar's treasury. In addition the prince may relate where to find master craftsmen to refine silver ore, and where the prince himself acquires silver ore."

"My prince is pleased to serve and to work diligently in all things for the abundant favor of the great sovereign," answered Fölkersahm. "His ships sail for foodstuffs and spices to his possessions in India, where the prince has his own island, with a settlement built upon it, in which some two hundred of his people live.[28] Its construction cost the prince dearly, for the wood had to be carried in ships from here. Ships too cost us a great deal because everything needed for their construction comes from foreign lands. I think that it would be better for the great sovereign to build his ships at Archangel." The duke sent a letter with a detailed explanation of the matter. The document has not been preserved, but we can easily guess at its contents.

HOLLAND AND ENGLAND

Relations with Holland, from which so many military officers and craftmasters volunteered for Russian service, were so important that in 1660 the Englishman John Hebdon[29] was sent there as the tsar's resident or commissar.

We have seen that relations with England were severed in 1649 in consequence of the execution of King Charles I, but continued with the pretender Charles II, to whom Russia gave assistance.[30] In 1654 William Prideaux, envoy of the English ruler Oliver Cromwell, sailed into Archangel.[31] The envoy gave the sovereign a letter which said that the great Parliament, despairing of correcting the many follies which existed in England during the reigns of previous kings, had changed the government and seated the best and wisest sovereign Oliver, who sent his most loving greetings to the great monarch the great sovereign lord Alexis Mikhailovich, and beseeched the return of privileges taken from English merchants.

When the tsar did not rise to ask after the health of the Protector, the envoy protested. "Although now in England we have a newly created government (a republic), yet our realm is by no means diminished. The Spanish, French and Portuguese kings and the Venetian republic honor our ruler, just as previously they honored our kings."

"Nonetheless the English kingdom has undergone a great change," was the answer. "This is the first dispatch from your ruler to his majesty the tsar, who is not aware of what business you were sent to conclude. Besides, the Venetian and Dutch rulers are no example for his majesty the tsar, and it is not fitting for you to speak of that." "I have never been in such a country," continued the envoy, "nor seen such 'honor' for myself. A bailiff sat at my right hand in the sled and took my sword from me!" "As custom demands in the Muscovite realm, so it is done," they answered him, "and it is not fitting for you to speak of the practices of a foreign country."

In his reply to Cromwell the tsar wrote "To Oliver, ruler over the realms of England, Scotland and Ireland, and the countries which border them. Insofar as you seek friendship and concord with us, so we accept this from you in concord and friendship. We wish to live in friendship, concord and correspondence with you who are the protector. We congratulate you on your sovereignty, in which God has placed you. Concerning that which your honor writes regarding merchants, we cannot now scrutinize this matter so soon after a time of war, but eventually you will have our gracious decree, such as will be conducive to peace, profit, friendship and amity for both states."

Affairs with Cromwell did not go further than these indefinite courtesies. The tsar's resident in Holland, the Englishman Hebdon, proved to be a supporter of Charles II to whom, when he was called to the English throne, Hebdon presented himself with a request that he release a detachment of three thousand troops to Russia. The king granted him full freedom to recruit this army and, informing the tsar of the matter (in the spring of 1661) wrote that he never could forget the tokens of brotherly friendship shown to him by Alexis during the time of the recent impious troubles, especially the decree whereby his unworthy subjects were deprived of their previous liberties within the Muscovite realm. Now that his good subjects had returned to their previous obedience, the king hoped the tsar would restore their privileges. The king's letter was sent with Hebdon's son.

The table attendant Prince Peter Prozorovsky and the nobleman Ivan Zheliabuzhsky were sent to England in 1662 to congratulate the new king on his accession to the throne.[32] The ambassadors were welcomed with the assurance that the king did not feel such goodwill to any other sovereign as to the Russian monarch. To all the assembled people he announced the favors shown him by the great sovereign, while to his privy lords and all his subjects he said repeatedly that no one save the Russian sovereign had shown him such goodwill when he was in exile. The king hoped somehow to repay the great sovereign for this favor. When the ambassadors sailed on the Thames all the ships fired their guns in salute, and where there were no guns crowds of people greeted the ambassadors with loud acclaim. The common people were ordered to line the London streets and cheer, while all the better-born were present at the reception.

The English peers[33] informed the ambassadors that when his royal highness was in exile the great sovereign had sent treasure to aid him. The illustrious king remembered this assistance and now was prepared to return the borrowed treasure to the great sovereign. The ambassadors asked that the great king give the great sovereign a loan of ten thousand puds of efimoks[34] in addition to the returned treasure, which the great sovereign in his turn would repay in annual shipments of hemp and potash, in terms to be set out by treaty. The English lords answered that this was an important matter which they could not decide quickly. At the departure ceremonies the king told Prozorovsky "With all my heart I would be glad to help my beloved brother, but I have no power, because I am newly come to kingship, and have acquired nothing. During my time of troubles my treasury was devastated. There is nothing left, and I live now in great poverty. If God grants that I strengthen my position and refill my treasury, I will be glad to share it with your great sovereign."

During his stay in London the second ambassador Zheliabuzhsky quarrelled with Hebdon. According to Zheliabuzhsky's report Hebdon received money from the royal treasury for the ambassadors' maintenance but kept it for himself, giving them bad food. In the ambassadors' lodgings he took the best rooms for himself and his children. He assigned fine rooms for Dr. Samuel [Collins][35] and his other foreign friends, yet allotted cramped little chambers to the secretary and nobles, and to the clerk he assigned a cubicle so niggardly that he hardly could squeeze into it.

Hebdon, the report continued, said that the boyars in Moscow did not work to the sovereign's benefit, nor did they know how to assess and deal with the foreigners who approached them. Wicked foreigners who live by deceit are the very ones the boyars enrich with the sovereign's goods and treasures. Even earlier, in the reign of Tsar Michael, the boyars Ivan Borisovich Cherkassky and Fedor Ivanovich Sheremetev rewarded wicked, deceitful foreigners.[36] Some claimed knowledge of silver mining, others claimed some other craft mastery. In this way they fraudulently obtained the money the boyars had given them. "The boyars have driven all merchants away from the Archangel wharfs," complained the English, "and now we have even less reason to visit. Such goods as once were imported from Muscovy now can be acquired in England. Hebdon undervalued the gifts the tsar sent to king. He spread rumors about the Russians, saying that they were drunks who consumed eleven barrels a day, and he called the second ambassador Zheliabuzhsky a grumbler whose stupidity was common knowledge to all London."

In turn Hebdon wrote to his brother-in-law in Moscow that Zheliabuzhsky's presence hampered the diplomatic process, for in his pride he refused to allow the king and magnates to meet with him. Further, when he departed across France for Italy the king and councillors praised Prince Prozorovsky for his courtesy. Hebdon's son wrote that the ambassadors were received with unprecedented honors because of his father's efforts, and that the king disbursed two hundred silver rubles to him daily. Only Zheliabuzhsky degraded the tsar's name through his haughtiness, whereas Prince Prozorovsky was held in high praise and honor by the king and magnates. Dr. Samuel Collins wrote that the whole court spoke only good of Prince Prozorovsky, and held Zheliabuzhsky to be a proud man who honored nothing and liked no one. When he left the furniture in his quarters was found ruined and all the rooms filthy.

In Moscow Prozorovsky and Zheliabuzhsky were assessed differently than in England. Not Prozorovsky but Zheliabuzhsky was entrusted to communicate with the duke of Courland on questions of seafaring. Not Prozorovsky but Zheliabuzhsky was commissioned to borrow thirty-one thousand efimoks from the English merchants. Zheliabuzhsky appealed to the merchants, setting out conditions for payment in Archangel in hemp and potash. The merchants replied that they were willing to lend the money if the agreement were cleared first with the "voevoda" of London (the lord mayor). "I will be happy to be of assistance to your great sovereign," the lord mayor replied. "I will speak with the merchants to determine who wants to give what, and I myself also will give what I can."

Zheliabuzhsky also appealed to the resident Hebdon, asking that he exert himself to gather cash for the great sovereign. Hebdon answered "We cannot borrow money at present. In the Archangel markets untruth and ill-will have begun to spread. Anything that is lent very likely will be lost. Even before, the repayment rate of loans was bad, and now there is no point even asking, given the present markets and goods. I cannot get efimoks anywhere, and anyway this is not my affair!"

Several times thereafter Zheliabuzhsky sent to the lord mayor and the merchants, who all promised to meet with him. At last they arrived and announced "We cannot give you any efimoks because the goods in Archangel have become expensive. We sell your goods more cheaply here in England than we buy them, and even then no one wants them. We have lost too much in loans to Muscovites, and we cannot get the debts called in." *Zheliabuzhsky.* You do not want to give efimoks because of some sort of intention to disoblige, and so you call it a complex matter. You have never lost a penny on a loan.

Merchants. Even as we speak we are taking great losses on the notes of debts and advances that we hold on Muscovite traders, and we have no judicial recourse. Furthermore, the officials and tax-collectors have made our voyages to Archangel more burdensome than in the past. If Vasily Shorin were still an official, and Klimshin a tax-collector, they would have driven off all the foreign visitors. We have not seen any other such iniquitous men in all the world.[37]

Zheliabuzhsky. None of this is my affair. I am requesting a loan for the great sovereign, and will give a note promising that it will be repaid from the tsar's treasury. You have debts outstanding among your brothers. Go now and call in these debts for the great sovereign. As for your complaints against those who burden and tax you in the markets, there will be an investigation and just settlement in all these matters.

Merchants. In Archangel we always petition about the debts and advances owing to us, and ask the governors for an order. The governors find just settlements for us in regard to these debts and advances, but in the matter of abuses by the administrators and tax-collectors they can do nothing. When the governors were in charge of the officials and tax-collectors, as was the case previously, conditions were better for us to travel with our wares.

Notwithstanding all of Zheliabuzhsky's exhortations the merchants flatly refused to loan money. The Dutch artist Artemy came by and tried to explain the situation. "On Hebdon's advice the merchants have refused to lend the cash. 'Do not give out any money,' he told them. 'If the tsar needed something here he would have sent you an official letter or would have written to me.'" The interpreter corroborated this.

In 1664 the famous ambassador Charles Howard, earl of Carlisle,[38] arrived in Moscow and in an unprecedented gesture brought his wife and son with him. In his letter King Charles apologized to the tsar for having delayed in sending a formal embassy, yet hoped that the choice of such a famous man as his relative the earl of Carlisle would demonstrate the special high reverence in which the king held the person of the great sovereign. Two boyars, Prince Nikolai Ivanovich Odoevsky and Yury Alekseevich Dolgoruky, with the lord-in-waiting Vasily Semeonovich Volynsky, were assigned to deliver the tsar's response. They were ordered to dress in gold robes with embroidered patterns and to wear golden chains and black hats for the occasion.[39] The ambassador presented the royal instructions, first, to inform the great sovereign that he might deign to confirm the former state of brotherly friendship and love with the king, and second, to ask the return of commercial privileges to the English merchants.

The Russians answered that the tsar greatly desired to maintain a state of brotherly friendship and love with the king, although they rejected the second issue. "The English traded duty-free in Muscovy for a hundred years and grew rich, but did not give luxury items and other suitable goods to the tsar's treasury at their [original] overseas price as was required. They imported and exported prohibited goods in secret, and carried third-party goods as their own so as not to pay duty. One of the merchants of the English Company arrived in the Baltic Sea in a warship and tried to rob the tsar's subjects traveling to Sweden to trade. We think," said the boyars, "that all this is unknown to the king, otherwise he would not be requesting the reconfirmation of previous charters."

"The king knows all this," answered the ambassador, "but now requests commercial privileges because he wants to reward those men who are true to him with the right to trade in Russia. There will be no deceit from such men in the Muscovite realm. They will sell luxury goods to the tsar's treasury at their overseas price, and will import fine goods, such as unstretched cloth."[40]

Boyars. If the English trade in Archangel with duties, this will cause no loss to his royal highness, and the tsar's subjects may trade in England. They will pay their duties without complaint or evasion, and from this exchange both states will profit, but if the English trade in Muscovy duty-free, there will be great loss for the tsar's treasury, and no gain.

After long negotiations and exchanges of letters the boyars informed Carlisle that "the great sovereign, heeding the most courteous and culti-vated plea of his brother, has instructed the English merchants[41] to send ten men to Archangel, and from Archangel to Moscow. They must be good men, certified as trustworthy, and pleasing to his royal highness, whom his royal highness should deign to choose anew. These ten men may buy quarters in Moscow. They will pay duty on their wares at rates equal to other foreigners while his majesty the tsar is at war with the Polish king and the Crimean khan. When the war ends his majesty the tsar will order that the English merchants draft an edict for his merciful sovereign consider-ation, as soon as possible."

The ambassador was dissatisfied. "If his majesty the tsar does not return our privileges," he said, "how can there be a strong foundation of friend-ship between the two great sovereigns?" "How can that matter, if the friendship was not broken by the king's refusal to lend money?" was the response. Carlisle was greatly exasperated by his lack of success, and in his irritation he allowed himself to use harsh expressions in conversations and in letters. Among other things he said that the Muscovite government intentionally asked to borrow such a large sum of money from the king in order to find fault at the refusal and thus avoid granting privileges to the merchants. The Russians paid him back in the same coin, saying flatly that he borrowed heavily from his own merchants, and that is why he worked so hard to restore their privileges.

Hoping to regain the commercial privileges, Carlisle offered England's mediation in reconciling Russia with Poland. Members of the tsar's council told him that the sovereign agreed, and that the ambassador might quickly dispatch his own courier to the Polish king. "I cannot send a courier," replied Carlisle, "because my previous matter of business has not been settled. Before anything else can be done we must restore the English merchants their privileges." "We have explained to you about the privileges," said the advisors, "and there will be no change in the decision."

"If there can be no change," answered Carlisle, "I will not send a courier to the Polish king, nor will I go myself, for there is nothing for me to do there. I beg the great sovereign to grant me leave to depart. Were his majesty the tsar now to promise me that he will fulfill the royal request, happily would I be his servant forever. The king sent me just for this purpose. When I return to his royal highness and present him the tsar's current answer, the king will say that an identical answer was given to Cromwell's ambassador, and even were he to send a courier he would return with the same response. I think that our king will send no further high ambassadors to his majesty the tsar. It is a pity that this affair could not be settled through me, for if it were settled by me I daresay that it would repay his majesty the tsar some ten or twenty times over."

None of the ambassador's declarations helped. A vexed Carlisle left for Sweden, sending word to England of the failure of his mission. In Moscow it was feared that Carlisle would bare his heart to the king, and they hastened to send the table attendant Vasily Yakovlevich Dashkov[42] to London to explain.

If Prozorovsky and Zheliabuzhsky were met with unprecedented honors, Dashkov suffered unprecedented dishonor. He was accorded neither transport, nor food, nor lodging, and to his complaints the English replied "You gave customary honors to our ambassador Carlisle, but you settled nothing of the matters for which he visited."

Dashkov explained that Carlisle did not conduct business properly. He interpreted everything in terms of the restoration of commercial privileges, calling these privileges the foundation of brotherly friendship and love between the two sovereigns, whereas the foundation of brotherly friendship between their highnesses must lie in their mutual goodwill, not in privileges. "Privileges cannot be a foundation for the priceless, invaluable and radiant sun of friendship and love between sovereigns, as the earth cannot be a base for the sun."

Hebdon presented himself to Dashkov with an offer of his services to his majesty the tsar. "You and I have not been instructed to talk, but mindful of the favor of the great sovereign I will tell you in confidence that Carlisle has concluded a treaty in Sweden which unites the Swedish king and ours against his majesty the tsar. English merchants will not go to Archangel, nor will they allow Dutch ships and those of other nations to pass. The English will sail to Riga, Reval[43] and Novgorod for Russian goods and will trade there free of duty. Our king told the House of Lords that the Russian sovereign's war with the Polish king will not soon end, and never will he have peace with the Crimean khan. This is a long time for our Company merchants to wait. Carlisle's errand cost the king many thousands, for which the Company will not reimburse him because the matter was not settled successfully. For the Muscovite venture Carlisle was given twenty thousand rubles from the royal treasury." Hebdon also boasted that he advised the Lords not to ally with Sweden against the tsar, proposing that they do Russia no further damage in this way, for they urgently needed the Russian imports. In the spring of 1665 the king gave Dashkov leave to depart, ordering him paid twelve hundred rubles because he had lived the whole time on his own resources.

When war broke out between England and Holland[44] the tsar sent a Scotsman in his service, Colonel Gordon,[45] to inform Charles II that the tsar had forbidden the sale of timber and other naval stores to the Dutch in Archangel. In 1667 our old friend Hebdon brought the king's response to Moscow, traveling in the capacity of royal ambassador-extraordinary. Hebdon proclaimed a list of crimes committed by the Dutch States which, forgetting the aid formerly rendered to them by Queen Elizabeth against the Spanish king,[46] not only began a war against England, but also boasted of it. The king instructed Hebdon to ask his majesty the tsar for the return of privileges to the English merchants, already promised to Carlisle. The king learned that many of the Dutch trading in Russia were false hypocrites, and thus ordered his agent to request his majesty the tsar that these Dutch be banished from Muscovy because of their frauds and deceptions and because of their enmity toward his royal highness. "By order of my king," Hebdon added, "I request that the Dutch be expelled from Muscovy. Yet now a rumor has arisen that my sovereign has concluded peace with the Dutch States. Thus I must leave the question of the expulsion of the Dutch to the will and judgement of the great sovereign."

Boyar Afanasy Lavrentievich Ordin-Nashchokin,[47] the overseer of foreign affairs, wrote the reply to Hebdon personally, as is evident from the heavy, obscure and precious style of the document. "Always is joy given from God to Christians, that they may abide in peace and increase their material belongings, and that the enemies of Christendom may thereby live in fear. At present in Muscovy, after great consideration, we have drafted commercial legislation to ensure that trade may proceed without quarrels and without offence. It is not fitting to allow entry to the earlier Company because it was the source of more quarrels than friendship. It has come to light that these foreigners traded in *undeclared and harmful goods*,[48] and that they made secret deals and burdened Russian people with many debts."

Naturally Hebdon was dissatisfied with this answer, and objected that the promise given to Carlisle was broken. Russia had sworn to return the English merchants' privileges as soon as the war with Poland was ended. Now that the war was over, it still refused to restore the privileges. No new considerations of any kind were admitted.

The vital question in English relations now was decided, and no other common interests remained. Then, when the Turks attacked Poland Tsar Alexis, through inexperience in European affairs, took it upon himself to invite all European sovereigns to aid Poland against the enemies of the Cross of Christ. With this goal Andrei Vinius,[49] a translator in the Chancellery for Foreign Affairs, was dispatched to England. The English told him that the king could not aid Poland for two reasons. First, the war with Holland occupied the whole of the English fleet of over seventy warships. Second, many English merchants lived in Turkey, and should the king intervene against the Turks the sultan would order all the English robbed or killed. Besides, an English ambassador lived permanently at the sultan's court.

In his daily log Vinius was the first to describe [to Russians] the form of government in England. "The government of the English kingdom or, as it is commonly called, Great Britain, is part monarchy (the rule of one man), part aristocracy (government by the most important people), and part democracy (government by the people). It is monarchical in that the English have a king, who has some power and command in the government but cannot act autocratically. It is aristocratic and democratic in that in time of great matters, such as declaring war, making peace or setting monetary requisitions, the king calls together the parliament or Sejm. This parliament is divided into two houses, one called the upper and the other the lower house. In the upper house meet the senators and highest nobility from all the land. Representatives of the common people from all the cities and towns meet in the other. Although the upper house makes decisions, no matter of business can be carried out without the approval of the lower house, on which all financial requisitions depend. For this reason the upper house may be called an aristocracy, and the lower a democracy. Without the approval of these two houses the king can take no action in matters of state."

FRANCE AND SPAIN

We have found that Tsar Alexis considered it necessary to inform the French king about his declaration of war on Poland. He also felt the need to inform Louis XIV about the successful conclusion of the war, to which end the table attendant Peter Ivanovich Potemkin and the crown secretary Semeon Vladimirovich Rumiantsev were sent to France in 1668 and presented themselves to the king at St.-Germain.[50] Louis told them that he greatly rejoiced at the successful conclusion of the war and prayed to Almighty God for the establishment of an eternal peace.

In their response the envoys informed the royal advisors of the objects of their embassy. (1) The great sovereign wished to live in brotherly friendship and love with his royal highness. (2) To confirm this friendship and love, the king should send his ambassadors or envoys to his majesty the tsar. (3) Merchants of both countries should be allowed to travel and trade in all towns.

The king's advisors replied to these suggestions with the following statements. (1) There must be firm and long-standing peace, unity and friendship between the tsar and the king and between their successors. (2) This state of peace and fraternal concord will spread the honor and praise of their highnesses into all neighboring states. (3) They shall ensure forever that neither will attack or cause loss or damage to the other. (4) Subjects of his majesty the tsar may travel to and trade anywhere in the French kingdom with full freedom, not paying anything to enter. They shall pay duties on their goods as do other foreign merchants. They may rent homes, cellars and warehouses without hindrance. They even may build quarters without impediment in order to deal in every variety of merchandise, by mountain and by water routes. They shall pay duties only on goods for sale, and they may export any French merchandise to whatever destination they wish. (5) Muscovites coming to live in France shall suffer no taxes or discrimination. They shall pay assessments as French merchants pay them. They may have a judge of their own to settle their litigations, and they may hold religious services in their own faith with all freedom. (6) French merchants and other ranks of French people may travel across Muscovy to reach all its neighboring states, including Persia. Their conditions of transit and freedom of religion shall correspond to those for Russians in France. No duties shall be charged for transit and for departure, and duties shall be charged on goods as they were for the English Company, namely one half the value, and thus Russians in France shall pay a duty of one half the value of their goods.

The envoys did not agree to these conditions or give any written answer. They merely sent a bailiff to inform the advisors that they were not instructed to negotiate commercial affairs, and that the king might send a separate embassy to Moscow for such matters. French merchants met with the envoys to discuss the conditions proposed by their government. "Go to Archangel to trade," Potemkin told them. "There will be no taxes or harassment for you, and your duty rates will be set equivalent to those of other foreigners." "Without a treaty and a resolution," replied the merchants, "it is not safe for us to travel such a long way." With this the matter ended.

Notwithstanding Louis XIV's manifest unwillingness to become involved in the affairs of Eastern Europe, in 1670 the tsar sent a letter informing him that Russian ambassadors and Polish commissioners had selected the king as one of the mediators to conclude their eternal peace. The other mediators were the German emperor, the Swedish and Danish kings, and the elector of Brandenburg. Finally in 1673 Andrei Vinius, whom we last saw in England requesting aid for Poland against the Turks, brought this proposal to Louis also. He found the king on campaign in Flanders, where the monarch told him that war with the Dutch prevented him from fulfilling the tsar's desire.

Even faraway Spain was not forgotten. As early as 1667 the table attendant Peter Potemkin traveled to Madrid with the tsar's letter. This document, announcing the successful conclusion of the war with Poland, was addressed to King Philip IV, although the envoy delivered it to Philip's successor, the young Charles II.[51] "The name of our forefathers," wrote the tsar, "is praised in all countries, and Great Russia increases in blessings from year to year. Many neighboring sovereigns have amicable and advantageous relations with us, but amicable relations with you, great sovereign, have been restricted unto this time, either because of the distance between our countries, or by the will of Almighty God, Who plans all things in ways incomprehensible to men, in expectation of a better time."

In his reply Charles stated that he was sending ambassadors to Russia forthwith, and until that time he ordered that all his seaports admit the tsar's subjects for free trade, hoping that the tsar would do the same for Spaniards. The way was paved, and in 1673 Vinius left France for Spain with the familiar invitation to aid Poland against the Turks. He brought the answer that Charles II, because of his relationship by marriage to the Polish king,[52] would aid him financially, though military aid was not feasible by reason of the great distance involved.

ITALY

Italy did not wait for an envoy, but brought itself to Russia's attention. The Venetian republic had its own war against the Turks, which was straining its resources. It sought aid everywhere. Well informed of the relations between Russia and the Christian population of the Balkan peninsula, and hearing of the tsar's military successes in Polish territories, Venice dispatched an embassy to Moscow in 1656. It requested that the tsar order the Don Cossacks to attack the Turks and so divert their forces, and also that he grant free trade in Archangel to Venetian merchants.

Just then Moscow had no time for the Turks. The Polish war appeared to be over, yet it brought a second war, the Swedish, in its wake. Russia's financial resources were exhausted, and the country hoped to use the Venetian embassy for its own purposes. It wanted to borrow money from the republic, which had a long-standing reputation for wealth. In the fall of 1656 the tsar sent the table attendant Ivan Ivanovich Chemodanov and the crown secretary Alexis Posnikov as envoys to Venice.[53] They sailed from Archangel in Dutch ships, and in accordance with Russian custom they carried goods from the sovereign and patriarch with them to sell to defray their expenses.

On the night of October 27 an Atlantic storm caught the envoys' vessel. Water poured into the ship, and the portholes of the upper-deck living quarters were pounded by waves. Much of the cargo was soaked. Water stood an arshin or more deep on the middle decks, and came to a man's waist on the higher levels.[54] A barrel of rhubarb from the sovereign's treasury was submerged.[55] A great weeping and wailing arose aboard the ship, as the envoys and all the sovereign's people began to pray. Then the storm subsided.

One disaster had passed, but another lay in wait. Off Lisbon the Russian party caught sight of fourteen ships. They took them to be pirates from the Barbary Coast and prepared for battle, but the little fleet proved to be merchants of various countries sailing from Spain. They warned the envoys that Turkish ships were plying the Mediterranean as far north and west as Livorno. In fact, while passing through the Narrows (the Strait of Gibraltar), the envoys met three pirate ships. Seeing the Turkish pirates prepare to attack, the entire Russian party offered up tearful prayers to the All-merciful Savior and His Immaculate Mother. The pirates, sailing with the wind and eager for a fight, pursued the ships at great speed and overtook them, but when they saw the official party on board, with its battle standards and defenses, they feared to attack, and disappeared into the night.

On November 25 the envoys arrived in Livorno, where they were met with great respect. A similar reception awaited them in Florence, where Duke Ferdinand de' Medici[56] came to visit. "Does your great sovereign," he asked, "welcome my subjects, my merchants? Does he allow them to buy caviar and other goods at Archangel? Still, I am glad to have the sovereign's favor and advice, and I will spare no effort to arrange things in my realm for the good of the great sovereign. To the end of my life I will be pleased to serve and to help him."

A general, the Pope's grandson,[57] accompanied the envoys through Ferrara. Coming up to a church he told them "This is the church of St. George, where the eighth council begun in Florence was concluded." "Was this that same eighth council," asked Chemodanov, "which St. Mark of Ephesus dispersed, not allowing it to be completed in Florence?" "I do not know why it was not completed in Florence, I only know that it was completed here, in this church," replied the general.[58]

In Venice a group of Greeks came to greet the envoys. "We rejoice," they said, "that God has permitted us to see the envoys of such a great sovereign of Eastern Orthodox Christians of our rule. Please allow us to visit your grace frequently. We have come to discover when it will please you to visit our holy church of the Greek faith. We will prepare ourselves in expectation of that time, and will chant prayers for the health of the sovereign and the tsarevich." "We will let you know when the time comes," answered the ambassadors.

Officers came from the government and announced that the doge was ailing in his legs, and thus the envoys would be received by the noble lords. The senior of them would sit in the prince's place, and the envoys should present their letter to him. "This is not possible," answered Chemodanov. "We have been sent to your prince, and our orders are to see him and to give the letter into his hands." "It is the same thing," said the officers. "Those matters which are written in the letter to the prince are ours to deal with. The prince does not deal with them and is not in charge of anything." "If your prince is not in charge of anything," objected Chemodanov, "if you rule the realm, you would have written your own names together with the prince's in your letter to his majesty the tsar."

They agreed to wait for the doge's recovery, and the reception took place on January 22, 1657. The envoys announced that the sovereign would permit Venetians to trade freely in Archangel with payment of customary duties. Concerning the main point, of sending the Don Cossacks against the Turks, they said "The great sovereign is ever zealous to free Orthodox Christendom from the infidel yoke, but at this time his majesty the tsar cannot undertake such an endeavor because he has gone to war against an enemy of his own. When, with God's help, he has dealt with this enemy, he will order a treaty concluded with you, on how to stand against the common foe of all Christians."

At last the envoys came to the main point for which they had been sent. They proclaimed the great deceits of the Swedish king, and announced that his majesty the tsar would not suffer his evil undertaking. "Thus let your principality and your noble lords demonstrate their love and goodwill to his majesty the tsar by sending aid to his troops in the form of a loan of gold pieces or efimoks, as many as possible, and as quickly as possible."

The prince and the noble lords did not well understand. How could this Muscovite sovereign postpone helping against the Turks to a later time yet request an immediate loan? They dispatched an officer to the envoys for an explanation. "Tell me," he asked, "how great a fortune will it take to persuade your sovereign to aid us against the Turk?" "Your words are foolish and unseemly," was the reply. "Should our great sovereign decide to send his army against the Turk, he will do so for the deliverance of Christians, not for money. By whose order do you say these idle words? Did the prince order you thus, or the lords?"

The officer pondered for a while and answered "I have said this on my own." When the matter was clarified, the Venetian government gave its response. "We have been fighting the Turks for thirteen years already. Our wits and our will do not weaken, but our treasury has suffered great losses. Thus it is with regret that we must refuse his majesty the tsar. We hope that, learning of our poverty, he will not become angry with us."

The envoys went to the Greek church, where they were met with great ceremony and tears of joy. After prayers at the ambo the clergy came away from the altar, and one of the deacons offered this speech to the envoys. "The Greek people, living in this most glorious city of Venice, pray thus to the Almighty. Grant, Lord, that the most radiant, invincible, powerful, glorious, pious and Orthodox defender of God's Eastern church, the pious zealot, the great sovereign tsar and grand prince Alexis Mikhailovich, comforter of the Christian nation, be in good health for many years. Like a radiant sun he rose to eradicate the darkness of unbelief, to maintain and unify the holy Christian faith, and to vanquish the enemies of God. Like a second Constantine he came to free the faithful Christian Greeks from the might of the pagan Turks. We pray Almighty God that the Muslims forever be enslaved and vanquished by the tsar's radiant sword."

After dinner the Greeks told the envoys "We travel frequently from Venice to Turkey to trade all manner of goods with the Turks, and many Turks have told us that God gave the Muscovite sovereign victory over the Poles and other realms. Those of us Greeks who live in Turkey hold this news in great fame. The sultan and the pashas have searched in their fortune-telling books and say that the time has come for Constantinople also to fall to the Russian sovereign. They live in great apprehension, and the gates of Constantinople have been bricked up for a long time. In their fear of Russia the Turks have begun to oppress us Greeks, but we trust in the mercy of God and in the protection of the great sovereign, that he may deliver us from the hands of the infidel."

Before he could help the Greeks the great sovereign had to free some of his own people from infidel hands. More than fifty Russians freed from Turkish captivity presented themselves to the envoy in Venice. They came for alms, and said that many of their fellow prisoners were traveling to Moscow by various routes.

The cordial reception given to Chemodanov in Florence drew the attention of the tsar, who in 1659 sent the courtier Vasily Bogdanovich Likhachev[59] there. This time the reception was even better. Taking the sovereign's letter the grand duke Ferdinand de' Medici kissed it and asked with tears "For what reason has your grand prince from the distant great city of Moscow, who is celebrated by all nations and peoples, sought for me, his servant, and sent me his gracious letter and gifts? He, your great sovereign, stands as far above me as does the heaven from the earth. He is renowned from one end of the universe to the other, and his name is feared in all countries. What might my poor self do to earn his great and extraordinary favor? I, and my brothers and son, are slaves of the great sovereign."

The envoys resided at the grand duke's palace. Likhachev, like Chemodanov, came directly to Italy from Archangel by sea, bypassing Western Europe. Thus it is understandable how struck he was by the miracles of nature and art in the Medici patrimony. "In the prince's court is a palace eight stories high, with two hundred and fifty rooms. In all of them are rich hangings, tables of slate embellished with gold, and plants. Some rooms are inscribed with gold. We saw a golden inkwell weighing thirty pounds, containing silver ore instead of sand, and armchairs covered in velvet. In the same court is a fish pond with live fish. The water is brought up some four sazhens. They have built a jordan [a conduit or pool], above which water continually leaps to a height of about two sazhens, in fine drops which glint like rock crystals in the sun. Around the prince's court are cedar and cypress trees and a great fragrance. At Epiphany [January 6] there are great fires, such as we have on St. John's Day [June 24]. Large apples and lemons ripen twice a year, and the winter in Florence is not even a month long."

The duke ordered a theatrical performance prepared for the envoys, at the cost of eight thousand efimoks. "The prince gave commands for a play. Chambers appeared, and after being there for a while the room sank downward, and in this fashion there were six changes. Also within those chambers there appeared the sea, with undulating waves, and in the sea were fish, and on the fish people were riding. Above the room were the heavens, and people sat on clouds. The clouds with people sank downward. They took a person from the ground by the arm and again ascended, and those who sat on the fish also were lifted. A man in a carriage also descended, and across from him in another carriage there was a most beautiful maiden, and the steeds[60] harnessed to the carriages moved their legs as if they were alive, and the prince said that one was the sun and the other the moon. Then many most wondrous youths and maidens came out from the curtain dressed in gold, and danced."

The abundance of the South astounded the Russians, and the Far North fascinated the southern monarchs with its vast wilderness and its primeval natural treasures. "The Florentine prince questioned us, and looked at maps of Siberia, taking notes of how many of each animal there are. They marvelled greatly at Siberia and its wealth of sables, that there are so many of them, and at the martens and foxes and squirrels and other animals. They wondered how was it possible not to overhunt them, for they have no wild animals, because the land is very hilly, and not wooded, and the forest all is planted. The Florentine prince's consort begged the envoy that two fur coats in the Russian fashion be made for her, as a gift for her newly married daughter-in-law. The envoy ordered the coats made of damask and taffeta, one with an ermine lining, and the other with squirrel. The princess donned them and marvelled at how well they were fashioned."

The Venetian government, perplexed by Chemodanov's demand, had yet to send a further embassy to Moscow. Then, when the Russian government had to prepare for war with the Ottoman Porte it remembered the republic and its celebrated war with Turkey. In 1668 the foreign merchant Thomas Kelderman[61] carried a letter from the tsar to the doge and senate in which the great sovereign expressed his amazement that the republic was not sending any news of itself. The letter also announced that the tsar had concluded peace with the Polish king and an alliance against the infidels. It related that Moscow had signed a commercial treaty with the Company of Persian Armenians[62] by which Persian goods would be carried exclusively through Russia. Finally, it noted that there was hope of the Persian shah turning his weapons against the Turks. In their answering letter the doge and the senate congratulated the sovereign and expressed their desire that all Christian sovereigns might unite against the Turks.

Mohammed IV's attack on Poland[63] gave the tsar yet another occasion to remember Venice. The Scotsman Paul Menzies, who has appeared before in this narration, rode from Vienna to invite Venice to join Russia's proposed alliance against the Turks. The senate responded with no more than a pious wish. "May God," they said, "help his majesty the tsar to smash the advancing foe and bring peace to Christian sovereigns."

MENZIES IN ROME

At last Menzies left Venice to deliver the tsar's letter to Pope Clement X[64] in Rome. "May it please you, Pope and preceptor of the Roman church, to inform us, the great sovereign, of the following. Are you prepared to perform your Christian duty to aid our brother, his royal highness, with your armies against our common adversary? If you wish to help, you must send us a letter forthwith, relating in what measures, at what time, and in which places this help will arrive, that we may conclude a treaty through common envoys. May it please you to write to neighboring sovereigns, urging that they assist his royal highness, and in particular to write to Louis the French king and to Charles the English king that they may conclude their war with the Dutch States and turn their armies against the common foe of all Christians."

When he arrived in Rome Menzies began by stating the conditions for his reception and departure ceremonies. The Pope must stand to hear the name and title of the great sovereign, Menzies demanded. He must accept the tsar's letter and offer his own, also standing. Before the letter was sealed it must be shown to the envoy to confirm that the tsar's title was written in its full and proper form.

The papal master of ceremonies then announced his own conditions. The Pope would remain seated during the entire reception and departure ceremonies, and the envoy must kiss the foot of his holiness. No one could direct the Pope to do otherwise. "My orders do not in any way include kissing the papal foot," said Menzies, "because our great sovereign does not follow the Roman Catholic rite. Furthermore in earlier times, when Greeks and Latins were united in faith, the Greeks did not kiss the Pope's foot. When Patriarch Joseph of Constantinople traveled to Ferrara with his metropolitans and bishops in 1438 to visit Pope Eugene IV the Pope kissed them in monastic fashion, and then the metropolitans and bishops and other ranks kissed his hand."[65]

"If," warned the master of ceremonies, "the emperor or any other Christian potentate arrives and will not kiss the papal foot, the Pope will not see him." "If that is the case," answered Menzies, "let the Pope instruct me to travel on."

Menzies was not allowed to depart, nor did the envoy kiss the Pope's foot. He merely "bowed according to the Roman fashion, really a genuflection to the knee, and immediately arose, and he did not bow his head." When Menzies began to present the tsar's letter to the Pope, the attendants pressed him down. The Pope remained seated to accept the letter, and handed it to the head master of ceremonies. "I rejoice," he said, "to see an envoy from your sovereign. On that which your sovereign asks of us in his letter, we will joyfully take action, and will quickly prepare our answer."

When the Pope finished speaking the master of ceremonies forced Menzies into a bow at the Pope's knees, and when the Pope stood and gave the blessing to all, Menzies was lowered to his knees. The envoy later spoke to Cardinal Altieri,[66] asking why they had lowered him by force. The cardinal replied that all envoys must follow the customs of the papal court and heed the masters of ceremonies.

Menzies also visited the former Swedish queen Kristina,[67] who had converted to Catholicism and lived then in Rome. "I am very pleased," said Kristina to the envoy, "that his majesty the tsar chose to communicate with the Pope. If I could take part in affairs of state in any way, I would do the same, because when I ruled over the kingdom of Sweden there was unity between us, which I will always remember."

The papal authorities began to write their response, and there they met an insurmountable difficulty. "The Pope," they told Menzies, "will write the great sovereign's name and title as they are given in the tsar's letter, *most great*,[68] which implies that he is superior to all other potentates, but we cannot call your sovereign 'tsar' because tsar and emperor are one and the same word,[69] and if we write 'tsar' the emperor and the other potentates will be angry with the Pope."

At this Menzies displayed letters from the Holy Roman emperor, Venice, and the electors of Brandenburg and Saxony, in which the sovereign was called tsar, but the Romans were not satisfied. The Pope sent to ask "What is a tsar?" "In the Slavonic language," replied Menzies, "the designation 'Russian tsar' is exactly equivalent to what the Pope, the Holy Roman emperor, the Turkish sultan, the Persian shah, the Crimean khan, the Indian mogul, the Abyssinian pretian, the Arabian zaref, the Bulgarian kolman, the Peloponnesian despot, the Babylonian caliph, and others each call themselves." "How does one translate 'tsar' into Latin?" Menzies was asked. "It cannot be translated," the envoy responded, "but see here. Without translation you can write all the titles of the sovereign in Latin letters that I have calculated for you!"

"If the present Pope does not sufficiently honor the dignity of his majesty the tsar," Cardinal Barberini[70] told Menzies, "do not be concerned. One of our group of senior cardinals will become Pope after him, whereupon the tsar's dignity will be honored fully. We senior cardinals will dispatch a letter to the great sovereign acknowledging the fault, and will write his name and title in full. For now let not the great sovereign become angry with us because by papal authority and papal word the Pope's nephew Cardinal Altieri rules and does everything his own way for his own worldly pride, and whatever he lays on the Pope's tongue is what the Pope says."[71]

At last Menzies was summoned to the Pope for a confidential audience. "Why do you not wish to accept my letters?" asked Clement. "Our great sovereign," answered Menzies, "wrote to you in the name of God and Christian duty about helping his brother the Polish king against the common foe of all us Christians, the Turkish sultan. You, the Pope and preceptor of the church of Rome, have not displayed your love to the great sovereign, have not deigned to call him tsar. You, as Pope and preceptor of the church of Rome, should work for unification, and not for destruction." "This is not possible," said the Pope, "because my brothers the previous Popes did not do it. We have already had a session with the cardinals, and they will not let me." "If you are in any way rude to his majesty the tsar," warned Menzies, "the sovereign will write about it to other Christian sovereigns." Then the Pope rang a little silver bell and ordered the chamberlain[72] who responded to bring a gold chain with the papal arms and a rosary made from lapis lazuli. Handing these things to Menzies, he said "I give these to you as a keepsake." Menzies was given leave to depart, with the promise that the Pope would appoint an envoy to Russia to negotiate an agreement about the tsar's title.

III

RUSSIA'S RELATIONS WITH THE ORTHODOX EAST

GREECE

We have seen the vitality which the needs of the Russian church, such as the correction of books and the Nikon affair, imparted to Moscow's relations with Greece. We have noted, too, the important role Paisios Ligarides played in the Nikon afffair, and that he wished to leave Moscow upon its conclusion. We do not know if it was voluntary or involuntary, but he remained in Moscow. In the summer of 1667 he petitioned the sovereign. "For seven years, great sovereign, I have served you in Moscow. I received a salary of eighteen altyns and four dengas a day, but I cannot support myself and my household on this." The petition was not granted, and it was ordered that Ligarides continue receiving his previous salary.[1]

In evidence of his service Ligarides presented a letter to the tsar in which wrote of a certain prophecy, found in the Life of Andrei the Holy Fool, which said that a fair-haired race would take possession of

Constantinople. Paisios, of course, applied this prophecy to Russia, and gave a similar interpretation to the phrase "Prince Mosokh the Russet," in which he saw the word Muscovite.[2] Nonetheless Ligarides was not fated to study the interpretation of prophecies peacefully in Moscow. In 1668 Patriarch Nektarios of Jerusalem wrote to the tsar saying "We have authentic news that Paisios Ligarides is no metropolitan at all, no hierarch, no preceptor, no prelate, no pastor, because many years ago he abandoned his diocese, and by the rules of the holy fathers was stripped of his episcopal rank. Among the Orthodox he is Orthodox, but the Latins call him their own. In fact the Roman Pope gets two hundred efimoks a year from him, and because Paisios gathered these alms for him, the Pope could send a fierce wolf in the person of his nephew against island of Chios."[3]

It is clear that the letter failed to provoke any action because soon after its receipt this instruction was given. "The great sovereign welcomes Metropolitan Paisios of Gaza and orders him given his salary and a food allowance of one hundred rubles. His house is to be inspected and all necessary repairs made. Furthermore, no duty is to be taken on wines which he buys in Archangel."

Whatever the truth of the matter, so as not to be troubled by further denunciations, Ligarides asked help from Logothete Constantine of Constantinople. He wrote that enemies slandered him and brought condemnations unjustly. "I have not spent my life in voluptuousness, drunkenness, and lechery," wrote Ligarides. "From my youth I have loved wisdom. At great effort and expense I have sailed the seas from love of learning. I have been slandered and called Latin-minded and heretic, but I do not obey the Latin rule. All I have in common with Latins is a love of learning. Like them I was and am an enthusiastic admirer of the ancient Athenian philosophers Libanios and Iamblichos, good servants of God.[4] Defend me, most learned of men! Let not ignoramuses become vain and hold high opinions of themselves. Be thou my intercessor and helper in both word and deed."

The logothete showed this letter to Nektarios's successor Dositheos, who grew very angry at Ligarides because of his harsh words against his enemies and persecutors, to whom Nektarios had belonged. At this point the tsar's envoy arrived with a request that the clerics pardon Ligarides and send him a certificate of absolution. They could not decline the tsar's request, so they forwarded the dispensation to Moscow. Dositheos vengefully wrote on Ligarides's letter to the logothete "If it were not for the tsar's pious entreaty you would recognize who is dead of soul and impoverished of spirit, he who abandoned his flock without a pastor for fifteen years, or he who lays down his soul for his sheep. Aesop's fable of the goat who cursed the wolf from a high place has been fulfilled in you, for in yourself you are insignificant and stupid, inhumane and shameless, only the place where you reside is the tsar's court. It is not too late for you to become chaste."

At the end of 1672 Ligarides set out for Palestine, but stopped in Kiev. He lived there for a long time, serving the tsar by reporting on local affairs. In this capacity he reported to Matveev in 1675. "By the grace of God and the tsar," he wrote, "I have in you a most gracious patron. Help me, then, with a little gift instead of alms, and entreat them to let me serve as prelate. A great deal of money is being gathered here from everywhere, but for whom and for what reason it is gathered I do not know. Be pleased to investigate this, O brilliant protector of Kiev! Make inquiries as to what use the metropolitan's revenues are put. Rumors are flying here that Bishop Methodius has been freed and installed as metropolitan of Kiev.[5] Keep close watch and do all that you can to ensure that this does not occur, for it would lead to great strife between the clergy and the laity. Even now discord still abounds, and his recent treason was the cause of great carnage. The great central cathedral of the Holy Wisdom[6] itself cries out, for whose repair he took fourteen thousand rubles from the great sovereign. About his other selfish acts I say nothing."

Soon after this the tsar's decree arrived in Kiev instructing Ligarides to return immediately to Moscow. He interpreted this as a sign of disgrace, and once back in Moscow he wrote to the sovereign. "The prophet-tsar David sang on his ten-stringed psaltery 'Hide not thy face from thy servant; for I am in distress, make haste to answer me.'[7] Even so do I dare to proclaim unto you, illimitable tsar, turn not thy radiant face from me, lest I perish in soul and body. I grieve especially because I do not know the reason for my recall."

In January of 1676 Ligarides turned to Matveev with complaints that he was dying of hunger and thirst, that his petitions were sent around from department to department as jokes, that he was in debt because of his great and difficult journey, and that he had neither priest, deacon, cantor nor subdeacon for his religious services. "You see to everything in this richest of tsardoms, and have forgotten only about me, a dignitary of the church." This brought him to the government's attention once more, and he was granted a food allowance as before. Ligarides's interests are revealed in part by the fact that he brought the monk-priest Vissarion, former head of the Kievan schools, to Moscow from Kiev "to aid him in zealous and assiduous service of the great tsar."[8]

GEORGIA

Another Orthodox Christian country was even more unfortunate and more oppressed by the Ottomans than Greece, and long had sought aid from its co-religionists in Russia. This was Georgia. After one unsuccessful attempt during reign of Tsar Boris the Muscovite state abandoned all thought of sending its army to the Caucasus.[9] Instead it helped with money, and sent its clergy to Georgia to supervise conditions of the church and liturgy, and to advise the local clerics.

Georgian Christianity made an unfortunate impression on the Russian clergy, who themselves could not always distinguish essentials from non-essentials and were strongly attached to form, to literal observance. "Your first point of divergence from the catholic and apostolic church," said the Russian clergy to the Georgian bishops, "is that your churches are not screened off from the altars. There are no royal gates[10] anywhere, and there never have been. The altars everywhere are bare and affixed to the wall. You serve in unsanctified churches. Not one single church has a cross, nor ever did. If there are icons in a church you stick candles on the plain wall, while the icons are hung separately. It seems to us that faith in the divine icons and in the holy cross has faded among you. Moreover you do not wear the cross on your persons. If anyone has icons they are hidden, though some carry little icons at their waists on a sash. You flap your hand around in the wrong way while crossing yourselves, and when you bow, you look at heaven and not at your icons.

"Your prelates and priests use the sign of the cross to protect themselves," continued the Russians, "and do not know how to bless other people. If one of your priests decides to celebrate the liturgy he brings his vessels and vestments with him in a sack, and no one has a Gospel or cross. Some priests arrive at the church and spread a cloth on the altar, then they take up the vessels and set to work in just a cloth jacket. When they have finished their work and the sanctum is covered, they robe themselves in their vestments and begin the liturgy. After the service they order their boy to gather the vessels and chasuble from the altar and put them into a bag for them. You bishops, like your priests, perform your duties wearing the chasuble on the neck, dangling in front, and when you begin the liturgy you put the chasuble behind.

"You baptize infants with only one immersion. Confessions to spiritual fathers are little known among you, as are communions. Only at death do you give communion, and even then without confession. Everybody enters your churches wearing hats, with sabers and staves, and your bishops also bring staves into church and up to the altar. Your people begin housekeeping without a wedding, and if children come they marry. If there are no children they abandon the old wife and take another. Also, you hold weddings during the fasts of Lent and the Annunciation."

In one place the Russian clerics witnessed a curious incident. Between matins and mass the local clergy entered the square carrying an image of St. George, which they placed on a pillar. On the church roof across from the image sat a peasant, who donned another image of St. George and began to speak to the whole assembly. "Listen to me!" he said. "Just now I spent the night in the church, and St. George spoke to me, saying 'oppress not my people, who believe in my name.'" The peasant then began to prophesy about the harvest, and about who would die that year. "What is this you have here," asked the Russians, "a holy man? Is he literate?" "No, he isn't," answered the Georgians, "but it runs in the family. If one dies, another member of the family starts to communicate St. George's words to the world."

We have seen that in the reign of Tsar Michael, Tsar Teimuraz of Kakhetia became a subject of Russia.[11] An ambassador from Teimuraz arrived in Moscow in the spring of 1647 and presented this letter to Tsar Alexis. "As I and my son and all the Georgian land lived as subjects of your father, so now I bow in homage to you, great sovereign. By the protection and beneficence of your father our Georgian realm was kept alive and intact. Now once again, if you do not regard us with favor and do not support us, our neighboring countries will destroy us utterly. 'You gave yourselves as subjects to the Muscovite sovereign and he betrayed you, he did not defend you,' they will say.

"Now I, Teimuraz the tsar, and my son David, give ourselves and the whole Georgian land to you in bondage. I will send my grandson Grigory as a bondsman to you in Moscow, but for my elder grandson Joasaph I would ask that you graciously bestow one of your sisters, an imperial princess, upon him in marriage. May it further please you that metropolitans be sent to us, as many as you may deem appropriate, for the Georgian realm belongs to God and to you, and its faith thus would be corrected as it has been in your own great realm."

Teimuraz and His Son David

At this time, and even more in the following year of 1648, Moscow had no time to spare on Georgian affairs.[12] In 1649 a new Georgian embassy arrived. "I wanted to send my grandson Nikolai (!)[13] to you, great sovereign," wrote Teimuraz, "but when the Persians heard of this they began to attack my country from three sides. For a year I could not send you my grandson, for the Persians do not let us pass to Shemakha. May it please you, great sovereign, to grant this favor, and dispatch your own people to bring my grandson to be your slave."

In 1650 Nikifor Tolochanov set out to Georgia with Russia's response to this proposal. The envoy brought a gift of sables to Teimuraz. The Georgian tsar bowed low yet expressed dissatisfaction. "Previously they sent me sums of twenty thousand efimoks at a time. Do you now bring nothing for me?"

"No money has been sent to you," answered the envoy, "because the great sovereign had no information about you, such as where you have been since your overthrow by the khan of Tiflis.[14] As your loyalty and service are made known to the great sovereign, he will be increasingly gracious to you."

"Look about you," responded Teimuraz, "and see how I have been devastated by the khan of Tiflis at the shah's order. In the past the sovereign's ambassadors visited me in Kakhetia. They viewed all the buildings, the monasteries and churches. Now mosques stand where once there were churches. May the great sovereign stand up for the house of God and for me, his slave."

Tolochanov revealed the main purpose of his embassy to Teimuraz, to take his grandson, the tsarevich Nikolai, with him to Moscow. "Will the great sovereign," asked Teimuraz, "give his sister to him in marriage?"

"We have no instructions about that," answered the envoy. "Who but God and the great sovereign can know such a great secret matter? If God wills, and the tsar is so minded, the marriage will take place, but if it is not the will of God and the thought of the tsar, how can it be? You need only let your grandson go with us, and carry out your duties to the great sovereign."

"If I send my grandson," continued Teimuraz, "and the sovereign does not deign to cleanse my country Kakhetia of its enemies, does not send troops, for what purpose is my grandson's journey?"

"We cannot send troops to you," answered Tolochanov, "because the mountains are covered with snow. They are high, with great clefts in them, and troops cannot cross them or convey their artillery and supplies. Your country is barren from the shah's depredations, and if our troops marched to you they would die of hunger in your lands. Instead the tsar will send treasure to you, more than you can imagine, if you now fulfill your obligations and send your grandson back with us. Besides this, the sovereign will send grand ambassadors to Shah Abbas advising him to give up Kakhetia as a fraternal gesture. If he does not yield, we think that the great sovereign will send his army across the Caspian Sea to attack and decimate the shah's cities. Whatever the tsar decides, you must perform your duties. If you send your other grandson Vlavursak with us also, the great sovereign will award him favor according to his gracious consideration."

"I will not give up Vlavursak to anyone," said Teimuraz. "I have no one else to give me a home, and no one to remember my soul in prayer."

"You have told us that the Tiflis khan destroyed you," suggested the envoy, "so if there is nowhere in Georgia for you to live, come yourself to the great tsar. We have been ordered to receive you and your subjects."

"When the time is right for me I will go to the sovereign's grace, but for now I will remain here," answered Teimuraz.

All these conversations ended with Teimuraz declining to send his grandson to Moscow. Tsar Alexander of Imeretia expressed his loyalty to the great sovereign more strongly, swearing fealty to Alexis in Tolochanov's presence. "Tsar Teimuraz did not send his grandson with you," said Alexander, "but if I had my son Bagrat and my brother Mamuk with me I would let both of them go to the great tsar. If it pleases the sovereign, let him send his viceroy to the city of Kutaisi. If I had someone to see to my patrimony of Imeretia, I would go myself to see the sovereign's most radiant eyes."

"I have committed myself," wrote Alexander in his letter to Alexis, "and so have my son and brother, all the clergy and privy councillors, the warriors and inhabitants of all the country, to live under the high hand of your great sovereignty as perpetual and unchanging subjects, to the second and third generation. May you, great sovereign, forbear to disdain me. May you defend me from infidel foes, lest the people of my country fall into unbelief.

"Previously the Dadianis were my subjects," Alexander continued, "but several years ago they seceded.[15] They became subjects of the Turkish sultan and live together with the infidels. They come to the aid of the infidel army, they ravage the countryside and wage war upon me. The Don Cossacks sail the Black Sea and wage war on Muslims, but do no harm to

Orthodox Christians. The Dadianis trick the cossacks, acting as if they wish to join them in making war against the infidels, yet once they have lured them into their country they capture them and sell them to the Turks. Some they send as gifts to the Turkish sultan, who rewards them. The Dadianis steal Christians from my lands as well as from their own to send to the Persian shah, asking aid from him. The Dadiani leader gave his own sister to the shah and renounced the Christian faith, for which he received money and aid from the shah. This same Dadiani leader sent another sister to Khan Rustem of Tiflis to induce him to turn his forces against me, and Rustem has sent his army against my country many times.

"Now I beg the favor of the great tsar, so that I might attack the Dadianis by boat from the Black Sea. In this manner I will take vengeance upon them for the ruin of my lands, and separate them from their infidel allies. I will establish them once more in the Orthodox faith, and bring them to live under my authority as before. The Dadiani leader sent word to me that he desires to be my subject again and would come to me himself if I would send him my son as a hostage. I sent my son to him, but he did not come to me, nor did he release my son. 'I will release your son to you,' he said, 'when you become the subject of the Turkish sultan.' Furthermore, when my brother went hunting the Dadianis captured him, and to this day they hold him prisoner.

"Should the great sovereign grant me his favor by helping me free my son and brother from slavery, when they are freed he may order them brought to Moscow or released to me, according to his sovereign will. He would favor me further if he ordered his seal sent to me, so that in all the land the tsar's command might be truer. Yet again the sovereign might favor me were payment sent for my privy councillors and military officers so that they not go hungry and horseless, but have the strength to stand against their enemies, and also were he to order military supplies sent me, to protect my land from enemies."

Georgian rulers began visiting Moscow in 1653 when Teimuraz's eight-year-old grandson Nikolai Davydovich arrived with his mother Elena Leontievna. Soon after the grandson came the grandfather also. When the sovereign's envoy Zhidovinov brought cash and sables to Teimuraz in 1656, he met him in Imeretia. "The Persian shah has driven me from my country," said the poor old man to the envoy, "so that now I live in Imeretia with my son-in-law Tsar Alexander, who gives me no aid. I am poor in all things, and dare not travel to my own country for fear of enemies. I will go now, with my wife, my grandson and granddaughter, and all my people, to serve the great sovereign in Moscow. Some three hundred people will set out with me."

In January of 1657 the secretaries of the Chancellery for Foreign Affairs interrogated three Georgians who arrived from Tushi to discover why they had come to Moscow. "We have come to petition the great sovereign to welcome us for the sake of our Orthodox Christian faith, and to take us under his high hand as subjects forever."

"Before this," asked the Russians, "of whom were you subjects, and who were your leaders? Was your faith Christian? How far did you live from Terek, and in what places? Do you have cities? How many military officers do you have, and what are your wars like? Who are your neighbors? Do you suffer oppression from the Persian shah, or from the Kumyks or the Cherkess?[16] Does grain grow in your land? Lastly, if the great sovereign graciously consents to take you under his high hand, by what terms do you wish to be his subjects?"

"We wish to give ourselves in perpetual bondage to the great sovereign," the Georgians replied. "Wherever he orders us to serve, we are ready. Our faith is Christian. We live in fortified places in the mountains of three countries, but we have no cities or leaders. Each of us sees to his own village. We have eight thousand troops. Our wars are fought with bows and spears, with everyone in armor. From Terek to Tushi is a four-day fast journey. Previously we were subjects of Tsar Teimuraz, but since the Persian shah ruined him we have lived on our own."

At last, in the year 1658, Tsar Teimuraz Davydovich himself arrived in Moscow. During his presentation the great sovereign ordered Teimuraz to approach the throne and desired him to rise. At this Teimuraz begged that the great sovereign give him his hand to kiss, but the great sovereign refused. "In the Gospels," he explained, "it is written 'Wherever men are gathered in My name, there am I also among them.' Let us give praise to all-merciful God, let us kiss upon the mouth in Christ's name, for you are of the holy Christian faith."

"Great tsar, I am your slave," said Teimuraz. "It is not fitting for me to kiss such an august and radiant sovereign on the mouth."

"By God's will you are our subject," replied Alexis, "but you are a tsar of our holy Christian faith, and by Christ's commandment we shall kiss upon the mouth." Then Teimuraz with great trepidation kissed the sovereign on the mouth.

The tsar charged Boyar Khilkov to translate for Teimuraz. "From what Turkish tsar came your war and devastation," asked the boyar, "and how long ago was this? What kind of exile did he force upon you, and what sort of ruin upon your country?"

Teimuraz. About thirty years ago the boyar Georgy Sios betrayed me. He converted to Islam, became a subject to the Turkish sultan Amurat, and sent his army against me. I led my own troops against him, and fought a war against the traitors and Turks, between my own land and that of Kartli. There were forty thousand Turks and traitors, and I had only about three thousand men, but God protected me. I defeated my betrayer and the Turks. I defeated the Turks not by force of numbers but by the power of the Cross.

Here Teimuraz showed the mark of a saber blow upon his cross. "Since then," he continued, "I have undergone no persecution from the Turk, nor have I had any exchanges of any kind with him."

Khilkov. At the time when you, Tsar Teimuraz Davydovich, petitioned the great sovereign to become his subject, what sort of ruin had the Persian shah loosed upon your country, and in what year was this?

Teimuraz. It was eleven years ago that I petitioned the great sovereign to become his subject. The present Shah Abbas had attacked my realm, and I fought against him. In that battle my son was killed, my daughter was taken by force, and two cities were destroyed. In the reign of the previous Shah Abbas I endured much devastation also.[17] Although my country suffered this ruin, I sent my mother and my younger son, the tsarevich Alexander, to serve as hostages to the shah.

"When my mother brought her grandson to the former shah," Teimuraz continued, "she begged him to accept her grandson as a hostage, and take tribute from our country instead of destroying it. The shah told my mother to send for her other grandson Leon also, and that he, the shah, would decide which grandson to keep as hostage and which to let go. My mother did this. She brought Leon also, but the shah did not release my mother or the children. He sent word to her saying that should she convert to Islam he would regard her as his own mother. She responded that she would never abandon the Christian faith. At this the shah put her under guard and ordered torture. First he ordered her nipples cut off, and then he had her pricked all over with harpoons of tempered iron, and cut at the joints. My mother suffered to the death for Christ from these tortures, and a Frenchman stole her body and brought it to me. The shah also had both of my sons castrated, and even now he keeps them with him.

"After this," Teimuraz went on, "the shah once more sent his army against me. I fought him and defeated him, after which I left for Imeretia and lived there for two years.[18] Then I joined forces with the Imeretians and Dadianis and drove the shah's men from my land and cleansed the land of their presence, but in that year the shah sent his troops again and I fled for a second time to Imeretia. The shah ordered that all Georgia be captured and devastated, to exterminate all vestiges of Christianity. Once more I drove out the Persians and began to rule my country as before. Then eleven years ago, in the reign of the present shah, two boyars betrayed me. They brought their daughters to the shah, converted to Islam, and led the shah's troops against me. I fought them, but they killed my son Davyd in battle, and drove me out. Because of this persecution I have lived in Imeretia since that time."

Khilkov. How large is your land, and how many inhabited and ruined settlements did you leave behind?

Teimuraz. My country is ten days' journey in length and the same in width. It has a total of seven large cities and many small ones, but they are ruined and empty. The boyars who betrayed me live in two cities, which are inhabited, but the other cities are all destroyed. A few people live in Krem, the capital, and others live in villages. Khan Rustem now rules over all my country. He was a Georgian, but converted to Islam.

Khilkov. How long ago did you bring the Dadianian and Gurian lands[19] under the high hand of the great sovereign? Did they swear fealty? Are they now subjects of the great sovereign as before? Whose men are they, and who governs them?

Teimuraz. For as long as the Dadiani tsar Leonty lived we endured incessant war and hostilities with him, but when Tsar Leonty died, my kinsman Vamyk was elected to take his place. He betrothed his daughter to my grandson Leonty Davydovich, and kissed the cross in fealty to the great sovereign with all his followers. Their land consists of four large cities, which stand in defensible places on the Black Sea. Five or six of their ships can set sail at one time, and the population numbers about forty thousand all told. Their wars are fought with sabers and pikes. They have arquebuses but only light artillery.

"The Gurian land is small," Teimuraz went on, "and has kissed the cross in fealty to the great sovereign. It lies between Imeretia and Dadiania. The Imeretian tsar Alexander governs the Dadianian and Gurian lands by council. They do not give him tribute, but accept his rule from friendship.

These lands lie beyond my country along the shah's borders. If it pleased the sovereign to order my land freed of traitors, I do not know whether the shah would support my traitors or not, for the shah's realm is not my concern. For myself, I gladly would become a subject of the sovereign were he to order my land freed and offer me his troops. Then I would gather an army uniting the sovereign's forces with my own and with the Imeretians, Dadianis and Gurians, and begin to take back my land. If the shah's forces attacked me, I would defend myself against them. When it pleases the great sovereign to let me proceed, let him write to the Imeretian ruler, and to the Dadianis and Gurians, telling them to give me troops for this purpose. Further, let him deign to notify the shah that I am true to the Orthodox Christian faith, and am a subject of the great sovereign. Then the shah will not attack and destroy my land, for the great sovereign will defend me."

Khilkov. The great sovereign has instructed me to ask how many military servitors you need. Through what provinces, and how far, must they travel to your country? Where will they get horses and grain, that they may not die of hunger on the long road, and then later in your forces? Finally, will not the Persian shah go to war on behalf of those who betrayed you?

Teimuraz. I need a good commander, and about thirty thousand mounted troops. Supplies may be had from Astrakhan on the way to my country, and once in my country there will be plenty for you. As to whether the shah will go to war for those who betrayed me, that I do not know. When I gave myself as subject to Tsar Michael Fedorovich, the father of the present great sovereign, he sent me his writ under a golden seal promising that the great sovereign would defend me from all my foes. Thereafter I received many documents from the tsar instructing me to send my grandson to Moscow. I sent my grandson, and now I myself have come to beseech that the great sovereign bestow his troops upon me. If the great tsar refuses to come to my defense, the Imeretian tsar and the Dadianis and Gurians will heed my experience and seek another sovereign to save them from Muslim persecution. All of us have but one petition, which is that the great sovereign grant us troops and come to our defense. Even the lawless cossacks petitioned the great sovereign to take them under his mighty hand. The great sovereign granted this to the cossacks for the sake of the Orthodox Christian faith. He deigned to take them under his mighty hand and to sever them from the Polish king. In my own country I was a tsar of the Orthodox Christian faith, and for this I gave myself as subject to the great sovereign, that he may be pleased to defend us.

The boyar Prince Alexis Nikitich Trubetskoy visited Teimuraz with the tsar's response to these requests. "The great sovereign," said the boyar, "is currently at war with the Polish and Swedish kings, and many of his troops are now stationed along those borders. For this reason, Tsar Teimuraz Davydovich, you must return to your country of Georgia and rule your tsardom as before, even though you are oppressed and in need because of your enemies. When the great tsar has dealt with his own foes he will send his troops to you, for he does not wish to see you persecuted and ruined. For now he has instructed me to give you six thousand rubles in cash, and three thousand in sables."

"It is the will of the great sovereign," acceded Teimuraz. "I made the journey here in hopes of gaining the sovereign's favor and protection, yet now he has dismissed me empty-handed. When I set out from my home at the great tsar's order, I was not told that all his troops were in active service. Had I supposed that the great tsar would not offer his troops in my defense, I would have stayed at home."

Trubetskoy. You say that the sovereign has let you return to your own land with nothing, but you are getting six thousand rubles and sables worth another three thousand. You can make the journey back your own country with this grant, and you need not anger the great sovereign in this way.

Teimuraz. Even one sable from the great sovereign is precious to me, but in the reign of his sovereign father I received grants of twenty thousand efimoks, and sables without number, even when I was not here. It would be better for me to give out the sovereign's grant to my own liking than to go to my own land and fall into Muslim hands. When the Turks, Persians, and mountain-dwelling Cherkess heard that I was going to the great sovereign they grew frightened. The Cherkess lay in wait along the road. They attacked me in the mountains and killed my men. I barely escaped. Having lost my troops I came to the great sovereign by stealth, day and night. I arrived and laid my head at the foot of the great tsar and pleaded for my grandson. When I saw his sovereign eyes I thought that I had risen from the dead, and that whatever I desired, I would receive. Now my journey and my petition have come to nothing. My traitorous mountain Cherkess laugh at me and raze my land to its foundations. If I am to be abandoned into false Ottoman hands and my Christian soul destroyed, it would be better for me to die here in the Orthodox Christian faith, for there is no reason for me to go to my own land. If the Ottomans destroy me, a tsar of the Orthodox Christian faith, and devastate my tsardom, whom will God call to account? What honor will there be for the great sovereign if they destroy me and my family and eradicate the Orthodox Christian faith? For this Orthodox Christian faith my little Georgian land and I have stood firm against the Turks and Persians, and have fought them without fearing the numberless Ottoman host. If only the sovereign would favor me and order his troops to accompany me!

Trubetskoy. The sovereign will order his troops to accompany you, and will write to tell the shah not to attack you and not to devastate Georgia. Go now and live as best you can in your own country, and later the great sovereign will send troops to you. Upon that you may depend without any doubt.

Teimuraz. If I cannot prevail upon the tsar's grace and receive aid now, when I am here in person, then later on, without personal contact, there is nothing to hope for. Once before the great sovereign wrote to the shah about me, but Shah Abbas devastated my land and drove me out.

Teimuraz departed. In 1660 he set out for Georgia with his grandson the tsarevich Nikolai Davydovich, the boy's mother, and the tsar's envoy Miakinin. When they reached Astrakhan they received terrible news. The Imeretian tsar Alexander had died of food poisoning. Sensing death's approach he set his son Bagrat on the throne and ordered him to marry Teimuraz's granddaughter. This was done, but the young tsar held the throne for only three months. Alexander's widow, who was Teimuraz's daughter, did not want to see her stepson as tsar. She captured him and put out his eyes, then married the Georgian Vakhtang, with whom she began to rule Imeretia. She was said to have done this after talking at length with the Catholicos.[20]

Unrest broke out, and Tsar Teimuraz fled to the Persian city of Tiflis. An Imeretian boyar named Eristov brought in the Turks, and exiled the tsaritsa and her husband to the Black Sea city of Apkhazit. Then another piece of news arrived, that Teimuraz had been taken and brought to the shah. Despite the troubles in Georgia, Tsarevich Nikolai left Astrakhan and settled in Tushi. In 1666 he returned to Moscow, and in 1674 again was allowed to depart to his homeland.

PERSIA

Georgia could not wait for Tsar Alexis to deal with his European enemies at his leisure before starting a war in faraway Transcaucasia. The Georgian tsars felt that the Muscovite ruler should defend them from the Persians, who were their principal enemies, but Persia and Russia had enjoyed friendly relations for many years and did not want them disrupted. In 1650

Mahmet-Kulybek, an ambassador of Shah Abbas, arrived in Moscow bringing a gift of four hundred batmans of niter from the shah [a batman was a Central Asian weight equal to 12 puds or 196.56 kg]. In a meeting with the boyars the ambassador began with long-standing complaints about thieving cossacks. He said that they had stolen trade beads valued at three thousand rubles, and two thousand rubles cash, from the shah's merchants at sea near Baku. These pirates were driven ashore where the local authorities confiscated their stolen property but did not return it to Persia. Thus the great sovereign should return the stolen goods and execute the cossack thieves. "When I was in Terek just now," said the ambassador, "I myself saw these cossack criminals, and when I came to Astrakhan, the khan of Shemakha wrote to tell me that pillaging cossacks had come again to his realm and robbed many of the shah's men."

"In the past," responded the boyars, "cossack lawlessness caused no quarreling and ill-will between the great sovereigns because the cossacks in question are not from Astrakhan, nor from Terek. They come from the Don to commit piracy, and they pillage and kill the tsar's people as well as the shah's. Now the cossack transgressors have been intercepted at sea and put in prison. All Persian goods found on them have been ordered given back to your representatives, whom the khan of Shemakha is sending to Terek, and the cossack thieves have been ordered put to death in the presence of your ambassador. So far, though, the khan has not sent anyone, making it his fault that the goods have not been returned. The governors of Terek wanted to execute the cossacks in your presence, but you did not agree." "This is all very well," said the ambassador, "but in an earlier letter the tsar promised the shah that there would be no more thieves." "There was no such thing in the letter," replied the boyars. "Our great realm is not without thieves, and where there are thieves, it is better to seek them out together."

Then the ambassador complained that the customs officials in Astrakhan and other cities were overvaluing goods in order to inflate the duties owed. During the reign of Tsar Michael they took lower duties, and more merchants came from Persia. The boyars reminded him that no loss had come to the Persians from the inflated duties because the higher the duty, the more expensively they sold their wares, passing on the customs charges to the subjects of the great tsar. Furthermore, they said, the shah was rich in niter. If he would order twenty thousand puds sent each year from his domains to the Muscovite realm, the great tsar would send copper or sables to pay for the niter. "Our sovereign," answered the ambassador, "will not stand in the great tsar's way in the matter of niter, nor of anything else. Let your sovereign lay this task upon me, and I will speak to the great shah."

At last the talk came to Georgia and Teimuraz. The ambassador explained the matter in this way. "Teimuraz's sister married the old Shah Abbas, and Teimuraz's daughter married the father of the present shah, Sefi.[21] Thus Teimuraz is our sovereign's man. The disputes between Teimuraz of Georgia and Rustem, khan of Tiflis, stem from the fact that they are closely related, of one lineage. They are descended from a grand prince of Georgia. Khan Rustem is now the shah's subject and a Muslim. Half the Georgian land follows him, and the other half follows Teimuraz. This engenders a feud between them. The shah is angry at Rustem because he plundered the Georgian land and killed the tsarevich. In his turn Teimuraz abandoned his own country and now lives with his son-in-law the Imeretian tsar, and does not write to the shah or petition him about anything. If he were to ask, the shah would order him to live in his own land as before. I will report on this matter to the great shah, and in goodwill for the great tsar the shah will return Georgia to Teimuraz and install him as its overseer once more."

The promise concerning the cossack brigands was kept. Thirty-nine of them were imprisoned in Terek, of whom three, Ataman Kondraty Ivanov Kobyzenko and two of his chief henchmen, were executed in the presence of ambassador Mahmet-Kulybek. Four died in prison, and the rest were sent to Moscow. Most came from cities in the eastern part of the Ukraine, three were Muscovites, one each came from Great Novgorod, Kostroma, Lukh, Romanov and Perm, one was Georgian, and three were said to be from Constantinople!

In 1653 high ambassadors set out for Persia, headed by the lord-in-waiting Prince Ivan Lobanov-Rostovsky and the table attendant Ivan Komynin. The ambassadors carried complaints against Khan Khosrev of Shemakha, who long had threatened war against Astrakhan and Terek on account of the cossacks. In 1652 he wrote to the governor of Astrakhan that the Grebensk Cossacks not only were robbing Persian merchants but had set up a fortified town in the Dagestan region and settled military servitors in it. From there they allegedly seized control of the Cherkess road.[22] Khosrev wrote the governor that by the shah's order he was gathering an army to take the cossack town, and then march against Astrakhan and Terek.

Besides this, Russian merchants complained that Khan Khosrev abused them in Shemakha, as did the officials in Gilian. They had held them for more than two years, oppressed and taxed them, and perpetrated all manner of offences, violence and damages against them. They beat them and robbed them, while Persian merchants went free and protected everywhere in the Muscovite realm.

Further, the shah had the habit of welcoming and helping Russian traitors. The tsar's subject Cheban, a murza of the Nogay Tatars,[23] left Astrakhan for Terek, and from there began to roam great distances through Kumyk lands, acting in disobedience of the great tsar. In 1651 the tsar's forces moved against him, Prince Mutsal Cherkassky and his musketeer captains joining with Nogay, Edisan and Cherkess leaders. When the sovereign's forces met up with Cheban they were betrayed by another subject of the great sovereign, his sworn bondsman Surkai, shevkal of Tarki.[24] Pooling his resources with Cheban, this turncoat began to attack the tsar's forces, while those troops did not dare to fight Surkai without the sovereign's order.

Then Surkai and Kaganali, a murza of the Andreevsk Kumyks, attacked the little Russian fortified town of Sunshinsk, near Baraguny, and also the tent villages[25] belonging to Prince Mutsal Cherkassky. Local towns sent troops to aid the shevkal, five hundred men from Shemakha and three hundred from Derbent, and with them two cannons. Allied with the Kumyks, the men from Shemakha and Derbent killed and severely wounded many of the tsar's troops, and took others prisoner. They captured the leaders of the Baraguny Tatars, burned Sunshinsk, and took more than three thousand horses, five hundred camels, ten thousand cattle and fifteen thousand sheep.

The great sovereign expressed his hope that all this was done without the approval of Shah Abbas, and his further hope that these incidents would persuade the shah to replace Khosrev as khan of Shemakha and punish him in order that there might be no more feuds between the two great sovereigns, and also would induce him to order the prisoners and all stolen goods given back. The high ambassadors also demanded that the shah give Teimuraz back his land and punish those who had been devastating Georgia.

In his rejoinder to all these complaints the shah ordered his privy councillors to tell the ambassadors "The late Shah Abbas ordered one guard post constructed on the Terek, and ordered no other cities built anywhere. Yet the subjects of your sovereign have built cities there without permission, and have robbed and killed our merchants. Consequently the dispute began from your side, and Khan Khosrev of Shemakha justifiably sent his people to burn out those cities. After Khan Khosrev died the shah ordered his successor, Khan Migir-Aley, and also Shevkal Surkai, no longer to quarrel with your sovereign's men. Furthermore, your sovereign must forbid his people to attack Persians who travel by sea. Shevkal Surkai, Cheban Murza and the leaders of the Baraguny Tatars transferred their allegiance to the great shah of their own will, and by our law whoever has come to us voluntarily may not be returned by force. If they themselves choose to serve your sovereign, the shah will not fight for them. Our officials have been ordered to return the bribes they have taken from Russians. When the great tsar orders Surkai's nephew and the Persian merchants there imprisoned to be released from Terek, the Russian merchants will be released from Shemakha.

"As regards Georgia," the privy councillors continued, "Tsar Teimuraz's wickedness forced earlier shahs to send troops into his land more than once to devastate it and drive him out. Teimuraz slavishly admitted his guilt to these earlier shahs, sent them his children, and had his provinces returned. This caused no ill will between the earlier shahs and the great Russian sovereigns. In past years Teimuraz again undertook indecent, contentious and evil deeds, and the shah sent troops against him, killing his son in battle and driving him out. If Teimuraz sends his grandson to the shah to acknowledge and atone for his guilt, once again he will receive his domain."

"From ancient times," objected the ambassadors, "the Russian tsars held not only the land where Terek and Sunshinsk are located, but also the land where Tarki lies. We were free to build cities there, for the late Shah Abbas himself invited Tsar Michael Fedorovich to do so. Concerning the robbery of merchants, nothing came to light during the investigation in Astrakhan. If the cossacks really robbed them, they brought that misfortune on themselves because they traveled in caravans together with Kumyks from Tarki and other felons. It is well known that the Terek and Grebensk Cossacks constantly dispute with the Kumyks. In the past merchants did not travel into the mountains without making arrangements with the Terek governor, and no one robbed them. The Kumyk shevkals and murzas have been bondsmen of our great sovereigns from ancient times, and earlier Persian shahs did not enter Kumyk territories. The present shah should not enter either, nor bring about bad relations with the great tsar over this.

Finally, the Baraguny murzas became subjects of the shah against their will. The Georgian land follows the Orthodox Christian faith of the Greek dispensation, and from ancient times the Georgian tsars have been subjects of our great sovereigns."

"No!" the shah's privy councillors retorted. "Teimuraz and all Georgia are subject to our Persian shahs. It is true that the late Shah Abbas promised Tsar Michael Fedorovich to protect Georgia out of brotherly friendship and love, and now if Teimuraz himself comes to the shah or sends his grandson, the shah will return his land to him. We will not carry any further report to the great shah concerning Teimuraz and Georgia, because he ordered us to answer you openly and in full, and to settle the matter without evasion, and all other matters also. Our merchants in Muscovy are not free, but held in confinement under guard, and wherever they want to go, guards follow them." "This is not done as oppression," answered the ambassadors, "but for safety."

The shah remained inflexible. Only one decision was changed: Abbas ordered the release of all Russian merchants held in Persia. One evening just before their departure the shah summoned the Russian ambassadors to join him in the cool of the garden. First they were treated to sugars and fruits. Then a golden vessel set with stones was brought before the shah, containing the grape drink called *chikhir*. The shah drank to the sovereign's health and asked the ambassadors "Does my brother, your great sovereign, have such a grape drink?" "The great tsar," answered the ambassadors, "enjoys many sorts of beverages, and he has drinks made from grapes, such as rumney, rhenish, and others, though none is exactly like this." Before the shah stood various flowers in a golden vessel. Abbas took up the blooms and asked "Are there such flowers in Muscovy?" "Indeed," replied the ambassadors, "the great sovereign has blossoms like this, peonies with curling petals and a multitude of other flowers of many different sorts."

Musicians played on domras, gusli, and violins[26] before the shah, who asked the ambassadors "How does my brother, your great sovereign, amuse himself? Are there such instruments in his realm?" "Our great sovereign," responded the ambassadors, "has many kinds of instruments, and many capable people who can play them, but the great tsar does not amuse himself with such frivolity. He passes the time with spiritual things. Organs play in his presence, giving praise to God with polyphonic harmonies, and he himself is skilled in many most wise philosophical sciences and valiant studies. He also is greatly inclined to the knightly arts of war because of his sovereign rank and propensities. He enjoys going into the field, and he orders his courtiers to practice the martial arts. They display their skills with pikestaffs before him, and shoot from bows and pistols."

The shah's stand regarding Georgia was only too clear. The matter could be pursued only by force of arms, and for Russia in the reign of Alexis Mikhailovich this was no possibility at all. When the Turkish war began, Russia joined Poland in trying to bring the shah into an alliance with themselves against the Turk, but the shah answered that he could not break his peace with the sultan without reason. Thus Moscow retained only a commercial interest in Persia. Persian traders constantly arrived in the capital with Eastern luxury goods, which were considered indispensable for the splendor of the tsar's court.

THE COMPANY OF PERSIAN ARMENIANS

In 1660 there arrived in Moscow an Armenian trader named Zakhar Saradov.[27] He brought great gifts for the tsar: a throne richly decorated with diamonds, rubies and sapphires, mother-of-pearl, Eastern turquoise, and Turkish enamel, valued at 22,589 rubles, a gold ring set with diamonds, a silver brazier with a little silver flask for heating aromatics, fifteen flasks of *sharap* from Shiraz, which the shah drinks, four little vials of attar of roses, three little phials of scent, a small phial or bottle of another spirit,[28] twelve zolotniks of Eastern perfume and twelve fronds of the palm tree, which the tsar carries in his right hand during the ceremony of the patriarch's Palm Sunday procession on a donkey.[29]

Officials interrogated the Armenian in the Chancellery for Foreign Affairs. Could he obtain textiles sewn with precious stones and other luxury goods in his country for the great sovereign, they asked. Could they acquire Indian birds and master craftsmen, artists to illuminate manuscripts in gold ink, master goldsmiths and silversmiths, and diamond cutters who cut many different types of stones?

The Armenian answered that he and his father could obtain all these things for the great sovereign because their agents traveled the whole country. They could order a rich saddle-cloth, which could be made for fifty thousand rubles. They could import birds from India which speak in the Indian language, but could not import animals because they must cross two seas. There were many skilled craftsmen in the shah's realm, and he, the trader, would summon them to Muscovy. He and his father were happy to work for the great Christian sovereign and to serve him in any way possible, not just for profit. The shah allowed them to trade duty-free, but the shah was of the Muslim faith and they were Christians. Thus they rejoiced to serve and work for the great tsar.

We have seen how during the reign of Tsar Michael the English and other Western peoples begged the Muscovite government for the right to trade freely along the Volga with Persia.[30] Now a similar situation arose but in reverse, related to the company of Armenian merchants who lived in Persia. In 1666 the Armenian Grigory Lusikov appealed to the tsar. "The shah granted our company the right to export raw silk from Persia by sea," he said, "across whatever country we wish. For many years we have carried it across Turkey, which grows rich from our customs duties. After talking with my partners I have come to you, great sovereign, to beg that you grant us leave to transport raw silk and other Persian goods across your nation of Muscovy, and thence by sea to Germany, and then allow us to return again with German goods and gold and silver coins from beyond the sea, through Archangel to Persia."

Lusikov continued in more detail. "If we sell silk in Astrakhan," he proposed, "we will pay a duty of five copecks on the ruble. If we do not sell it, let the silk be valued at twenty rubles per pud, take five copecks per ruble of its value, and let us go on to Moscow. If we sell it in Moscow, take a duty of five copecks per ruble, and if we do not sell it, value it at thirty rubles per pud, take duty of five copecks per ruble, and let us go on to Archangel. If we sell it in Archangel, take a duty of five copecks, and if we do not sell it, value a pud at forty rubles and take a duty of five copecks per ruble and let us go on across the sea to Germany. On whatever Persian goods are destined for German hands, take from us a duty as is customary. Also take the usual duty on those German goods which we bring to Archangel. Your subjects will profit greatly from this trade in silk and other wares. All foreigners who now sail to Turkey to buy this silk and other wares will come to Archangel instead, and their customs duties will bring great revenues into your treasury."

In May of 1667 Ordin-Nashchokin and the company signed an agreement based on the conditions set out in their offer. At the Armenians' request the Englishman Bryan[31] was named the company's agent in Moscow. As their agent he was obliged to send trustworthy men to Astrakhan, Novgorod, Archangel and other border cities and deal honorably and truly with the great sovereign and his boyars, councillors and officials, in every petition and commercial matter relating to the company, to present petitions assiduously and to notify them of all dealings and offences, without making any allowances for the company's enemies, and to send written reports about company affairs to its members in Persia, whenever a messenger was available. For these services the company promised to pay Bryan a percentage of its sales at the rate of a grosha per ruble. If the company brought silk or other goods to the agent himself for sale, they promised pay him from these goods at the rate of one grosha per ruble value. If he sold the goods or exchanged them for others, they were to pay him a second grosha per ruble.

CONSTRUCTION OF SHIPS FOR THE CASPIAN SEA

The treaty was written in May, and on June 19 the great sovereign released instructions regarding the construction of ships for the Caspian Sea. The tsar decreed that ships be constructed in the village of Dedinovo, in the district of Kolomna, to be launched on the Caspian Sea from Astrakhan.[32] Boyar Afanasy Lavrentievich Ordin-Nashchokin and the conciliar secretaries Dokhturov, Golosov and Yuriev administered the project, working through the Chancellery for Novgorod.[33]

The same day the foreigner Jan van Sweeden[34] informed the chancellery that Captain Lambert Holt and four companions had been hired for a term of four years. Colonel Cornelius van Bockhoiven was sent to the Viazma and Kolomna districts to survey the forests, and the Marselis family received orders to produce their very best iron for the shipbuilding project in their factories at Tula and Kashira.[35] Orders went out to hire carpenters and smiths from among the fishermen of Dedinovo village, as volunteers. No one was to be forced to work against his will. Yakov Poluekhtov was assigned as chief supervisor for the ships' construction.

The new venture did not go as quickly as planned. The government wanted a ship ready by the spring of 1668 but on October 1 of 1667 Poluekhtov forwarded a deposition from the elder of Dedinovo saying that he had no carpenters interested in building ships. On the same date a separate message from Poluekhtov said that the director of taverns had refused to contribute anything toward the ship project on grounds that he had no money.[36] Moscow ordered Poluekhtov to hire carpenters in Kolomna and Dedinovo, but the supervisor sent a new report on October 27. There were no carpenters in Dedinovo willing to hire on to the enterprise, nor were there contractors. The ship project was stalled for lack of carpenters. The central authorities sent a memo to the Chancellery of the Royal Household directing all Dedinovo carpenters to sign on without misgivings, promising that the terms of their hire would not be reduced, and that the shipbuilding would not be forced on them against their will. They were urged not to believe troublemakers. The tsar's charter was sent to Poluekhtov authorizing him to search beyond Dedinovo and have the local officials of nearby villages provide thirty carpenters, whom he was to pay at a rate of four altyns a day.

The work began on November 14. In January Poluekhtov reported "The carpenters and smiths each have been given salaries of four altyns per day, but the days are short and cold. The shipbuilding is not going well, but I dare not raise wages without orders." The government approved an additional two altyns per man and warned Poluekhtov to watch that the men did not idle. Even these thirty carpenters proved too few, nor was this the only shortage to plague the venture. The ship needed cables and tow-ropes yet while there were rope masters among the peasants of the episcopal village of Gorodishche not one contracted voluntarily. The authorities sought a canvas master for the sails, but could not find one. The foreigners insisted that the ship needed a carved crown, but a woodcarver could not be found anywhere.

The people of Dedinovo grew tired of their uninvited guests. The village elder with a crowd of people drove Colonel van Bockhoiven from his home, then assigned him new quarters far from the construction site. The Moscow authorities demanded that Dedinovo supply twenty more carpenters and ordered the colonel to live nearby. They directed the bishop of Kolomna to give rope and cord masters. They ordered the Armory to send a master carver to Dedinovo and the Chancellery of Artillery to send the crown smith Nikitin. These efforts were no more successful than earlier tries. The Chancellery of Artillery replied that the smith Nikitin was making a tongue for the great bell of the Kremlin's Dormition cathedral, and no one else could do the job. The Armory said that it had no master carver. The authorities then ordered the sailmakers and lathe operators brought from Kolomna, the smiths from Pereiaslavl-in-Riazan, and the artist and carver from the Grenade Department. When none were found there, they sent to the Chancellery of Musketeers instead.[37]

Meanwhile spring had come. It was May. Poluekhtov reported that the ship was launched, and would be finished on the water, and that the yacht and sloops soon would be completed. Then, in June, he sent new complaints, protesting that the Kolomna bishop Misail had not provided the required rope masters. "I sent eight master craftsmen," the bishop responded, "but Poluekhtov beat and tortured them. He put them in a storage cellar, refused to give them hemp and food money, and tormented them by starvation."

The Kolomna liquor storehouse, which supplied the money for the ship construction, had run out of funds. They sent to Zaraisk and Pereiaslavl-Riazansky to deduct it from the customs receipts. They found an icon painter and carver and sent them to Dedinovo, where the carver was directed to carve the crown, and the icon painter to apply the colors.

Summer was coming to an end and the ship still was not completely finished. On August 7 the tsar sent a charter to Poluekhtov ordering herbaceous designs to be carved and gilded on the ship's stern, cancelling the order for an eagle and crown, and demanding lions on the prow. The tsar ordered these done with great haste so that the ship might leave Dedinovo in the month of August. Poluekhtov protested that the main cause of delay was Bishop Misail. Eight rope masters were too few, yet the bishop refused to provide more. The authorities wrote sternly to the bishop, and again ordered Poluekhtov to have the ships ready for departure in the month of August without fail.

August came and went. Mid-September arrived. Poluekhtov reported that the ship, a yacht, two sloops and the boats were finished, completely ready. Only the large cables on which the ship and yacht depended were not done, because there were only eight craftsmen, and Bishop Misail had not sent any more. A third letter went to the bishop, and another order to Poluekhtov. "Sail the ships to Nizhny Novgorod with Colonel van Bockhoiven and their captains. Take able men for helmsmen and oarsmen, men familiar with navigation on the Oka river. Take them from the town quarter and the post-horse station of Kolomna. Once in Nizhny Novgorod set the ships in the backwaters to protect them from the fall and spring ice, and guard them carefully." Van Bockhoiven was supposed to finish any uncompleted work on the ships in Nizhny Novgorod. Then on October 19 a letter came from Dedinovo. The Kolomna post-riders had disobeyed the tsar's command, and refused to provide helmsmen and oarsmen for the ship. The ship could not sail on the Oka, as the water was too shallow.

Here again Poluekhtov quarreled with van Bockhoiven, and they began to denounce each other. Bockhoiven wrote that the Oka was too shallow for the ship's draft, whereas Poluekhtov said that the river was running deep and it was perfectly possible for the ship to sail. Instead, he said, the colonel refused to exert himself on the sovereign's behalf and preferred to drink and carouse with his clerks. He wanted the vessels to winter over in

Dedinovo. The Moscow authorities tried to resolve these complications by informing Poluekhtov that if departure were delayed he faced disgrace and punishment, and liability for any extra costs relating to the ships. They wrote to Bockhoiven saying that if he did not sail for Nizhny Novgorod immediately he must return his salary payments for all the past months. Even this did not help. Bockhoiven protested that there was hard frost since November 4 and large floes of ice had begun to float down the Oka, while Poluekhtov sent a report by the hands of the elders of the Lovetsky villages swearing that on November 2 the Oka was navigable. Whatever the true situation may have been, the ship spent the winter in Dedinovo.

On November 20 ship's captain David Butler and fourteen companions appeared at the Chancellery for Foreign Affairs. They had crossed the sea from Amsterdam to serve the great sovereign at van Sweeden's call. On March 2, 1669 Butler and his crew, together with a native of Astrakhan who had Caspian Sea experience, were sent to Dedinovo to examine the ship and see whether it was fit to sail. They returned to announce that the ship and yacht were seaworthy. On April 25 the ship, by sovereign decree, was given the name of *Orel*, or *The Eagle*. Captain Butler was ordered to affix carved eagles to the bow and stern, and to have eagles embroidered on the banners and pennants. Butler in turn presented the Chancellery for Foreign Affairs with a list of guidelines on how a captain should keep order among his men and lead them. The articles were approved and at last, at the beginning of May, *Orel* set sail from Dedinovo. On June 13 it left Nizhny for Astrakhan. The cost of constructing the ship, a yacht, two sloops[38] and a longboat came to 9,021 rubles. This unfortunate beginning was followed by an equally unfortunate end, when Stenka Razin burned the ship in Astrakhan.[39]

MORE ON THE ARMENIAN TRADING COMPANY

Razin's brigandage, disagreement within the Armenian trading company, and the death of Shah Abbas II all hampered fulfillment of the agreement with the Armenians. In addition Ordin-Nashchokin, who negotiated the trade treaty, retired. Matveev took his place, and in July of 1672 he summoned commercial representatives, two good men from each hundred,[40] to meet in the Chancellery for Foreign Affairs. There they listened to a reading of the 1669 treaty with the Armenian company and considered the question of whether the Armenians, who in accordance with the treaty began to import raw silk and other goods into Muscovy, to Archangel, Novgorod,

Pskov, and Smolensk, and then took these goods across the sea, would disrupt trade for the merchants of Moscow and all other Russian cities.

"In the reigns of tsars Michael Fedorovich and Alexis Mikhailovich," the representatives answered, "many traders from the realm of Persia–Persians and Armenians, Kumyks and Indians–came with silk and other Persian goods and traded in Moscow and Astrakhan and other cities, always with Russian merchants. Nowhere did they trade with Germans, Greeks, or other foreigners, nor did they travel across Muscovy to the German lands.[41] It was the Russian merchants who traveled across the sea to Astrakhan and to Persia with all manner of Russian and German goods. They exchanged these Russian and German goods for silk and other Persian wares, and sold them to the great sovereign's treasury, and the treasury in turn sold them to the Germans for efimoks.

"The merchants also sold silk directly to the Germans for efimoks, and gave the efimoks to the treasury in exchange for smaller coins. This trade provided no small gain for the treasury, there was work for Russian merchants, and a wealth of taxes entered the treasury from them and from the Persians. If the Armenians now trade directly with the Germans they will demand a treaty with them. They will trade silk to the Germans for efimoks and for gold pieces, and also for goods imported from overseas, which previously Russians bought from the Germans and sold to the Persians. Thus by this agreement gold and silver coins and imported goods will go across Muscovy to Persia. There will be profit for Persia and loss for the great sovereign's treasury, for Russian merchants will lose their business and become impoverished."

Late in 1672 Grigory Lusikov came again to Moscow and heard the following speech from Artamon Sergeevich Matveev. "In 1667 the great sovereign welcomed you Armenians, and permitted you to come with silk and other goods, as it was written in the contract. Ample funds were prepared for the purchase of silk, which has suffered great losses because of long idleness. In this way you have broken your treaty. State now whether you have brought silk with you according to the treaty, and how you will compensate the tsar's treasury for the losses it has suffered."

Lusikov. Christ did not come to destroy the law of Moses but to fulfill it, although there are rumors that Russia wants to change the terms of the silk trade.

Matveev. It is true that Christ came to earth for our salvation, and did not come to destroy the law but to fulfill it. These words of yours regarding the replenishment of the tsar's treasury are seemly. Say now by what means you will compensate the tsar's treasury for its losses.

Lusikov. The treaty did not demand that we put our silk in the tsar's treasury. Because of the cossacks' raiding I have not brought silk with me, nor do I know how to compensate the tsar's treasury for its losses.

Matveev. There was no reason for you to leave your goods behind because of cossack raids. A man's safety is more important than his possessions, yet you yourself came. You could have brought the silk, but you did not do so. Thus you caused loss for the tsar's treasury and broke the treaty.

Lusikov. If you buy silk for the treasury, by that act the treaty will be broken, because there is no such clause in the treaty.

Matveev. If such quarrels arise between the great tsar and the German sovereigns that you cannot be allowed to proceed overseas, you will have to trade in Archangel and in other Russian cities, and sell your wares either to the tsar's treasury, or to Russian merchants.

This new clause was not in the first treaty, and Lusikov sent his response in writing. The Armenians agreed, he said, only if the price of silk could be set, and only if any goods lost to thieves on the journey from Astrakhan to Moscow would be compensated from the tsar's treasury. The Russians agreed to setting prices, but offered a more complex resolution concerning the theft of goods. If there were thievery on the Volga, they suggested, the Astrakhan officials were to send word to the nearest Persian border town so that merchants might choose not to travel to Astrakhan with their silk and other wares. If in spite of all the care and attention of the Armenians the goods sank or were lost by some other means, no duties would be taken on those goods. Moscow agreed to the Armenian demand for a constant Russian guard on the merchandise during transport, adding that if goods under this guard were lost the owners might seek justice against the watchmen. If an investigation was impossible, they must rely on sworn testimony.

"In winter," protested Lusikov, "when we reach camp we go into shelter. In our absence the Russians can do whatever they wish with our wares because we are not accustomed to winter. We cannot remain outside in frost."

On the question of pricing silk destined for the treasury they agreed that a pud of *lezhei* silk would cost thirty-five rubles, and one of *ardash* would cost thirty.[42] Lusikov gave his pledge. "Neither company members nor other subjects of the Persian shah will travel to European countries across

Turkey or by any other route, and if foreigners come to Persia to buy silk, the Armenians will not sell it to them. All silk will go to Russia."

On May 21, 1673 Matveev summoned the leading merchant Vasily Shorin[43] and his partners and informed them of the tsar's decree. In future Russian merchants and their agents would not be allowed to travel from Astrakhan into Persia. Persian merchants were to trade with Russians in Astrakhan only, and would not be allowed to enter the cities upriver until a time yet to be determined by ambassadors from both realms. These new regulations were instituted because the khan of Shemakha robbed an agent of the leading merchant Astafy Filatiev, and also other agents, of their merchandise and possessions. If nothing were done the khan would continue to rob Russians in revenge for the pillage of the shah's envoy and merchants in Astrakhan during the time of Stenka Razin's rebellion.

In the Chancellery for Foreign Affairs in Moscow the Russian agents begged the great sovereign with many pleas and petitions to send search warrants to Astrakhan and other cities along the lower reaches of the river. The tsar's officials refused because in the time since Razin's rebellion many merchants bought Persian goods in Astrakhan, which they then took to Moscow and other cities. Russia feared that if search warrants were sent the envoy and merchants in whose hands they found such goods would claim them as their own, and great altercations would ensue. If the leading merchants agreed to obey the instruction not to go to Persia, but rather to trade in Astrakhan, they were to send a signed statement to that effect to the Chancellery for Foreign Affairs.

The leading merchants sent the statement. "Russian merchants have suffered great injury and oppression and slavery at the hands of the shah's officers in all the cities of the shah's domain. The khans take the better merchandise—sables, strips of belly-fur, cloth, walrus tusk ivory, and mica[44]—by force, without paying. They hold it for half a year or for a whole year, and after long petitions they pay half or a third of the price. They hold some other goods until they are spoiled or rotten, and then return them with great dishonor and insult. In many cities they attack Russian merchants and cripple them with sticks without cause.

"In Shemakha in 1650," the leading merchants continued, "they seized the Russian merchants and held them under lock and key until 1656, as a result of which the Russians suffered damages of more than fifty thousand rubles. In 1660 the shevkal of Tarki robbed the leading merchants Shorin, Filatiev, Denisov and Zadorin of more than seventy thousand rubles' worth of merchandise. In 1672 the same shevkal robbed an Astrakhan resident, the Armenian Nestor, of more than five thousand rubles, yet every year the shevkal's merchants travel to Astrakhan and trade freely. If they were detained in Astrakhan, the shevkal would stop robbing Russians. Because of these offenses in the shah's territories Russian merchants fear to travel there. Likewise Persian merchants should not be allowed beyond Astrakhan, for they take away business from Russians and cause great loss for the tsar's treasury. At present Persians and Armenians, Kumyks, Cherkess, Indians and Astrakhan Tatars all come to Moscow and to other Russian cities. They sell their wares to anyone, not just to the wholesalers. They retail them at high prices, and they buy the finer Russian goods for low prices. Instead of the two or even three duties which are taken from Russians, these foreigners pay only one duty. The purchase of Persian goods is costly for Russians of all ranks, and the sole profit is for the Persians."

After reading this statement the officials sent to question Lusikov. Would not the shah become angry if Persians were not allowed to travel from Astrakhan to Moscow, and would not the Persians petition to the shah against the Armenians, when by treaty they alone could travel to Moscow and other Russian cities?

Lusikov answered that at present Persian merchants did not journey personally to Russia. Previously they took goods on loan from the shah's treasury, giving bribes to the treasurer in exchange for an inventory under the shah's seal which allowed them to trade duty-free. Since the signing of a treaty with the Armenian Company, though, Persian merchants no longer obtained their merchandise from the treasury. The Persians would not petition against the Armenians because the shah had granted them a charter for the export of silk to Russia, and this charter could not be changed.

"Teziks come from the shah's territories to the Russian realm with the merchants," Lusikov added, "and others come on their own. They set up little markets and usually they trade in tobacco. They live this way in Moscow and other cities for years, and there is no profit from them.[45] Some six years ago they plotted and abducted a young nun from Moscow, who converted to Islam and married a Tezik. Now the Teziks taunt us Armenians, saying 'See how Christians turn from their faith!' If the great sovereign ordered all Teziks sent from wherever they are back to Persia, this would be agreeable to the shah. We Armenians will not trade in tobacco and abduct Russians, because we are Christians."

RUSSIA'S RELATIONS WITH THE PEOPLES OF ASIA

So far we have been tracing the relations of the Muscovite state, on the verge of becoming the Russian empire, with the states of Europe and Asia, that is with peoples belonging to the Christian or Muslim civilizations. Yet from its very beginning Russia continuously had nomadic neighbors, peoples who came out of the steppes of Central Asia and exerted a powerful influence on Russia's history. The Pechenegs and Polovtsians disappeared.[1] The terrible Tatar enslavers became subordinated to their previous Russian tributaries, although they did not cease to turn their eyes toward Constantinople in hopes that the successor of the caliphs would deliver them from the Christian tsar.

Through all this change of peoples the steppe frontier did not change its character. Nomads roamed about and jostled one another, as once the Polovtsians pressed against the Pechenegs, and the Tatars crowded out the Polovtsians. Now, though, they did not face Kievan Rus, but rather the powerful Muscovite state, and it is interesting to retrace their initial relations with Moscow. At first they tried to maintain their independence, right of movement, and predatory way of life, but soon, willingly or unwillingly, they were subject to Moscow, entered into service relations with it, and transformed themselves from wild Polovtsians into the tamed tribal allies known as Black Hoods.[2]

KALMYKS

As early as 1645, still during the life of Tsar Michael, two Kalmyk taishas[3] sent their ambassadors to Moscow offering to obey and serve the Russian sovereign in all good will if in return the tsar allowed them to go to Astrakhan, Ufa and other cities for various kinds of trade. Upon his accession to the throne at the end of that same year (1645) Alexis Mikhailovich sent Colonel Kudriavtsev of the Moscow musketeers to the taishas, to persuade them to turn to the sovereign's grace without war or bloodshed.

Kudriavtsev left Ufa on March 22, 1646 on the last winter passage, riding the spring floods across grassland and steppe. He took four weeks to reach the Kalmyk tent villages. On April 21 he came upon Chief Louzang[4] in his encampment on the little river Kiim, and ordered him to send word to his brother and nephews and the other taishas to convene in one place and heed the words of the tsar's envoy. "Our chiefs will not come to me for such a meeting," answered Louzang. "Give me the sovereign's letter now, and relate to me his gracious words."

Kudriavtsev rode up to him and gave him the letter. "Wait," ordered the taisha. "When we have discussed everything among ourselves, we will inform you of our decisions." Kudriavtsev had waited a week when his mission ended in a surprising fashion. Louzang sent his people to beat and rob the envoy, after which they carried him off to another settlement, this one belonging to Louzang's nephew Naamsara,[5] who sent the Russian to another uncle. This uncle held Kudriavtsev for three weeks and then sent him back to Naamsara.

On June 17 the Kalmyk taishas traveled down the Or river and summoned the envoy to their presence, where he made them this speech. "You know well that from ancient times you owed obedience to the great sovereign tsars but in 1613, forgetting the mercy of Tsar Michael Fedorovich, you attacked Astrakhan and killed Russians and Nogay. You captured the leaders of the Edisan Tatars and the men of their territory with their wives and children, you carried them off to your own ulus, and to this day you have not released them. Then you attacked the Nogay murzas on the Terek river, but were beaten in the mountains by Kumyks and mountain cossacks.[6] This did not stop you, since you came then to Saratov and other cities downriver. Tsar Michael Fedorovich refused to tolerate such vexations, and sent his commander Pleshcheev against you. This commander met you beyond Saratov and killed many of your people. Others he took prisoner, and he brought great ruination upon you for your crimes. At last you sent to the great sovereign to petition him to take you under his mighty hand. The great sovereign Michael Fedorovich exchanged his wrath for mercy, and directed that you no longer be fought and destroyed.

"Now his son, the great sovereign Tsar Alexis Mikhailovich, has sent me to you with his gracious word," Kudriavtsev continued. "You must cease your crimes, serve the great sovereign, leave Astrakhan and Ufa and the other cities, and return to your nomadic ways in your former remote nomadic territories. You also must give your oath through me, according to your own faith, that you will release the Edisan Tatars, and give hostages to Astrakhan and Ufa from among your taishas or from the highest ranks of your ulus. Insofar as you fulfill all this, the sovereign will reward you in his mercy, and will allow you to engage in trade and crafts free of duty."

"We do not remember," answered the taishas, "whether in past years the Kalmyk clans owed obedience to the Muscovite sovereigns or not, nor do we remember how, or whether, the previous sovereigns rewarded them. We only know that our fathers, and our uncles, and we ourselves, and our brothers and nephews, have never given our obedience to the Muscovite tsars or to Tsar Michael, nor has any sovereign reward ever been sent to us. We did not send our ambassadors to ask to become slaves. We sent to request peace with the sovereign. We do not want to war against his cities, nor do we want him to send his forces against us. We merely want him to let us trade near his cities.

"Besides," continued the taishas, "not all the chiefs attacked Astrakhan. Only two did so, and their purpose was not to attack the sovereign's patrimony. They went to meet with the leaders and people of the Edisan ulus, who asked our taishas to take them under their protection. Our leaders did so, they did not take them at saber-point. They are God's people, and now they roam the steppe in their own bands according to their own will. If they want to go to Astrakhan we will not hold them, but we will not give them up against their will. We did not attack Saratov and other cities, and if someone came from us by stealth, we do not know about it because we do not all range in the same place. As to the commander Pleshcheev killing our people and taking them prisoner, such things have happened in all ages. In war men kill and take prisoners.

"The sovereign orders us to leave his cities and return to our former distant migration routes, but we do not range near his cities. The land where we roam is God's land, and empty, and we are God's free people. We move by our own will and not to order. We do not desire to serve the sovereign, although even without taking oath to him we wish him no ill. In earlier years we served no sovereign and gave no oaths. If you kiss the cross to swear that your sovereign will make no war against us, we will order our leaders to swear their own oaths that we will not begin a war. We will not give hostages, because this is not our custom. We have no Russian prisoners, because we do not go to Rus. Trade is a private matter. If the sovereign wishes us to bring merchandise, we will trade, but we have others to trade with besides the sovereign's men, and we will pay taxes to no one."

"In that event," said Kudriavtsev, "the sovereign will force you to fight on two fronts. He will attack you with firearms, and will order your

enemies, the other Kalmyks from far away,[7] to march against you also."
"So you have come to threaten us!" retorted the taishas. "Had you not been
sent from Moscow we would imprison you in Bukhara for such words.
Even if your sovereign is going to make war on us, he should not threaten
battle and ruin, for it is in God's hands whom He will aid."

The Kalmyks actually discussed killing or selling the envoy, but several
dissented. They took Kudriavtsev on their distant migrations, where he
suffered great hunger and was forced to eat all sorts of filth. During this
time the envoy saw the Nogay and Edisan murzas and tried to persuade
them to return to Astrakhan. "We betrayed the sovereign," was the answer,
"and we cannot go back. The people of our ulus do not wish it. Yet if we
follow our ancient migrations near Astrakhan the Kalmyks will come and
take us. If the Kalmyks crowd us out, we will go to Astrakhan."

"In all this the murzas deceive their people," wrote Kudriavtsev. "They
have forgotten the sovereign's kindness and they attribute all sorts of evil
to the Kalmyk taishas. If it were not for them the taishas would know better,
for the murzas tell of all manner of Russian customs and speak ill of them."

Kudriavtsev tried to learn whether all Kalmyks were agreed to go to war
against the Crimea together with the Russian people, but the taishas
refused. "We await war against us from the faraway Kalmyks," they said,
"and the Crimea is remote from us, an unknown place. Nor can we go
together with Russians. Your Russian campaign is difficult, you go on
foot. Where we can go in a day, Russians take a week. We also are afraid
of the Russians, that they might do something to us." Having kept
Kudriavtsev with them for nearly five months, the Kalmyks finally let him
leave the steppe.

The Kalmyks stayed in their new nomadic route along the Yaik, Or and
Sakmara rivers, which were controlled by the tribute-paying people of the
Ufa district.[8] They robbed, killed and captured these tribute-paying people
in raids. They burst into the Kazan and Samara districts and destroyed
Russian and Bashkir villages.[9] The Bashkirs paid them back in the same
coin. Captives accumulated on both sides and negotiations went on about
their exchange, while the Muscovite government incessantly repeated to
the taishas that they should return to their old migration routes along the
Black Sands[10] and the Irgiz river, and not occupy the land between the Yaik
and the Volga.

The taishas answered as one, saying that they were never in bondage to
anyone, and never feared anyone but God. "The land and the water belong

to God," they said, "and formerly the land in which we now wander with the Nogays was Nogay land, not the sovereign's, nor were there any Bashkir settlements there. When we came here we dislodged the Nogays, and the Nogays went to roam near Astrakhan. As we took the Nogay and Edisan murzas near Astrakhan by the sword, so now we move together with them along these rivers and natural boundaries because they have become our bondsmen. Why should we not rove in these places? We have no other land in which to roam, and your sovereign has no cities here."

So spoke the Kalmyks, but soon they changed their tune. In 1657 four taishas wrote these words to the tsar. "The great governor of Astrakhan has begun sending envoys to us without cease. They give us no peace, they all ask hostages of us. We Kalmyks have given them our kinfolk as hos-tages, and in the presence of military commanders and a crown secretary we swore an oath with our ulus. We taishas even signed a written treaty, hoping in the future to be favored by you, great sovereign. Also, as we swore our oath, they told us that we would be rewarded."

The Kalmyk envoys presented their conditions. (1) The great sovereign must order the taishas given a reward, and three more uluses for their own. Seeing the sovereign's mercy and favor toward themselves, they would bring those uluses under the tsar's protection. (2) The sovereign must allow them to migrate up both sides of the Volga from Astrakhan in the summer, and nowhere shall they be blocked from crossing the river. (3) The sovereign must grant them freedom to trade in the cities near their migration routes. They shall be subject to no taxes or oppression from the governors, and safeguarded in all things. (4) Should the sovereign order them to war against the Crimea, he must send servicemen from Astrakhan with them.

The last clause was very important under the contemporary circum-stances of the Muscovite state. In 1661 Crown Secretary Gorokhov[11] was sent to the Kalmyk taisha Daichin to request him to write an order to the Crimean khan to break off relations with the Polish king and refuse him aid, saying that if he did not break with the king the Kalmyks would go to war against the khan's domain. It would be best of all, said Gorokhov, if Daichin-taisha would advance against the Crimean territories in the present summer. There was much wealth there now, brought from Poland, which the Kalmyks might take for their own. The great tsar pledged magnani-mous favor to the taishas and all the Kalmyks for their service, and in the sovereign's cities the Russian people, seeing the Kalmyks' honest and loyal service, would be of one soul with the Kalmyks.

"The great sovereign asks service of us," answered the taisha, "yet sends us little reward, although I was told that I would receive a reward like that previously given to the Crimean khan." "You should not speak like that," objected Gorokhov. "You are in a position of subjection and obedience to the great sovereign. Already you have received much reward, though so far no service has been required of you."[12] "The Kalmyks obey the great sovereign," replied the taisha. "They wage war on the Nogay bands subject to the Crimea. We used to dwell near Azov and along the Kaban river. Now if we are to fulfill the commands of the great sovereign we must send our men against the Crimea. After the spring floods I myself will go, with my sons and nephews. I will make camp on the Don beside the cossack stockades, and from there I will raid into the Crimea. We will issue strict instructions to all our ulus and Tatar allies to avoid any quarreling or flares of temper with the great sovereign's people, lest the Kalmyks suffer evils from the Russians, or, most evil of all, from the Bashkirs. The Kalmyks are always the victims of every possible wickedness from the Bashkirs."

"Last year," responded the crown secretary, "you complained, as a result of which the table attendant Somov was sent to Ufa. He was instructed to search thoroughly among the Bashkirs and take anything stolen from you and send it to you in your ulus. The worst of the Bashkir thieves were ordered put to death, and the others were fined. To avoid execution the ringleaders and destroyers of your tent villages, Gaurko Akhbulatov and his company of thirty men, ran away. They now live with your son Monchak-taisha,[13] and your son, heedless of their offenses, offered them a great and generous welcome. On their arrival he gave two horses and a camel to each man, and no few cattle and sheep, doing this in falsity, violating his own oath. Let him send these Bashkir thieves back to Astrakhan, and if he does not want to yield them, we no longer will protect the Bashkirs from Kalmyk depredations."

Daichin fell silent for a little. "I know nothing of this," he then said. "When you meet with Monchak-taisha, speak to him about it. Monchak is a ruler in his own right, and I am old. The men of my ulus will be his, and my personal advisors and I will direct them to him. Once you have met Monchak, make all haste to Moscow and proclaim our loyalty and obedience to the great sovereign. Should our Kalmyk affairs become important to the sovereign, let the sovereign order Kazbulat, the Circassian murza,[14] to see to things in Astrakhan, because he is familiar with our Kalmyk affairs."

The crown secretary went to meet with Monchak in his tent village. The first matter of business upon his arrival there was to send men from Ufa to negotiate secretly with the runaway Bashkirs. Why had they betrayed the great sovereign and fled Ufa? What advantages did they expect to find in the Kalmyk camps? The Kalmyks were their long adversaries, and could be expected to wreak vengeance upon them for the spilled Kalmyk blood.

At Gorokhov's arrival in Monchak's domain the taisha assured him that he was not estranged from his father, and that he fervently desired to fulfill the great sovereign's orders. The Edisan Tatar leaders said otherwise. They visited the crown secretary in the taisha's name, saying "The great sovereign asks our service but has sent little reward. When the sovereign gives us what is granted to the Crimean khan, forty thousand rubles, we will serve him, but without this we will not serve him. Instead we will go to war along the Volga against the great sovereign's cities and his people."

"You say this because you have forgotten the fear of God," Gorokhov answered the Tatar leaders. "You have no choice save to labor in the great tsar's service, because you were born his bondsmen." "We served and strove," said one of the Tatars, "and we brought the Kalmyks into the great sovereign's fold, yet received nothing. Now you have brought us nothing, so we will rob you and all the sovereign's men with you, and this way enrich ourselves. The Crimeans have sent us an envoy, and henceforth we will serve the Crimean khan." Having spoken this, the Tatars went out with great noise.

The crown secretary quickly sent an interpreter to learn if it were true that there was a Crimean envoy in the tent villages. The interpreter reported that an aga[15] from Azov was there, telling the ulus that the recent union of Russia and the Ukraine[16] would bring evil to Muslims. Gorokhov, together with Kazbulat the Circassian murza, went to Monchak. The taisha ordered the building in which they met locked and no one allowed in, for secret negotiations were beginning.

The crown secretary told the taisha of the arrival of the Edisan leaders and of their story. The taisha said that he had not sent the Tatars, but that they were extremely embittered at not having received anything from the sovereign. They were promised princely status and rich reward, but nothing was forthcoming. Still, it was not yet too late to satisfy them.

"In the Kalmyk horde you taishas rule over both Kalmyks and Tatars," said the crown secretary. "The great sovereign sends his reward to you and conducts negotiations with you about his affairs. It is not fitting for the Tatar leaders to be rewarded equally with you. Furthermore you must know that the Tatars and their leaders are not well inclined to Kalmyks. They obey you only in fear. Because they are Muslims they favor the Crimeans, while they seek the ruin of Kalmyks and want to sever you from the mercy of the great sovereign. The Tatar wise men[17] say that according to their scriptures the Tatars and Crimeans will be brought to ruin by the Kalmyks, and now your father Daichin sends his army against the Crimea. You should consider whether the time has come for you Kalmyks to possess the Crimean territories. It is proper for you to be of one mind with your father and not listen to the dissenting Tatars."

"In our Kalmyk lore too it is written that the Kalmyks shall rule the Crimean domains," answered the taisha. "On the island [sic] of the Crimea there is a mountain called Chaika-burun. It is written among us that this mountain is full of gold, and that we Kalmyks are destined to have this gold. Well do we know that the Tatars are ill-disposed toward us, and that Muslim is well-disposed only toward Muslim, yet we cannot rely on the Russians. We suffer much harm every year from the Yaik Cossacks,[18] from Russians of the cities along the Volga, and from Bashkirs. The Russians do not know our Kalmyk customs, and therefore troubles abound. Further-more the Crimean khan sends ambassadors to us every year, promising us great treasure, and saying that if we Kalmyks capture the tsar's cities for him, they shall be entirely our own. We neither heed nor aid the Crimean khan, but what resources have we to war against the Crimea? No treasure is sent to us, while every year Moscow sends forty thousand gold pieces to the Crimean khan, although the Crimeans ravage Rus.[19] How much worse are the Kalmyks than the Crimeans, that you do not give us as much treasure?"

"The Crimean khan offers you the sovereign's cities," the crown sec-retary answered, "but this is not possible. Not only have the Crimeans never captured our cities, they have never taken even the smallest villages from us. You want large treasure, but first you must demonstrate your service. It is an act of service now for you to send the Crimean envoy to Moscow. For this you will receive great reward, and the envoy will meet no ill." "This is absolutely impossible," said the taisha. "This would be a shameful deed, and never again would anyone send ambassadors to us." With this the conversation ended.

Gorokhov succeeded in summoning several of the runaway Bashkirs to talk. To the question of why they fled, they answered that they could not endure the taxation in the form of tribute furs. "You lie!" said the chancellor. "You were subject to no taxes, and how do you expect to live here! Do you really not know that the Kalmyks are your foes, and will seek vengeance against you?" "We know," replied the Bashkirs, "but there is nothing we can do. We dare not go back, for we fear being put to death. Somehow we will bring the Kalmyks around through our service and industry, because we know not only the main roads but also all the little paths, and the crossings on the big and small rivers." "It would be terrible of you to do this," said the chancellor. "Not only are you traitors, now you even want to lead the Kalmyks to destroy our villages and hamlets!" "From this we think to find some benefit for ourselves," said the Bashkirs, "because, after all, we have given up our own homelands." "You would do better to return to the great sovereign," said the crown secretary. "He will welcome you." "The very thought is terrifying," answered the Bashkirs. "We have run away, and robbed the sovereign's people. Some we even have killed." The crown secretary reassured them of the sovereign's mercy and regaled them with food and drink. The result was that the Bashkirs promised to think things over and return at another time.

After two weeks with Monchak, Gorokhov pressed the taisha to decide about campaigning against the Crimea. The taisha replied that first they must settle the matter of the Bashkir raids. Not long ago the Bashkirs had driven off two thousand of the Kalmyks' horses. How then could they enter into active government service? "Then why," asked the crown secretary, "did you take in the runaway Bashkirs? Give them up to the great sovereign." "Who would become his own enemy," Monchak answered angrily, "by releasing men from his authority? If you keep asking for the Bashkirs, we will send no men against the Crimea." The matter ended with Monchak saying to Gorokhov "Order wine and food brought from your camp. I want to drink with my close advisors. I will drink away these angry words and nevermore remember them."

The crown secretary hastened to meet this good suggestion, and in fact there were no further angry words. The Kalmyks pledged under oath to go to war against the Crimea. Signing the written oath, Monchak said "As the pages of a scroll are glued together, so let the Kalmyk and Russian peoples be united forever."

The pledge was met, and war began on the Black Sea steppes between the Turko-Tatar and Mongol tribes. Monchak pursued his enemies, the Tatars and Bashkirs, and reported to Moscow on their relations with the Crimea. In 1664 he notified the great sovereign that for the last six or seven years the Ufa Bashkirs and Kazan Tatars had sent representatives to the Crimean khan to remind him that they shared his religion and previously were subjects of the Crimean khans yet now, living among Russians, many were abandoning the Muslim faith. Thus they desired the khan to take them under his banner and march together with them against the sovereign's cities.

The taisha further reported that the Astrakhan Tatars and all Muslims in general were in communication with the Crimean khan and the pasha of Azov. Shevkal Surkai of Tarki and the Kabardinian rulers supported this alliance. They planned to build a city on the Crimean side of the border near Mazhara, an ancient Hungarian fortified town between Astrakhan and Terek,[20] to prevent free passage between these cities. The khan planned to send his princes with many soldiers to meet the Tatars, stationing them between Cherny Yar and Tsaritsyn so that ships could not take supplies and merchandise to Astrakhan and the other cities downriver. They also took some ships for plying the Volga and attacking the Yurt Tatars[21] and Nogay who lived near Astrakhan.

SIBERIA

So far we have touched upon only those Kalmyks who threatened the southeast borderlands, on the Ufa and Astrakhan (or far) side of the Volga, but others caused much greater trouble for Siberia.[22] A broad expanse of territory in Northern Asia was occupied by Russians during the reign of Tsar Michael. The use of firearms allowed these sparse detachments to overcome the scattered tribes of natives with ease, and compel them to pay fur tribute. Then in the 1620s uninvited guests appeared in the southern steppe regions of Western Siberia who could not be dealt with so easily. These were the Kalmyks.

Under pressure on two fronts from the Mongols and the Kaisak-Kirghiz,[23] they moved along the upper reaches of the Irtysh, Ishim and Tobol rivers and peacefully settled in lands which Russians already considered their own. The arrival of the Kalmyks was particularly dangerous since Russia's control of Siberia was only recently consolidated. The natives, compelled to pay tribute at gunpoint, sought the first opportunity to escape this imposition, and the descendants of Kuchum[24] still wandered the steppes with claims to the lands of their fathers and grandfathers. These peoples accepted the Kalmyks as liberators and loudly voiced the hope that soon the Russians would be no more than a memory in Siberia. While it is true that the Kalmyks had no firearms, the natives dreamed that somehow they would prevail, attacking the Russians during a fierce storm or blizzard when it was impossible to shoot from guns.

The natives' hopes went unfulfilled. Bows and arrows could not drive men with firearms out of Siberia, though the archers made several attempts. Villages of the Tara and Tiumen districts were reduced to ashes in 1643, and the city of Tara was besieged twice. The Kalmyks could not withstand the defenders' firearms and failed to take the towns, but the Russian pursuit of pillagers on the steppe was equally unsuccessful. For several years there was hardly an autumn in which the Russian settlers were not anxious through word of Kalmyk plans, and peasants along the Irtysh abandoned their villages to take shelter in the towns and stockades.

In September of the year 1651 a new monastery burned, which the elder Dalmat built on the Iset river, and Russians living in the monastery were killed or taken captive. This was the work of Tatars led by princes of the line of Kuchum. In 1659 other descendants of Kuchum ordered the Kalmyks into the Baraba steppe, destroying five communities and taking seven hundred people into captivity. The following year brought further ruin for the region.

What did the men with firearms, the Russian cossacks, do? When they could, they exterminated the plunderers, but were hampered by a severe shortage of manpower. The city of Tara provided no more than sixty cossacks to defend the entire Baraba steppe! In 1662 a revolt sprang up on the Iset river, the Bashkirs, Cheremiss and Tatars turning against the Russian settlements and destroying many of them. The Voguls of Verkhoturie also arose, crying "Our tsar has taken arms against Rus!"[25]

The Kalmyks were there, of course. Tatars, Bashkirs, Mordvinians, Cheremiss and Chuvash took the town of Kungur and burned out all Russian peasant homesteads on the Sylva river.[26] Rumors flew that the Tatars, after taking Kungur, had built a fort and learned to shoot in the German fashion, with salvaged shot. Othersrelated that all Tatars of the Ufa, Pyshma and Yapanchinsk districts, as well as the Verkhoturie Voguls, offered their loyalty to the princes of the Kuchum line, to attack the districts of Tobolsk, Tiumensk and Verkhoturie by way of the Iset and Pyshma rivers. Finally, it was said that the uprising occurred in consequence of a pact with the Crimean khan.

OSTIAKS

In 1662 it also became apparent that things were not well among the Ostiaks. Their princes and common people were meeting frequently in council with Prince Yermak, and they were buying young people to sacrifice to the deity of the Sosva region, something previously done only when they were thinking of changing allegiance.[27]

At the beginning of 1663 the Sosva Ostiak Umba was captured and confessed that his brother-in-law had come to him from Perm to summon Ostiaks of the Berezov region to treason. The Berezov Ostiaks told him that they were ready to join in attacking the town of Berezov and killing the tsar's servicemen. They agreed to mutiny as early as the spring of 1662, they said, in the season of low water, but did not reach Berezov because they could not convince the Samoyeds[28] to join them in treason. Now they had reached an understanding with the Samoyeds and with all other Ostiaks from the Cherdyn and Pelym regions, and were decided to attack Berezov in the spring of 1663.

At Umba's direction the Russians questioned other Ostiaks and discovered a wide conspiracy. In 1661 the Ostiaks still were in correspondence with their leader Tsarevich Devlet-Girei of the family of Kuchum, and determined to make war on all Siberian cities in summer of 1663. They planned for the tsarevich to attack Tobolsk with Kalmyks, Tatars and Bashkirs, and when the city was taken and the Russians killed, the tsarevich would sit in Tobolsk to rule all Siberia. They would take tribute from all the cities, while the chieftain Yermak Mamrukov of the Obdor Ostiaks would rule in Berezov with Ivashka Lechmanov.

These pretenders to the Berezov principality were captured, brought to Berezov, and tortured. They confessed and were hanged, with fourteen other ringleaders, at the order of the Berezov governor Davydov. The Tobolsk governor Prince Khilkov wrote in anger to Davydov "You did not carry out the sovereign's orders! You hanged highborn Berezov Ostiaks without due cause, for their idle cupidity in aspiring to become thieves and to collect the regional tribute. By sovereign edict you were ordered to search out treason among the Ostiaks. Those found to be involved in treasonous activities should have been sent to me in Tobolsk. You should not have executed them yourself."

It is impossible to determine to what degree Khilkov was correct in his accusation against Davydov. It is known that in the winter of that same year, 1663, Samoyeds burned the Pustozersk fortress and killed the commander and all the servicemen, while in Mangazeia they killed the tribute collectors and traders.

In the end the Ostiaks failed to rise in organized revolt. In the south, Russian soldiers and cavalrymen attacked Bashkirs and their allies wherever they could find them. Yet because of their inadequate manpower and the wide expanse of the land in question, the tsar's detachments could not pursue the scattered tribesmen and prevent their regrouping.

At the end of 1663 the Bashkirs of the Ufa district, the Nogay and Kazan roads[29] and the Ik river region, sent word to the Ufa governor Prince Volkonsky. They said that they wanted to live under the protection of the great sovereign in perpetual bondage as they had done earlier. They wanted their hostages transferred from Kazan to Ufa and for the governor to send someone to reassure them of the great sovereign's mercy.

Volkonsky promised them that the great sovereign, gracious and with no thirst for blood, generously would forgive the faults of the guilty were they so to petition him with their souls cleansed of all deceit. When they received this pledge the Bashkirs sent chosen representatives to Moscow. In the Chancellery for Kazan, before the boyar Prince Yury Alekseevich Dolgoruky and the crown secretaries, the representatives swore an oath on the Koran to break with the Kalmyks and Nogay, to return that winter to their former domains in the Ufa district, to serve the great sovereign faithfully and righteously, and to return all captives and all stolen property.

At the acceptance of the oath the Bashkir representatives stood in the sight of the great sovereign's eyes, "like the radiant sun," and received a charter on two pages, in Russian and Tatar script. The Ufa governor wrote to the Bashkirs on his own account to say that the people of Ufa, servicemen and merchants, no longer would oppress them. No one would take their spare carts except on crown business, and no one would attempt to rule them in their homeland.

Volkonsky wrote to the Ufa Bashkirs asking them to persuade the Bashkirs of the Siberian and Osinsk roads to submit to the tsar as well. If any such attempts were made, they had no effect. In July of 1664 the Bashkirs appeared at Fort Neviansk (on the Neiva river, as it flows into the Tura) where they burned a monastery and the neighboring villages. Cavalry and soldiers chased the brigands, but half a day from the Ufa river they overtook only a paltry band of twenty men. Meanwhile the great Bashkir army, hearing soldiers after them, fled over the Urals. They changed to their unencumbered spare mounts and scattered through the forests and swamps, where the soldiers and cavalrymen could not follow because their horses were exhausted from the earlier chase. The following year Tatar bandits appeared in the same places, where tributaries flow into the Tura river. The moment they saw soldiers and cavalrymen pursuing them these brigands too "melted into the swamps and river marshes and got away, discarding all their clothing, saddles, cookpots and axes."

Further east the frontier city of Kuznetsk suffered great perils, cut off from Russian settlements to the northwest by unruly Teleuts or White Kalmyks.[30] In 1636 it endured a siege from a joint band of Teleuts and Kalmyks. The natives used guile rather than force. One day the Teleuts approached Kuznetsk and proposed to set up the customary market outside the town. The unsuspecting townsmen went out to the marketplace and were killed. Later the Teleut leaders swore fealty to the great sovereign and sent tribute, but then rose up again, joining the Kalmyks and the so-called Saian Mountain Tatars[31] in devastating the Kuznetsk district.

KIRGHIZ AND OTHERS

Krasnoiarsk suffered even more from the Kirghiz than did Kuznetsk from the Teleuts. The inhabitants dared not show themselves outside their walls, and begged Moscow to send troops, or else permit them to abandon the unfortunate town. The native tribesmen who lived near Krasnoiarsk and paid tribute to the tsar either fled, unable to endure their position between the two opposing forces, or rose in revolt and killed Russians.

In the last years of the reign of Michael Fedorovich the government finally took strong measures, mustering servicemen from various Siberian cities, and taking the Kirghiz in check. Pressured in turn by Russians demanding obedience and tribute, the Kirghiz turned to the Kalmyks and Mongols for help. The Mongol khan, or as he usually was called at that time, the Altyn khan,[32] had sworn to become a loyal subject of Tsar Michael, but did so merely to wheedle rich gifts. He had no objection to aiding the Kirghiz, but not disinterestedly. He also wanted to win the tribe to himself.

Once the Kirghiz and the other tribute-paying natives, such as the Tubins, Altyrs and Kerels,[33] had settled the Krasnoiarsk district they found themselves between two wildfires. In 1652 the Altyn khan descended upon them, demanding obedience and tribute. The Krasnoiarsk governor warned him that the sovereign's troops from four cities would go after him with firearms. The khan took fright and departed, though without renouncing his claims to the tribes. When the Mongols began to gather on their migration routes envoys from the Krasnoiarsk governor came to the tribes to demand that they stand firm and immovable, and not go over to the Altyn-tsar.

The Kirghiz, Tubins and other tribesmen remembered their oath and did not transfer their loyalty to the Altyn khan, but the Russians saw with horror that they had acquired thirty Russian rifles, fifteen Kalmyk arquebuses, and a great deal of powder and shot. Asked their origin, the tribesmen answered "People bring them to us from Tomsk and trade them for other goods."

Worst of all, the envoys noted that the tribesmen's marksmanship was no worse than that of Russians. "In future," wrote the governor of Krasnoiarsk to his colleague in Tomsk, "no good can come from the Kirghiz, Tubins, Altyrs and Kerels, because they fear the Altyn-tsar and obey him. They tell my messengers 'From the time we were bound to our lands not one Mongol tsar, nor tsarevich, nor the Mongolian nor Kalmyk taishas have sent troops against us, but now the Altyn-tsar marches against our land with five thousand men! Should the Altyn-tsar or his son ever march against us there will be no way to withstand him, because he lives across the Saian mountains only ten days' journey from us.'

"Furthermore," continued the governor, "if the Altyn-tsar or his son brings a large force to war against the sovereign's borders, not only can we not send men from Krasnoiarsk to rescue the loyal tribesmen, we also will have no one to guard Krasnoiarsk fortress. I have only three hundred and fifty servicemen, and from these I must send some around the various settlements every year for grain supplies, others to Moscow for the sovereign's disbursements, some to the tribute territories to collect the tribute, and still others to the way stations, for news, and to distant guard posts. In all some three hundred or more men are sent out. Only fifty men or fewer remain in Krasnoiarsk for the whole summer, and of those half have no weapons, for there is not so much as one arquebus in the sovereign's storehouse. No good can come from the local Tatars, the Kachins, Aryns and Yastyns,[34] whose nomadic routes lie near Krasnoiarsk, because they have kin and clan ties to the Kirghiz and Tubins. They marry them and give their daughters to them in marriage, and they are of one mind."

The misgivings of the Krasnoiarsk governor did not come to pass, but in 1657 it was the Tomsk governor's turn to tremble before the nomads. The son of the Altyn khan unexpectedly fell upon the Kirghiz with four thousand men, smashed their defences and forced them to submit to him, after which he made directly for the Tatars of the Tomsk district. The Mongol tsarevich followed the example of his predecessors, the thirteenth-century conquerors, by taking all the young men of the Kirghiz and Tatars into his army, which quickly doubled in size from this influx of troops. He already had concluded a treaty with the Teleut leaders, in which both sides agreed to attack Tomsk at the same time. Then news of the death of his father forced the tsarevich to return to his steppe homeland.

There followed ten peaceful years, interrupted only by the traitorous Kirghiz leader Yereniak's raids. Then in 1667 Krasnoiarsk was besieged by the Kalmyk taisha Senga, who had joined forces with Yereniak. A junior boyar came from Tomsk to the Kalmyk tent villages. "Do you, Senga-taisha," he asked, "send your men, or do they go of themselves to Krasnoiarsk?"

There was no response. The taisha did not ask after the health of the great sovereign, and took the tsar's gifts of cloth and silks without right, dishonorably. Yereniak did not cease threatening the tribute territories, warning that he and the Kalmyks would attack again if the tribes did not pay their tribute to Taisha Senga. The Kalmyks secured their control over the Teleuts, though some of them fled to Tomsk. Senga demanded their extradition and grew very angry when this did not occur. "For many years," he told the envoy of the Tomsk governor, "I have asked the great sovereigns for my own people, the White Kalmyks,[35] and the great sovereigns have not granted me this. They do not give me my people. If they do not intend to give them forth, they should not send envoys to me from Tomsk, for I will make war on Tomsk."

Tomsk, Yeniseisk, Krasnoiarsk and Kuznetsk dwelt in constant anxiety because in addition to the Kalmyks and Kirghiz the Tubins had arisen, as had the Altyrs and especially the Teleuts, who gave Kuznetsk no peace. At last in 1674 the Tomsk governor Prince Danila Boriatinsky received an order to unite the forces of four cities and subdue the traitors by force of arms. They began with the Teleuts, "and in all the battles those who betrayed the sovereign were killed in great numbers."

The Tobolsk governor, too, was forced to deal with Kalmyks who migrated to the Ishim river. The governor entered into negotiations with their taisha Dunduk and persuaded him to submit to the authority of the great sovereign. In the summer of 1674 the musketeer colonel Ivan Arshinsky rode to Dunduk to observe the land occupied by the Kalmyks and to demand hostages. Arshinsky was met very courteously, and matters could not have gone better. Dunduk convinced the envoy of his devotion to the great sovereign. Arshinsky passed nine days in the tent village, and on the tenth Dunduk summoned him to say "We need advice on how best to write a letter to the great sovereign."

While a clerk wrote the letter the taisha conversed with Arshinsky. "I am sending two of my people with a letter to the great sovereign in Moscow," he said. "Last year I also sent a man with petitions to Tobolsk and to Moscow, in the company of the Tatar Avezbakei, who is in the tsar's service, but the authorities delayed letting my man go from Tobolsk to Moscow. They made excuses from day to day, and on the road Avezbakei told him they had taught my son to read and baptized him."

Having said these words, Dunduk gave a shout and ordered his Kalmyks to bind Arshinsky and all the Russians with him and strip them naked. "My justice has fallen upon you for the faults of Avezbakei," the taisha told Arshinsky, "but do not fear. They will not beat you to death." At this the Kalmyks broke camp and took to the road. They carried with them the bound Russians. Once across the Ishim, Dunduk ordered Arshinsky brought before him and told him "The property I took from you was my own, not yours or that of your companions. Go seek your own goods from Avezbakei. I gave him twenty horses and ordered him to bring merchandise from Moscow, but he brought nothing and did not come to me himself." Arshin-sky and his thirty comrades were released to go on foot to Tobolsk, but the Kalmyk leader took pity and gave them half a pud of groats for the road.

EASTERN SIBERIA

Even while the old Russian settlements beyond the Urals felt the danger of Kalmyk-backed native uprisings, when long-time subjects of the great sovereign such as Bashkirs, Cheremiss, Chuvash and Mordvinians rose against the Russian people, at that time Russians in the far reaches of Northern Asia tirelessly sought new land for settlement, new tribes on which to impose tribute, and new trade routes. Embassies of the great sovereign even appeared before the Son of Heaven, in the Middle Kingdom.

The establishment of a Russian presence in Eastern Siberia took place with much the same scant resources as in Western Siberia, and with little planning or unity of action, for the crown's supervision weakened with distance. At the end of Michael Fedorovich's reign Russian cossack officers, stationed with their cossacks in the Bratsk fortress on the upper Lena, subdued the Buriats,[36] compelling them to pay tribute to the great sovereign, and reinforcing their troops with small groups of craftsmen and freelance volunteers.

At the same time Ataman Ivan Kolesnikov,[37] sent from Yeniseisk with orders to explore "around Lake Baikal and to seek silver ore," established a fortress on the Angara river and demanded tribute from the Buriats. They refused on grounds that they paid tribute to the upper Lena fortress. Kolesnikov, seeing the refusal as recalcitrance, made war on them and ruined them. The Buriats grew agitated and acted in a manner hostile to the Russians. "What is this?" they asked. "Why do two representatives come to us from one sovereign? Those from the upper Lena fortress carry our tribute to the tsar, and the others from the same tsar war against us, kill us, take our wives and children prisoner, and drive off our livestock and horses. How can we be under the sovereign's protection?"

Whatever the truth of the matter, by now the rebellious Buriats had to be subdued by force, with firearms. Instead of fleeing the government troops, the angry Buriats went to war by the thousands, coming together from many clans. The desperate struggle continued until 1655 when at last the exhausted Buriats were forced to recognize the sovereignty of the newcomers.

Meanwhile Kolesnikov, the man responsible for the Buriat uprising, found success on the Baikal against the Tungus people,[38] who promised to lead him to the silver ore. In 1647 Kolesnikov returned to Yeniseisk and presented the governors with the tribute he had gathered from the new Baikal lands. In addition to furs valued at a thousand rubles, Kolesnikov announced that he had sent four of his cossacks with Tungus guides to seek silver ore. The messengers went into Mongol territory, where Prince Turukoy bowed to the great sovereign, promising obedience for himself and twenty thousand of his subjects. The prince said that indeed not too far away, in the lands of the celestial emperor (in China) there was gold and silver ore, which was brought to him. In proof he sent to the great sovereign a nugget weighing four zolotniks, and a cup and plate made of silver. Other detachment leaders and tribute collectors came from Yeniseisk to Baikal to relieve Kolesnikov. In 1661 Irkutsk was founded.

Detachments of Russian troops came from Yeniseisk to occupy the land and pacify the tribes along the Angara, Baikal, Vitim, Shilka and Selenga rivers. More troops marched north from Yakutsk to the shores of the Arctic Ocean, east to the Sea of Okhotsk, and south to the Amur. The savages of

Northeast Siberia bore the sovereignty of the newcomers as unwillingly as did those of Western Siberia, and arose at the first opportunity. In the 1640s the natives near Yakutsk[39] rebelled, but were subdued by the forceful measures of the local governor Peter Golovin. In 1645 the Yukagirs[40] arose in the Far North on the Indigirka river. Their prince Peleva and his followers killed a Russian serviceman and snatched away their hostages, who were kept in the Russian winter encampment.[41] The servicemen Gorely and Kataev, sent against them from Yakutsk, punished Peleva and took new hostages. Then in 1650 the Yukagirs of Alazeisk turned traitor, killed two servicemen, robbed the sovereign's treasury, and murdered many merchants and craftsmen. Kataev marched against the traitors from the Alazeisk winter storehouse upstream along the Alazeia river, where at last they ran the Yukagirs to earth. They were living in a large stockade, some two hundred adult men armed with bows, as well as youths and reindeer, all gathered in the same stockade.

The Russians built two stockades of their own, one forty and the other twenty sazhens from the Yukagirs. There was shooting from both sides, but where the Yukagirs wounded, the Russians killed. Later the Russians made six screen shields, rolled them out, and marched behind them to the Yukagir stockade. The savages took fright, for they had no means to withstand a siege. "Do not kill us," they cried, "we will give hostages and pay the sovereign's tribute, only now we have no sables. This autumn we have not worked, for we feared you cossacks. We all have been living in the stockade." The Russians desisted and took the leaders as hostages.

The Russians already had reached the Kolyma river. In 1649 the junior boyar Ivan Vlasiev, who was stationed there, gathered a party of servicemen and traders under the leadership of Nikita Semeonov and sent them further to the northeast, to the upper reaches of the Anui river, to demand tribute from the still-untamed tribesmen. They found the savages and routed them in the usual way. The prisoners said that beyond the mountains was another river, the Anadyr, which flowed near the headwaters of the Anui. The trader-volunteers immediately petitioned Vlasiev to send them to this new Anadyr river beyond the mountain ridges to seek new tribes to pay tribute and bring under the sovereign's protection. Vlasiev sent them off under the leadership of Semeon Motora, but the venture was plagued by rivalry. The serviceman Stadukhin, having heard the savages' words, also headed for the Anadyr.

DEZHNEV'S VOYAGE

Even earlier, in the summer of 1648, the serviceman Semeon Dezhnev set out from the mouth of the Kolyma by sea to discover new lands. "After the Feast of the Intercession of the Virgin [October 1]," wrote Dezhnev, "I was carried helplessly by the will of the sea, and at last was thrown ashore on the headlands beyond the Anadyr river.[42] We numbered twenty-five men in all on the journey, and we all set out into the hills, not knowing where we were going, cold and hungry, naked and barefoot. In this way I, poor Semeika, reached the Anadyr with my companions in exactly ten weeks. We struck the river downstream near the sea, but we could not get fish, and there was no forest,[43] and because of hunger our poor company ran away one by one. Only twelve men remained with me of the original twenty-five, and we set out in boats upriver along the Anadyr and came to the Anaul people.[44] We captured two of their men in a fight, and took tribute from them."

There Dezhnev met up with Semeon Motora, who reached the Anadyr overland, and they went on together. Stadukhin then came along after Dezhnev and Motora to threaten the same natives who already had paid tribute to Dezhnev. One day the savages sitting in their stockade observed a curious scene. A squabble broke out between Dezhnev and Stadukhin. "What you are doing is wrong," said Dezhnev to Stadukhin. "You are killing the natives indiscriminately." "These are not tribute-paying people," the other answered. "If they are payers of tribute, go to them, summon them forth from the stockade, and gather the sovereign's tribute from them." Dezhnev went to tell the savages to come out without fear and offer tribute, and one of them set out sables from his yurt. Stadukhin's eyes lit up at the sight of the sables which Dezhnev took. He threw himself upon him, tore the furs from his hands, and struck him about the face. After this Dezhnev considered it better to stay as far as possible from Stadukhin.

In 1652 Dezhnev and his companions left from the mouth of the Anadyr and took to the sea in boats. Their main business there was to battle walruses and gather their tusks. "The animals lie around in great numbers," wrote Dezhnev. "They cover the promontory along the seaside for half a verst and more, and inland for thirty or forty sazhens." Dezhnev ventured as far as a promontory he called the Great Stony Nose.[45] "This headland extends far out into the sea," he reported. "The Chukchi people live on it, and on the islands opposite live people called the Zubaty [the Tusked Men], because they all wear two fair-sized ivory teeth through their lip."[46]

The Russians could not establish even a single walrus enterprise at the mouth of the Anadyr, for they also had to struggle with the Koriaks.[47] "We attacked them," wrote Dezhnev, "and found them living in fourteen yurts in a fortified stockade. God gave us aid, and we defeated them and took their wives and children, but the men themselves got away. The well-born men also got their wives and children away, because they are a numerous people. They have big yurts, so that ten families may live together in one yurt, while we were few in number, only twelve men in all." At Dezhnev's news a musketeer captain was sent immediately from Yakutsk to secure the rule of the great sovereign in the new territory and to look after his financial interests there.

LAMUTS AND TUNGUS[48]

Even as the Russians were gaining control of these new territories they had difficulties holding the older ones because of a revolt by the savages on the Yana and Indigirka rivers. In 1666 the Lamut people besieged a Russian stockade on the Indigirka. The Russians fought them off, but the savages did not pay tribute for a whole year. At the beginning of the next year the Lamuts "gathered together in a great thieves' assembly. They came up to the stockade by night and began to hack with axes at the walls, the tribute storage buildings, and the gates. Others set ladders against the walls over the warehouses. The servicemen and traders fought back, killing three of their leaders and seriously wounding many others." The Lamuts took fright, threw down their weapons and fled. The Russians could not pursue them because there were only five servicemen and ten traders in the outpost, with no weapons, shot or powder, and nowhere to get any.

In the spring of 1647 a detachment of Russians under the command of Semeon Shelkovnik came to the Ulia river, which flows into the Sea of Okhotsk. From the mouth of the Ulia they sailed to the mouth of the Okhota. To take the Okhota the Russians had to storm the Tungus people, who had mustered over a thousand men. The Russians then established an outpost, which the Tungus besieged. A second Russian detachment had to hurry to rescue their comrades. The Russians had great difficulty taking the Okhota because the native tribes fought hard in defense of their territory, and knew how to unite in large forces. In 1654 they burned the Okhotsk outpost, freed the hostages and drove away the Russians, who declared that "the natives make it impossible for us to live on the Okhota."

Another detachment of servicemen arrived from Yakutsk and built a new outpost. Once it was established the Russians began an offensive against the natives, capturing their stockades and taking the main leader of the uprising, Komka Boiashinets,[49] as one of the hostages. From this time the Tungus people of the Okhota region traveled by foot and by reindeer to make their submission to the sovereign.

In 1665 there was yet another new disturbance among the Okhotsk Tungus. The tribal elder Zelemei, leader of a tribute-paying clan, came to the Russian fortress with his companions to warn the commander Fedor Pushchin. He said that groups of Tungus who did not pay tribute were on to the Okhota inciting the tribute-paying people to revolt. The newcomers were settled two days' journey from the fortress, where they awaited the next delivery of the sovereign's treasure to Yakutsk, for their goal was to kill Russian servicemen. Pushchin, hoping to avert this danger, dispatched fifty servicemen and traders to summon the Tungus who did not pay tribute to the Okhotsk fortress. They were ordered to bring them through kindness and courtesy, not with brutality.

Not one of these messengers survived. They perished at the hands of the very Zelemei who first warned Pushchin of the danger. Zelemei rose in revolt with all the tribute-paying natives of several clans and stealthily killed Russians, lying in wait for them on the road. Zelemei, it is said, made this speech to the tribute-paying Tungus. "Foolish people!" he said. "You are ignorant. You do not know the Russians' routes, or you could live as I, Zelemei, live. You know how many Russians I have killed, even though I see poised above me such an innumerable host that I bow to the Russians. You see this, and in your eyes the Russian people seem even better. Well, the Russians deceive us. They tell us they await more men in the Okhotsk fortress to exchange as replacements every year, but never was there any large number of men in the fortress. Therefore, since these reinforcements are not come, we can kill the others and rescue our hostages. Later, when more Russians reach the Okhota, we can lay in wait on the roads and not let them pass.

"Even as we exterminate Russians on the Okhota," continued Zelemei, "so we will destroy all Russians on the Maia and along the other rivers. In future, for our preservation and safety, we will summon the people of China because they are not far distant. We will pay them a modest tribute, in due portions, not like the amounts forced upon us in recent years. We have written many petitions to the great sovereign about this yet have received no considerations at all, nor has there been a decree of any kind about it."

The danger was worse for the Russians because only thirty men remained in the outpost, all of them elderly, or very young, or sick with scurvy, while there were sixty hostages and the fortress was in bad repair. Nevertheless the crisis was resolved without great misfortune, for the Tungus could not bring themselves to attack the fortress while their hostages were there. They tried every means to deceive the Russians and lure out the hostages, but in vain.

Pushchin ordered several suspicious Tungus found near the city captured for questioning. The savages did not give themselves as a gift into Russian hands. Two Russians were killed, while five Tungus died and three were taken prisoner. The prisoners admitted that they had come to kill the servicemen, take the outpost, and free the hostages, for they saw that there were few cossacks in Okhotsk, and that the fortress was poorly maintained.

The captives were hanged, and Pushchin immediately ordered new fortifications built, with wooden guns set along the walls to terrify the natives, and a new hut constructed for the hostages. These measures produced the desired result. The Tungus gave way and apologized for their crimes, which they attributed to anger at the insults inflicted upon them by Russian servicemen.

THE AMUR RIVER REGION

Even before the Anadyr and Okhota rivers were tamed men from Yakutsk explored the great river Amur. As early as the reign of Tsar Michael rumors spoke of a numerous agricultural and grain-growing population living by the Shilka river. This was said to be the home of Prince Lavkai, who owned deposits of silver ore in two places near the mouth of the Ura river, one on a cliff and the other in the water. Downstream on the same Shilka river were said to be deposits of copper and lead, and a wealth of grain of all kinds.

When he heard this report in 1643 the Yakutsk commander Peter Petrovich Golovin sent the chief secretary Vasily Poiarkov[50] to the Ziia and Shilka rivers to collect tribute for the sovereign, to seek out new tribes not yet paying tribute, and to find silver, copper, and lead deposits as well as grain. One hundred and thirty-three men went with Poiarkov. They sailed downstream on the Lena from Yakutsk, then upstream on the Aldan. From the tributaries of the Aldan they went by portages to the tributaries of the Ziia, which flows into the Amur. From the mouth of the Ziia Poiarkov sailed downstream on the Amur, believing that he was sailing on the Shilka. The Amur, in his words, began at the mouth of the Shingal.

Poiarkov reached the mouth of the Amur and wintered there. When summer came he went by sea to the mouth of the Ulia river, and from the

Ulia by portages reached the Maia, a tributary of the Aldan. By this and the Lena he returned to Yakutsk, bringing a rich tribute of sables, but having lost eighty men of his company. Of these, twenty-five were killed by the Duchers[51] along the Amur, and the others died of starvation on the road.

Poiarkov showed the Yakutsk commander places along the Ziia and Shilka (really the Amur), and along their tributaries, where in his opinion they should establish stockades. "There," said Poiarkov, "we can go on campaign to bring the settled farming tribes under the tsar's mighty hand, holding them in perpetual bondage and collecting tribute. There will be great profit for the sovereign because those lands are rich in men and grains and sables, and there are many animals of every variety. Much grain grows there, the rivers are full of fish, and there will be no shortage of food for the sovereign's troops."

Together with Poiarkov's magnificent tales of the Piebald Horde (as the peoples of the Amur Basin were called) there were terrible stories from his companions about Poiarkov's conduct during the campaign. "He beat and tortured the servicemen unjustly. He robbed them of their grain allowance, drove them from the stockade, and told them to go eat dead natives. To avoid a pointless death the servicemen ate the dead bodies of many natives and servicemen who had died of hunger. They ate about fifty people. Poiarkov beat others to death with his own hands, saying 'These service-men are cheap! A corporal costs ten dengas, and a rank-and-filer two groshas.' When he sailed along the Ziia river the local inhabitants did not let him come ashore, calling the Russians foul cannibals. In the spring, when the snow retreated from meadows at the mouth of the Amur and the grass was clear of ice, the remaining servicemen began to dig grass roots to eat, but Poiarkov ordered his men to burn the meadow to force the servicemen to buy their supplies from him at a high price."

Whatever the truth of these stories, Poiarkov's tales of the richness of lands along the Amur were not forgotten. In 1649 an old adventurer named Yarko (Yerofei) Pavlovich Khabarov presented a petition to the Yakutsk commander that he would set out for the Amur, leading a party of seventy servicemen and traders. He would finance the expedition himself, provid-ing money, food, ships, guns, powder and shot. The commander agreed, and Khabarov set out. He used a new route, by the Olekma, a tributary of the Lena, and then the Tugir, a tributary of the Olekma. From the Tugir he went by portage to the Urka, a tributary of the Amur.

Here he found villages[52] and a town belonging to the famous prince Lavkai, but the villages were deserted and the town abandoned. The town was large, with five towers, deep defensive ditches, passages under all the towers, and hidden ways to the water. There were stone buildings in the city, which had large windows glazed with paper. Khabarov went from the Urka river downstream along the Amur to another town, and it too was deserted! He sailed further down the Amur, found a third town, and again it was deserted!

Khabarov stopped to rest in the deserted town, setting out a guard. That very day the sentries notified him that five tribesmen had appeared. Khabarov sent an interpreter to ask who they were. The eldest announced that he was Prince Lavkai, with his two brothers, his son-in-law and a servant. He asked in turn who the Russians were, and whence they had come. "We have come to you to trade, and we have brought many gifts," answered the interpreter.

"What deceit!" Lavkai retorted. "We know that you are cossacks! Before you arrived a cossack named Kvashnin came among us, and he told us about you. He said that there are five hundred of you now, and that after you many more will come. You want to kill all of us and steal our possessions, and take our wives and children captive, and so we fled."

Khabarov told the interpreter to persuade Lavkai to render tribute to the great sovereign. Lavkai's brothers and son-in-law said they had no right to impose tribute, but Lavkai commented "Let us observe further what sort of people these are." With this the princes departed and returned no more. Khabarov followed after them, finding a fourth and fifth city, all empty.

Khabarov went no further. He returned to the first town, left some of his troops there, and returned to Yakutsk in May of 1650 with his account. He reported that along the renowned great Amur river dwelt the Daur people,[53] who lived by agriculture and husbandry. There were many fish of all kinds in this great river, as many as in the Volga. Along the shores were wide meadows and plowed fields, vast dark forests, sables and many animals of all kinds. Great treasure awaited the sovereign there. Grain grew in the fields, barley and oats, millet, peas, buckwheat and hemp. If the Daur leaders submitted to the sovereign, the profit would be great, for grain no longer need be imported to the Yakutsk fortress. Instead grain could travel from Lavkai's cities on the Amur across a portage to the Tugir to a new stockade which Khabarov had established. This was a journey of only about a hundred versts, and from the Tugir stockade it took a mere two weeks to float downstream on the Tugir, Olekma and Lena to Yakutsk. The Daur territory promised to be more profitable than the Lena region, one of the most beautiful and abundant places in all Siberia.

Khabarov's tales produced such an effect that a hundred and seventy volunteers immediately flocked to his side. The governor of Yakutsk gave him twenty cossacks and, still in the year 1650, sent Khabarov to the Amur with three cannon. This time the men found no empty cities, for the Daurs had determined not to allow the newcomers to settle among them and take tribute. Before he reached Albazin, the first of Lavkai's cities, Khabarov met the Daurs in the open. He fought them from midday until evening, and drove them away, at the cost of twenty Russians wounded.

The Daurs abandoned Albazin, which then was occupied by the Russians. Their chief Gugudar desperately repulsed the Russians from his three-part town.[54] To the demand for tribute for the great sovereign Gugudar answered "We pay tribute to the Chinese tsar, what tribute have we for you? Do you want the furs that we toss to the last of our children?"

"Then the Daurs shot arrows at us from the city, as though they were sowing seeds in a cornfield," wrote Khabarov, "but even the fiercest Daurs could not stand against the terror of the sovereign and our military prowess." Khabarov took the town, after more than six hundred of the enemy laid down their lives there. Four Russians were killed and forty-five wounded.

In other places all over Siberia Russians had grown accustomed to the idea that when the tribal leaders, the chieftains, fell into their hands as hostages the whole clan submitted and paid tribute. With the Daurs it was not so. Khabarov unexpectedly succeeded in capturing one Daur village, swearing the inhabitants to loyalty and taking their leaders hostage, but soon he discovered the villagers were fleeing. "Why have you betrayed the great sovereign," Khabarov asked the hostages, "and sent your people away?" "We have not sent them away," was the answer. "We sit here among you, and they have their own counsel. It is better that we alone, who have fallen into your hands, should die for our people, than for you to kill us all."

Khabarov built an outpost at Achansk to pass the winter and was besieged there by the local Duchers and Achans.[55] The Russians had little trouble fighting off these savages, but in the spring of 1652 another sort of enemy appeared. This was the Manchurian army, sent by order of the viceroy of the Chinese emperor. The Manchurians approached the Achansk stockade with guns and rifles, but the Russian troops and Russian guns proved superior in this first meeting. Let Khabarov himself tell us about the battle.

"On March 24, at first light, the renowned force struck, the imperial Chinese army, its men all mounted and clad in armor. They came out of cover across the Amur river against the town of Achansk, against us cossacks. Our Captain Andrei Ivanov, the tsar's serviceman, alerted the city. 'Brother cossacks,' he shouted, 'make haste to your stations and cover yourselves in strong armor!' At this the cossacks rushed about in the city and onto the city wall, clad only in their shirts. We thought it was cossacks from the city firing their guns and weapons, but it was the Chinese army firing their guns at our cossack town. We cossacks fought with them, with the Chinese army. We fought from the walls from dawn to the setting of the sun.

"Then the Chinese army threw themselves against our encampment, and would not let us cossacks cross the town. They covered the city wall with their banners, and cut down three sections of our city wall all the way to the ground. Their prince Isinei[56] called out to the Chinese soldiers 'Do not put these cossacks to the sword or to the torch. Take them alive.' Our interpreters overheard Prince Isinei's words and told me, Yarofeiko.[57] Once we heard the words of Prince Isinei we cossacks donned all our armor, and I Yarofeiko and my servicemen and free cossack volunteers all prayed to the Savior and to Our Lady the Immaculate Virgin and to St. Nicholas the Miracle-Worker, the zealous servant of Christ, and bade each other farewell. Then I, Yarofeiko, and Captain Andrei Ivanov and all our cossack host, said these words. 'Let us die, brother cossacks, for the Christian faith, and let us make our stand for the House of our Savior and for the immaculate saints and for Nicholas the Miracle-Worker. We cossacks will do our duty to the tsar and grand prince Alexis Mikhailovich of All Russia, and we will die to the last man against the sovereign's enemies. We will not give ourselves alive to these, the Chinese emperor's men.'

"When the emperor's men galloped toward the breached walls, we cossacks rolled a great bronze cannon to the breach and fired it at the imperial army. We shot from the city from small arms, and fired other iron cannon at the Chinese and there, by the grace of God and the sovereign's good fortune and by our own efforts, we killed many of the Chinese dogs. Then, as the Chinese recoiled back from the breach from our fire, our servicemen and free cossack volunteers marched out in armor, one hundred and fifty-six men strong, in a sortie against the Chinese outside the city, while fifty men remained in the city.

"As we left the city in this sortie the Chinese bought up two iron cannon to attack the city, and by God's grace and the sovereign's good fortune we cossacks captured those two guns from the Chinese army. Some of the higher-ranking officers in the enemy's force had firearms, and we killed those men and took their weapons from them. At this a great terror fell upon the Chinese. Seeing our indomitable force, all the remaining Chinese fled from the city before our weapons. After this we moved around the city of Achansk to see who was killed. Six hundred and seventy-six of the Chinese officers and soldiers were killed outright, and of our cossack forces ten were laid low by the Chinese, while seventy-eight of our cossacks were severely wounded in the fight."

Khabarov wrote in a poetic manner but it is evident that he thought prosaically. He realized that he could not expect the powerful Chinese tsar to allow the cossacks to hold sway in his territories, nor could he expect a second victory should a more numerous Chinese force come to Achansk. Less than a month after the Chinese attack Khabarov and his companions left their stockade and sailed up the Amur. Even before this the riverside peoples were disinclined to cooperate, and tribute was gathered only by force. Now local captives told of hostile plans, of new dangers. "Our people," they declared, "do not want to give you tribute, they want to fight you. They say 'Where they stop to pass the winter and establish an outpost, there we will gather an army of ten thousand men or more, and we will strike a devastating blow.'"

On the way Khabarov encountered a detachment of cossacks sent from Yakutsk to help him, but the force was too small to be effective. With its few men and its single cannon it did not allow Khabarov to return downriver where, in his expression, the whole land was up in arms.[58] On August 1 Khabarov went ashore at the mouth of the Ziia river and asked his cossacks "Where shall we build our town?" "Where it is suitable and where it will make a profit for the tsar, there let us make our town," was the response.

Most, but not everyone, answered thus. About a hundred cossacks thought differently. They "gathered up their homespun coats and their belongings" and set off from the shore in three boats, which also contained the sovereign's coffers and the guns, lead, powder and armor. The mutineers threw one of the guns from the boat onto the shore, and heaved another into the water. They also threw part of the remaining treasury into the water, and took the rest with them. They captured some thirty volunteer cossacks as slaves, though two of them, not wanting to sail with the rebels, leaped from the boat into the water dressed only in their shirts.

The mutineers, numbering one hundred and thirty-six men, sailed down the Amur, terrorizing the natives who lived by the shore. Two hundred and twelve men stayed with Khabarov. They remained at the mouth of the Ziia for six weeks, calling the tribesmen whose hostages they held, but the natives would not approach. "You deceive everybody," they said, "and now your people sail down the river and ravage our land."

Khabarov sent four cossacks to Yakutsk to inform the local governors that the mutineers made a mockery of the sovereign's service, drove away those of other faiths, and troubled the land. He would be unable to gain control of the region with the men remaining to him because the land was populous and the natives had firearms, yet he dared not leave the Amur without the sovereign's order.

There was no response until 1653. Then the nobleman Zinoviev came to the Amur with remuneration from the sovereign in the form of gold pieces for Khabarov and his companions. Khabarov handed over the tribute to Zinoviev and returned with him to Moscow, leaving Onufry Stepanov as "steward of the new Daur land of the great river Amur." Stepanov accepted the post reluctantly because Khabarov's recent adventures did not make a future on the Amur sound attractive.[59]

In September, having taken counsel with his troops, Stepanov sailed downstream on the Amur. Upriver there were neither tilled fields nor forest but Stepanov found grain along the shores of the Shingal, a southern tributary of the Amur. From there he set sail further down the Amur and wintered in the country of the Duchers, from whom he collected tribute. In the summer of 1654 he set out once again to the Shingal for grain. He traveled upstream safely for three days, then on June 6 he met a large Chinese military force equipped with good quality firearms, who were moving by horse and boat.

Despite a Chinese cannonade against the Russian vessels the cossacks drove the enemy from their ships to the shore, where the Chinese made a stand. They took up position in an old fortification and began to fight from behind its earth walls. The Russians tried to storm this embankment but were beaten back, and were forced to sail away to the Amur without grain, hastening upstream on the great river. Their captives related depressing news. The Chinese emperor[60] had ordered three thousand troops stationed for three years where the Shingal joins the Amur, to keep the Russians out. There was nowhere to obtain grain along the Amur because the Chinese emperor had forbidden the riverside tribes to sow grain and ordered them all to move closer to him on the Naun river, taking a tributary to the south from the Amur.[61]

Leaving the Shingal, Stepanov fortified his camp at the mouth of the Kamara river,[62] where it flows into the Amur from the south. There, on March 13, 1655 ten thousand Chinese soldiers appeared at the stockade and shot burning arrows to set fire to the outpost. On March 24 they attacked from all four sides. They brought carts protected by leather-covered wooden shields, ladders with wheels on one end and sticks and iron pegs on the other, firewood, pitch, straw, iron boat hooks and various other assault gear. The cossacks managed to beat off the attack, and the special equipment fell into their hands. After this failure the Chinese remained at the stockade until April 4, bombarding it day and night. At last, seeing that there was nothing to be done, they went away.

This defeat of the Chinese army by defenders of the Kamarsk stockade cleared the Amur and Shingal for Stepanov, who once again ventured there for grain. Then in 1656 a decree arrived from the Chinese emperor ordering all Duchers to leave the Amur and Shingal region. Stepanov came to collect tribute and grain, but found no one and nothing! "Now everyone in the army has grown hungry and thin," wrote Stepanov to Yakutsk. "We feed ourselves on grass and roots, and await the sovereign's command."

BAIKOV'S EMBASSY TO CHINA

The Chinese placed great obstacles in the way of Russian expansion, forcing the Muscovites to try to initiate peaceful diplomatic relations with the mighty Chinese emperor. On the first attempt, in 1654, the junior boyar Fedor Baikov was sent from Tobolsk to China to gather information on its markets and goods and on other local practices. Baikov traveled from the junction of the Irtysh river with the White Waters[63] to the Chinese empire, past the Kalmyks and Mongols, over mountains, and through lands which provided little food or water.

Baikov traveled in Chinese territory for two months before he reached the first city, Kokokotan.[64] They had to travel for ten days, two weeks, three weeks, even a month between the Mongol taishas, on whom they depended for supplies in the waterless waste. It was twelve days' journey from the city of Kokokotan to the frontier town of Kapka, across land held by the taishas of the Mugali nomads, who served the Chinese emperor. From Kapka the ambassador came to the emperor in the city of Kanbalyk (Peking) on his own horses and camels, having been given no provisions or transport.[65] He walked for seven days. On the way he saw eighteen cities, some of brick and others of adobe. Bridges built of very intricately wrought dark grey stone crossed the river.

The Russian party reached Kanbalyk only in March of 1656. Two of the emperor's privy councillors met the ambassador half a verst from the city and treated him to tea made with butter and milk. Baikov refused to drink, because it was Lent.[66] "At least take the cup," begged the courtiers. The ambassador took the cup, held it for a moment, and gave it back.

The ambassador was lodged at first in a house which had only two rooms. Later he was given more spacious quarters. The next day the emperor's councillors came and said that the celestial emperor instructed them to receive the gifts sent by the Russian sovereign. "It is customary everywhere," replied Baikov, "for the ambassador himself to make the presentations, first of the sovereign's gracious letter, and only then of the gifts." "Your sovereign has his order of ceremonies, and ours has his own," answered the privy councillors. "Emperor does not give orders to emperor." At this they took the gifts by force. The next day councillors came to tell the ambassador that he was to bring the tsar's letter to them in the chancellery. Baikov refused. "I was sent to Tsar Bogda,[67] and not to his privy councillors in the chancellery." "The emperor commands you to be punished for not heeding his decree," the privy councillors were told to say. "Even if the emperor orders me torn to pieces, I still will not go to the chancellery, nor will I give you the sovereign's letter," declared Baikov. The Chinese returned the gifts as a sign of their emperor's wrath at this obstinacy, and with this the affair ended. Baikov returned with nothing more than tales of a wondrous country, seen by Russian eyes for the first time.

Because his embassy was received with such disfavor, the tsar made no second attempt, nor did hostile actions cease from the Chinese side. On June 30, 1658 forty-seven boatloads of Chinese troops attacked Onufry Stepanov as he sailed down the Amur to the Shingal. The Russians suffered a complete defeat. Stepanov perished together with two hundred and seventy cossacks. Two hundred and twenty men escaped to the shore and in one boat, and the sovereign's store of tribute sables fell into the hands of the Chinese. With this unfortunate encounter the cossack expeditions to the Amur from Yakutsk came to an end.

Long before Stepanov's death the tsar ordered that Russian outposts on the Shilka and on the upper reaches of the Amur be secured, to give his men places from which to work their way further downstream along the great river as opportunities arose. With this goal Afanasy Pashkov, the governor of Yeniseisk, restored the abandoned outposts of Nerchinsk, near where the Nercha river joins the Shilka, and Albazin on the Amur.

Even this much could not be accomplished without a clash with the Chinese. The Albazin cossacks took tribute from tribes which the Chinese emperor considered his subjects, and several of the natives, discontented with the Chinese, went over to the Russian side. In 1667 the Tungus prince Gantemir came from Chinese territory to Nerchinsk, offering himself to the sovereign's protection with all his sons and brothers and villagers, forty in all. He promised to pay a tribute of three sables per man. Gantemir acted in anger at the loss of a lawsuit resulting from the unfairness of a Chinese judge.

The Chinese governor of the Shingal region learned where Gantemir had gone, and in 1670 sent this letter to the Nerchinsk commander Arshinsky. "If you would send us your envoys," he wrote, "to negotiate with us face to face about how much tribute to take from which peasants, there would be no reason for us to quarrel with the great sovereign. Consider, if someone pays the great sovereign tribute and then flees, surely would you not seek him even if it took ten, twenty or a hundred years?"

Arshinsky immediately sent four cossacks to the emperor in Peking with a proposal for a military alliance and free trade between both states. The cossacks returned to Nerchinsk very pleased with their reception. They brought a letter from the emperor to the tsar. "My traders have been to the Shilka river, and on their return they told me that Russians now live by the Shilka in Albazin and make war on our border folk. I, the celestial emperor, wanted to attack these Russians, but was told that the people who live there are yours, O great sovereign. Instead of ordering war I sent to learn whether they are indeed your people, O great sovereign, who live in the Nerchinsk fortress. The Nerchinsk commander sent me envoys and a letter on your authority, and I now know that it is true that the commander and servicemen live in the Nerchinsk fortress by your great sovereign order. Therefore I say that if they no longer make war on our borderlands and do no evil, and word is given on this, we will live in peace and joy." This document occasioned a new embassy from Moscow to Peking.

SPAFARY'S EMBASSY TO CHINA

At the beginning of 1675 a translator from Moscow's Chancellery for Foreign Affairs, a Greek named Nicholas Gavrilovich Spafary, was sent as ambassador to China.[68] He took a different route than Baikov, journeying to Yeniseisk and Nerchinsk, and reaching the imperial city of Beijing (Peking) only on May 15, 1676.

The Chinese officials likewise told Spafary that Emperor Kangxi (the second of the Manchurian dynasty)[69] would not accept the sovereign's letter from him. "Such arrogance, contrary to the laws of all nations!" said Spafary to the Chinese. "It is a marvel! All wonder how such a custom began among you, that ambassadors may come before the khan, but may not bring the sovereign's documents."

The Chinese explained the origins of the custom to him. "Long ago the ambassador of a certain state came to us," they said. "He brought a multitude of gifts and loudly professed great friendship and love for us. Our emperor, rejoicing, immediately ordered the ambassador and his letter brought before him. Then as they read the letter they saw that it greatly dishonored our emperor, and the ambassador too spoke in an unseemly fashion. Since that time it has been our established custom to take the letter from the ambassador first, and read it through. Only then, depending on the suitability of the letter, will the emperor receive the ambassador or refuse him. The khan himself cannot change this custom. It is only out of friendship to the great tsar, and contrary to our custom, that he has ordered two privy councillors to accept the letter from you, but that they should bring you along with the document, do not even dream of such a thing!"

Spafary repeated that he would not give the letter to the chancellery.[70] After this two mandarins visited the ambassador, bringing with them an elderly Catholic monk of the Jesuit order named Ferdinand Verbiest, of a Spanish-Netherlands family.[71] The Jesuit was to serve as a translator, because Spafary could speak Latin. After more prolonged arguments about its acceptance, Spafary dictated a Latin copy of the tsar's letter to the Jesuit, so that the Chinese would know that nothing in it disparaged the honor of their emperor.

"I am glad," the Jesuit told the envoy in an aside, "to serve the great tsar for the Christian faith and to exert myself in all ways on his behalf. Yet it grieves me that an embassy has come from such a renowned sovereign, for the Chinese are barbarians and do not give proper honor to any ambassadors. In speech and in writing they term gifts sent to them from other sovereigns as tribute, and in their replies they write as master to servant. They say that all other people on earth see with one eye and only they, the Chinese, with two." The Jesuit entreated Spafary before an icon not to repeat or write these words to anyone before he left China because foreigners here suffered many deprivations for Christ, and at present were under suspicion. He promised to send the envoy a book in Latin describing Chinese customs and the reception of ambassadors.

The copy of the tsar's letter did not help. The mandarins announced that they trusted only the original document and seal, when they saw them in their hands. "Once the hair that grows on the head begins to turn grey it is impossible to change it. So too is it impossible to change our customs. You shall give the letter to two privy councillors, who are to the emperor as two arms on the body, while the emperor is the head."

A Chinese frontier commander in communication with Nerchinsk told Spafary "Some years ago, when Baikov was here, the cossacks marched along the Amur and attacked our people. We said to Baikov 'How can we trust you? You come with an embassy, while the cossacks make war upon us!' Baikov explained to us that the cossacks were bandits and made war without the tsar's authority, and so the emperor's army killed all the bandits. After that the emperor's Tungus subject Gantemir ran away to Nerchinsk with his people, at which the emperor ordered me to take six thousand men and ten guns and march against the rebels and Gantemir. I set out with the army, sending a Daur scout ahead to Gantemir to find out what sort of people he had joined. Gantemir captured the scout and sent him to the Nerchinsk commander. He and Gantemir told the scout that they were not bandits, but men of the great sovereign, the white tsar, and that by his order they had built two fortresses, in Nerchinsk and Albazin.[72] They also said that the great sovereign desired to live in friendship and amity with the great emperor and that commerce between both states should be promoted.

"This Daur scout returned to meet me and my troops when we were two days' march from Nerchinsk. Hearing that there were no bandits in Nerchinsk, only men of the white tsar,[73] and that they had let my man come back peaceably, I proposed to the emperor that it is better to approach such people in friendship than in war. The emperor ordered me to send to Nerchinsk for servicemen because he wished to write a letter to the great tsar to learn the truth for himself. Besides that, everyone after Baikov who came here from Russia to trade–Seitkul, Tarutin, and others–said they brought letters from the tsar, but after we let them enter China we found they carried no such papers.[74] They deceived us, and because of this we cannot believe you now unless we see the tsar's original documents."

The commander gave assurance that they had not reported to the emperor about the proposed violation of that ancient custom, that he accept the letter from hands of the envoy, for such custom is holy. The Jesuit maintained that the commander was lying. He said that they had reported to the emperor three times already, and that the emperor ordered a search made in ancient books to see if there were no similar example. The emperor had no objection to accepting the letter, but the privy councillors stubbornly insisted on the old custom, afraid that neighboring rulers would think they had done this in fear of the Russian sovereign. Above all they did not believe the copy of the letter because in their own letter they had written to the tsar as lord to inferior, and they feared to find repercussions from this in the tsar's letter. Not to raise suspicions the Jesuit said this while looking at the draft, as if he were reading it aloud.

During all this time there were terrible heatwaves. Half of the servicemen accompanying the envoy were sick from fevers and bad water. The gates of the ambassadorial lodgings were locked and no one could pass them, while the sentries sold provisions at three times the going rate.

At last the Chinese got down to business and agreed that the envoy would bring the letter not to the chancellery but to the palace, where the privy councillors sat in council. He would lay the documents on the imperial seat, and two councillors would take them immediately to the emperor. After this ceremony the envoy was to bow before the emperor. Spafary bowed quickly, and not all the way to the ground. The mandarins told him to bow all the way to the ground, slowly, as they did. "You are bondsmen of the emperor," answered the envoy, "and know how to bow, but we are not bondsmen of the emperor, and we will bow in our own fashion."

After three bows the mandarins told Spafary to walk quickly to the emperor, for it was their custom that when the khan summoned, they responded at a run. "It is not my custom to run," answered the envoy, and approached slowly.[75] When he was before the emperor Spafary bowed once to the ground and sat down on a cushion. From the emperor's seat to the place where the envoy sat was about eight sazhens. The khan's seat was about a sazhen in height from the ground, octagonal, made of gilded wood, and was approached by three gilded steps. The emperor was a young man with a pock-marked face. He was said to be twenty-three years old. Both sides of the chamber were lined with the emperor's brothers and nephews, sitting on the floor on lengths of white felt.

When the envoy arrived they brought tea for the emperor's relatives and all the privy councillors, served in large yellow wooden cups. The tea was Tatar, not Chinese, brewed with butter and milk. Music played affectingly, and a man shouted something in a loud voice. After tea the music and the shouts ceased. Everyone rose, and the emperor stepped down from his throne and returned to his private chambers.

Spafary was very insulted that the Son of Heaven had paid him no attention. The grandees assured the envoy that at their second meeting the emperor would engage him in conversation. Finally, after a long wait, the Russian embassy again was summoned to the palace. The envoy and his suite bowed ten times and sat down on cushions before the emperor. Two Jesuits came and stayed kneeling while the emperor spoke quietly to them. When he finished the Jesuits went to the envoy, ordered him to kneel, and said "The great autocrat of all the Chinese state, the khan, asks 'Is the great sovereign, the autocrat of all Russia, the white tsar, in good health?'"

"When we departed from the great sovereign," Spafary answered, "we left him well and happy in his person and his realm. Our great sovereign sent his hopes that the great Sacred Khan may likewise enjoy many years of health and fortunate sovereignty, as our most well-beloved neighbor and friend."

Once more the Jesuit interpreters went to the throne and returned with new questions. "His imperial greatness poses three questions. How old is the great tsar? How tall is he? How long ago did he begin to rule?" "The great sovereign," answered Spafary, "is about fifty years old.[76] He is of full height, and his life is adorned with all manner of virtues. He began to rule more than thirty years ago."

Next there came queries about the envoy himself. "How old are you? The emperor has heard that you are a learned man, and instructed us to ask whether you have studied philosophy, mathematics and trigonometry." The emperor asked about this because he himself studied trigonometry and astronomy with the Jesuits. After these interrogations they brought in tables laden with sweets such as Persian apples[77] and various comfits, watermelons and melons. Later they brought grape wine of the very best quality, like good rhenish, which the Jesuits made for the emperor every year. Only the envoy and his suite were regaled with wine. The Chinese grandees drank tea.

Spafary passed the entire summer in Peking. The envoy and his suite had brought a great deal of merchandise, on the crown's behalf and their own, to sell and exchange for Chinese goods. Their trade went badly, for only one shop sold damasks, satins and velvets. The other shops would sell nothing to the Russians because the grandees, interpreters and merchants agreed at what price to buy Russian goods and at what price to sell their own. At the end of the summer they began to speak of departure.

Spafary demanded a copy of the imperial letter to the sovereign in Latin in order that he might know that there were no sharp words in it. He declared that he would not leave without it. At this the Chinese explained some of their customs to him in no uncertain terms. (1) Every ambassador who comes us in China must describe himself as coming from a lowly and humble place and ascending to the high throne. (2) Gifts brought to the emperor from any foreign sovereign are termed tribute in our records. (3) Gifts sent by the emperor to other sovereigns are called payment for service. The emperor uses these same expressions in his letters to other sovereigns as well. "You should not be surprised that we have such a custom," said the grandees to the envoy. "As there is one God in heaven, so there is our one earthly God, our emperor. He stands in the middle of all lands, in the center among all sovereigns. This ritual never has been and never will be changed among us.

"Report our words on three matters to the great tsar," the mandarins continued. "(1) He must give up Gantemir. (2) Should he send us another envoy, he shall direct him not to resist anything he is instructed to do. (3) He must forbid those of his people who live within our borders to harm any of our people. When the great tsar fulfills these three conditions, the emperor will fulfill his wishes. Otherwise no one may come from you, from Russia or from the frontiers, to us in China, for trade or for any other purpose."

With this Spafary was dismissed. He left without the imperial letter, for he had not consented to the insulting expressions, slighting the honor of the tsar, which the Chinese had included. The envoy took away most unfavorable impressions about the Chinese. "In commerce there is no more sly and crafty people in the whole world, and nowhere do you find such thieves. If you do not guard yourself they will cut the buttons off your clothing. They are all rogues!"

The Jesuits, dissatisfied with Emperor Kangxi, complained of his inconstancy and inability to govern. They painted a depressing view of China's future, shaken by revolts. In general the Jesuits were very candid and pleasant toward the Russian envoy.[78] Among other things they asked him for icons for their church, for remembrance. "For our part," said the Jesuits, "we will pray to God for the great tsar. The Russians who come to China always come to our church, but not seeing Russian icons they do not trust us, thinking that we are idolators and not Catholics."[79] Spafary gave them an icon of the Archangel Michael in a gilded silver frame, and two candlesticks to place before the icon.

V

OVERVIEW OF THE REIGN OF ALEXIS MIKHAILOVICH

Spafary's embassy to China was one of the last items of business in Tsar Alexis's celebrated thirty-year reign. The publication of the great Code of Laws, the annexation of the Ukraine, the exploits of Russians in Northern Asia, broadening diplomatic relations from the Western Ocean to the Eastern and from Madrid to Peking, the Nikon affair, religious schism, the Razin and Solovetsk rebellions,[1] all were major developments. They justify the use of the term "celebrated" for his reign, although the fame was dearly bought. Alexis Mikhailovich received a burdensome inheritance from his father.

The reign of Michael Fedorovich, Tsar Alexis's father, appears at first glance to be a period of tranquility for the Muscovite state, a pause in the recent domestic strife and foreign wars. Cossacks no longer fought against the crown, and "eternal" peace was concluded with Poland and Sweden, yet all this was but the calm before the storm. During the Time of Troubles the humbler segments of the urban population had acquired habits which were far from eradicated during the reign of Tsar Michael.[2] The cossacks were forced to abandon government-controlled territory, and the petty tsars, the pretenders whom they brought forward, had played out their role, yet in their steppe homelands the cossacks were not at all weakened. They continued to benefit from the friendship of the Ukrainian population and to maintain ties with them. They had merely to block passage to the sea from the Don and present themselves to an enterprising leader, and they could overrun the state, carrying masses of the common people with them in their wake.

The barbarian peoples who lived within the borders of earlier tsardoms such as Kazan, Astrakhan and Siberia, also awaited their chance to rise against the Russian tsardom. They continued to maintain ties with the Crimea and Turkey, forever anticipating that Muslim authority would be restored along the shores of the Volga. Even the wretched inhabitants of the northern Siberian tundras did not lose hope of restoring their independence under the banners of local leaders. Nor did the treaties of "eternal" peace with Poland and Sweden come without difficulties. Russia could not forget Smolensk,[3] for the honor of the new dynasty demanded the return of Russian territories given up by the dynasty's founder.

It was assumed that Michael's successor might postpone war indefinitely in order to gather his forces, yet when the time came circumstances allowed no possibility of delay. Even before the end of Michael's reign there arose an opportunity to take the Ukraine under the tsar's aegis to save it from Catholic persecution. The cossack movements did not cease, they merely continued under the banners of religion and Rus ethnic identity.[4] The chance to take over the Ukraine came again to Michael's son, this time with the added threat that if the cossacks could not agree to Moscow's conditions they would give themselves as subjects to the Turks. War with Poland appeared inevitable.

What resources did Tsar Alexis have for this western war, which already had been fought unsuccessfully three times? We have seen[5] that in the second half of the sixteenth century the forces of the Muscovite state, although victorious in the East, having subjugated whole tsardoms there, appeared inadequate for a collision with their Western European counterparts. The reign of Ivan IV ended with a cry of despair that the state had no resources to maintain the army it needed to rebuff its fearsome foes. The reign of his successor began with just such a cry.[6]

One result of this despair was the binding of peasants to families in crown service, an act which clearly demonstrated that the Muscovite state of the sixteenth and seventeenth centuries was in the same economic circumstances as Western Europe at the beginning of the Middle Ages, or as colonial America, compelled by the inadequacy of its free labor force to buy black slaves. The more clearly Muscovy perceived its grievous economic situation, the more oppressive measures it enacted to meet the most basic needs of the state, those of external defense, and the more urgently it strove to establish ties with the rich and powerful Western European states, to imitate what made them rich and powerful. Thus it is not surprising that even Godunov, who enserfed the peasants, was known for his love of foreigners and their customs.

After the Time of Troubles the new dynasty, finding itself in the same circumstances, had no choice but take as its own the traditions established by earlier sovereigns. In the reign of Tsar Michael Moscow was filled with foreigners granted privileges to found various industrial enterprises. Foreigners entered Russian service in droves. Beside the old noble cavalry and musketeer infantry a new army was created, following the foreign model and using foreign nomenclature such as cavalry, dragoons and soldiers.[7]

Alexis Mikhailovich

The hire of foreigners and equipping the new army took money, and there was no money. Russia's merchants were poor. They could not withstand the foreigners who gathered Russian commerce in their hands. The taxpaying classes were burdened with levies, which they were forced to take extreme measures to avoid. Whole districts were abandoned. The taxes fell with all their weight on those who remained,[8] and on top of this the people still had to support the local governors and officials. In such circumstances Alexis Mikhailovich took the throne!

During the reign of Tsar Michael the taxpaying classes had spoken out strongly, though legally, of their displeasure. Under the young Alexis this displeasure found expression in the Moscow riots of 1648 when the people could blame their misfortunes not on the tsar but on the boyar who ruled in his name.[9] To calm popular anxiety the crown quickly took steps such as the Law Code of 1649, the end of pledged dependence[10] as a means to avoid taxes, and the end of privileges for foreign merchants. The mutiny planned by pledged dependents lost its advantages and failed. The towns of Solvychegodsk and Ustiug had their revolts a little later, and Novgorod and Pskov later still. All this made difficult times for both government and populace.

Meanwhile, even as Moscow blazed with riot and fire, Khmelnitsky triumphed over the Polish commanders in the south and took the Ukraine.[11] Khmelnitsky asked Moscow to accept him as subject while the tsar was struggling to put down revolts in Novgorod and Pskov. These revolts died away because of isolation, as the fire of a burning building dies away when there are no others nearby to catch the blaze, but only two years later war with Poland had to be waged. The impoverished government exhausted its resources preparing for the war. At first success justified the sacrifices, but soon came plague, war with Sweden, further disturbances in the Ukraine and unrest among the barbarian peoples in the East. The treasury was drained to the dregs. Troops deserted because of hunger and cold. The state tried to resort to credit, but its copper coins fell in value and the Muscovite mob again took to the streets.[12]

The truce signed at Andrusovo ended the hardships of the Thirteen Years War,[13] yet the state could not remain calm for long. The Andrusovo treaty was concluded in 1667, the very year that Razin's insurrection began. Then in 1668 Briukhovetsky mutinied. Cossacks killed Muscovite commanders and troops in Ukrainian cities,[14] while in the North the Solovetsk rebellion flared. In 1671 the Razin revolt was crushed, but in 1672 the Turks took the city of Kamieniec and kept Moscow in a state of constant alarm until the end of the reign. After all this, the slowness and indecisiveness of government instructions regarding troop movements should cause no surprise, nor should the scarcity of troops and their poor condition, as a result of which large numbers existed only on paper, and not in fact. The only wonder is how the impoverished state survived such a series of blows, such a series of wars.

In fact foreign observers wondered that the Muscovite state recovered so quickly after defeats such as Konotop and Chudnovo.[15] The answer seems to lie in the government's ability to concentrate its power, and in the unity, regularity and continuity of its instructions. The local authorities moved slowly, avoiding fulfillment of orders. Indeed, they were incapable of fulfilling any. Eventually their sloth, evasiveness and incompetence drew complaints to Moscow, where the great sovereign repeated his command that the officials personally accomplish their task without resting. The response always was that something necessary could not be found anywhere. The next command was to look there, or there. Again there was delay, followed by an order threatening disgrace and fearful punishments. Eventually the task was done. In this manner they began to build a ship, with nothing prepared. We have seen how they built it, but build it they did!

In all this there were still elements of good fortune. It is true that during the reign of Tsar Alexis the Muscovite state reeled under successive blows. This is what is important, that the blows followed one another instead of falling all at once. The Novgorod and Pskov uprisings came a year after Moscow's, when everything in the capital again was quiet and important changes implemented. By then, with the population of the central regions pacified, the government could concentrate all its attention on the Northwest. Similarly Razin's insurrection did not begin until the war with Poland was over, in 1669. The next year Briukhovetsky rebelled, but by that time Razin had left for the Caspian Sea and thereby gave Moscow respite to put its Ukrainian affairs in order. Razin led his second revolt only after all was calm in the Ukraine, when consequently a large part of the military forces could be moved eastward. Similarly the Turks did not begin to threaten Russia until the situation with the eastern cossacks was settled.

These favorable circumstances somehow allowed the Muscovite state to resolve the various serious ordeals it faced in the second half of the seventeenth century. Nonetheless these ordeals, following so swiftly one after the other, could have acted destructively on a far more robust nature than that of Tsar Alexis. Moreover, Alexis suffered not only political misfortunes but also domestic afflictions.

THE TSAR'S FAMILY SITUATION

The tsar had six daughters and five sons from his first marriage to Maria Ilinichna Miloslavskaia. All the sons were notable for their frailty. Two of them, Dmitry and Alexis, predeceased their father and mother, and in March of 1669 Tsaritsa Maria died. After her, the same year, followed a third son named Simeon.

On January 22, 1671 Tsar Alexis married a second time. His new bride was Natalia Kirillovna Naryshkina, ward of the conciliar noble Artamon Sergeevich Matveev. We have met Matveev often in past volumes, for he was one of the men closest to the tsar. The paucity of unofficial sources, such as memoirs, does not allow us to discover how Matveev, a crown secretary's son, drew near the tsar and became his friend. If it were permissible to guess, in all probability this occurred through the offices of Morozov.[16]

Matveev, like Ordin-Nashchokin, Rtishchev and other prominent individuals of Tsar Alexis's reign, was distinguished by a love of foreign novelties.[17] His home was decorated in European fashion, with pictures and clocks. His wife did not live in seclusion like most high-ranking Muscovite women, and his son received a European education.[18] Matveev even put together a troupe of actors from his household servants, who entertained the sovereign with theatrical performances.

In politics as well as taste Matveev, like Nashchokin, looked to the West, yet he sharply distinguished himself from Afanasy Lavrentievich in his conduct. Nashchokin, as we have seen,[19] moved quickly, not caring if he offended anyone along the way. He quarreled with the aristocracy and was forced to leave his service career prematurely. Matveev stood equally close to the tsar, yet did not thrust himself forward. For a long time, a very long time, he held the modest rank of colonel and regimental commander of the Moscow-based musketeers,[20] and he maintained good relations with the nobility. Although later, as we have observed,[21] he was overthrown during the reign of Alexis's successor, it was not the great dignitaries who overthrew him. They (at least the most illustrious among them) were loyal to Tsaritsa Natalia Kirillovna, and hence to Matveev.

Near the end of the reign of Tsar Alexis, Matveev was head of two of the most important chancelleries, those devoted to Ukrainian and Foreign Affairs, with the modest title of conciliar noble. Only in 1672, at the birth of the tsar's son Peter, was Matveev promoted to lord-in-waiting together with the tsaritsa's father Kirill Poluektovich Naryshkin, and not until October of 1674, on the occasion of the baptism of the tsar's new daughter Feodora, was Matveev made boyar.

DEATH OF A TSAR

On September 1, 1674 (New Year's Day in the old Russian calendar) the
sovereign "presented" his eldest son, thirteen-year-old Tsarevich Fedor.
In a special ceremony on Red Square the tsar's son was introduced
formally to the whole Muscovite state and to the foreigners. After the
ceremony the tsarevich wished his father and the patriarch a happy new
year and made a speech. After Fedor the boyar Prince Yury Alekseevich
Dolgoruky made a speech to the tsar, the tsarevich and the patriarch. The
same day some foreigners, the sons of the Ukrainian cossack leader
Samoilovich[22] and the Lithuanian envoy, saw the heir in Archangel cathedral. The sovereign sent Boyar Khitrovo to them to present the tsarevich
and to say "You have seen for yourselves the radiant eyes of the sovereign's
heir, and how he is grown. Write specially of this to your governments."

In 1676, between the twenty-ninth and thirtieth of January, between
Saturday and Sunday, at the fourth hour of the night, Tsar Alexis
Mikhailovich died in the forty-seventh year from his birth. He had blessed
his eldest son Fedor as his successor. Besides Fedor only one son remained
from the old tsar's first marriage, the tsarevich Ivan, and one from the
second, Peter. Alexis also left daughters, Evdokia, Marfa, Sophia, Catherine
and Maria from his first marriage, Natalia and Feodora from his second.
Three of the sovereign's sisters were still living, Irina, Anna and Tatiana
Mikhailovna.

CHARACTER OF ALEXIS MIKHAILOVICH

At the very beginning of our narrative of the activities of Tsar Alexis we
noted the similarities of his nature with that of his father, and also noted the
differences.[23] During his thirty-year reign these similarities and differences grew clearer. Alexis was indisputably the most attractive personality
ever seen on the throne of the Muscovite tsars. Foreigners who made his
acquaintance could not escape the enchantment of his gentle, humane and
good-humored nature. These character traits stood out the more sharply,
and attracted the more attention and sympathy, because of the dark circumstances of Alexis's reign. "It is astounding," said foreigner observers, "that
despite the unlimited power which the tsar holds over his people, power
approaching complete slavery, still he has not infringed upon anyone's
possessions, nor upon anyone's life, nor upon anyone's honor." The
unaffected, paternal bearing of the Russian autocrat toward his subjects
must have struck the foreigners particularly strongly, since in Western

Europe this type of relationship already had disappeared. This was the age of Louis XIV!

A profound religious faith permeated the tsar's entire being, which imparted a particular mildness, a particular attractiveness to his actions. Yet although he recalled his father in the gentleness of his nature, Alexis resembled his famous son[24] in vitality, receptivity and passion. He was very hot-tempered, and when a man near him incited his wrath Alexis dealt with him personally, humbling him with his own hands. This was the custom of the times, and was not considered an infringement of honor.

An ambassador of the Holy Roman empire, [Augustin Baron von] Mayerberg, was greatly impressed by the character of Tsar Alexis, and described the following incident. When news of the defeat of Khovansky and Nashchokin reached Moscow in 1661[25] the tsar convened his advisory council and asked what was to be done. By what means might Russia defend itself against this fearsome enemy? The tsar's father-in-law Boyar Ilia Danilovich Miloslavsky burst into speech. "If it please the sovereign," he cried, "give me command of the army and I will soon bring the Polish king to Moscow as a prisoner." Nothing irritated Tsar Alexis as much as bragging and over-independence. He lost his temper. "How dare you, you peasant, you paltry little man, boast of your military skill? When did you march with the armies? What victories have you had over our enemies? Or are you mocking me?" These words did not end the matter. The furious tsar slapped his elderly father-in-law in the face, pulled out some of his whiskers, drove him from the room with kicks and slammed the door.

In another incident the great sovereign had himself bled and, feeling better, proposed to do the same to all his court. Willingly or unwillingly everyone agreed except for the tsar's maternal uncle Rodion Streshnev, who excused himself on grounds of age. Alexis flew into a rage. "Perhaps your blood is more valuable than mine? Perhaps you consider yourself better than everyone else?" Again the matter did not end with words, but when his rage was spent the tsar sent rich gifts from the palace to Streshnev, that he might forget the beating.

When a distinguished provincial administrator committed an offense Alexis also lost his temper, and wrote a long angry letter to the guilty party. Even then the tone of these letters always was moderated by the tsar's attempts to show the culprit his sin before God, his responsibility before the tsar of tsars. The angry, threatening tsar vanished, and the man was seen, a man worried by the fault and its consequences, who tried to present their full significance to the offender. Within the angry expressions we hear the sympathy of one human being for another.

Thus in 1668 Alexis sent the household officer Golovkin to question the boyar Prince Grigory Semeonovich Kurakin. "Why did he not march to Nezhin and to Chernigov in accordance with the great sovereign's command? How is it that he was not moved by the plight of the people of God and of the sovereign who were besieged there, at the end of their resources? How will he answer for them on Judgement Day? How could he, a boyar, have forgotten our Savior Jesus Christ's miraculous power, which gave victory for the sake of his tears and diligence? Why has he become so conceited? Why is he so puffed up? He heeded rogues and foolish talkers who think first of themselves and only later of what is right. Why did he remain so long at Glukhov? Not only his staying but his very going there was improper, for surely he could have written a letter to the city about surrender. He was supposed to go directly to Nezhin and Chernigov to free the region and wage war, yet he wrote that since he had not succeeded at Glukhov he could not go. This lofty design was enraging and loathsome to God, and so indeed he began to make his own plan apart from God's, and placed reliance in his own strength and good fortune. The people of Nezhin and Chernigov lament that it pleased the sovereign to rescue them, but they were lost by his boyar. God will call him to account for them. It were better for him to carry out his charges with tears and diligence and humility before God. As he began, so should he end, and not by force and glory.

"The sovereign is greatly astonished," continued the message, "that having received such fame from the Lord God for his tears he, a boyar and commander, should so lose himself. It would have been better for him to take the city of Glukhov and pour out much blood, than for the sufferers in Nezhin and Chernigov perish to no purpose in a slow and miserable death, yet by ill chance his efforts failed. What now will happen? First, he angers God. He trusted in worldly force. He wanted to take the city and caused much bloodshed to no purpose. Second, he loses men and brings terror and fear upon the people. Third, he rouses the anger of the great sovereign. Fourth, he earns shame and disgrace because he lost men to no purpose. Fifth, the praise and honor which God has granted him in this world will be stripped from him miserably by this shameful affair and his delay near Glukhov. Instead of praise he will be subject to all manner of reproaches and embarrassing talk. All this is written to him in the hope that he, the boyar, may receive the blessings of the holy Eastern church, and that the interest of God and the sovereign may be accomplished through good military leadership, while he, the sovereign, regards his boyar with favor and wishes him honor and takes pity on him in his old age."

Alexis used even stronger words in a letter to Prince Grigory Grigorievich Romodanovsky. "To the enemy of the Cross of Christ and the new Ahithophel, Prince Grigory Romodanovsky. May the lord God reward you for your purely satanic service to us, the great sovereign, just as he rewarded Dathan, Abiram, Ananias and Sapphira.[26] They swore falsely to the Holy Spirit, as you clearly have amended God's will and our sovereign decree. Just as Judas sold Christ for bread, so you sold God's will and our edict and mercy with a lie. You were ordered to send reinforcements to the regiment of Table Attendant Semeon Zmeev for the urgent business of God and our sovereign self. Indeed you ordered them sent so well-organized and fortified, and so well maintained by all our favor, that when they came to your troops after only five versts' march not only did you not send them on to where they were ordered by our initial command, you took them with yourself, enticing them with our great reward and secretly promising to send them to their homes for your own thrice-cursed profit. Thus as you turned your mind from the business of God and our sovereign self, so will the Lord God turn his mind from you, and your wife and your children will weep such tears as orphans weep when they are beaten for no fault.

"You, thrice-cursed and infamous hater of the Christian race, our faithful traitor and most true son of Satan and friend of devils, because you did not send our troops you will fall into the abyss of hell, from which none has ever returned. Remember, O cursed one, by whom have you been favored? By whom rewarded? On whom do you depend? Where can you hide? Whither can you flee? Whom do you disobey? Against whom do you act slyly? You are patently false to Christ himself and you turn your back on His interests! Know you not that endless torment awaits him who honors Him falsely, and who spends his days before his sovereign in craftiness and guile and alters orders without fear? At last we have seen, our envious and true transgressor, how you accomplished that matter by artful and malicious design. As for your comrade, the foolish and worthless little prince, we order torture,[27] and the bumpkin Klimka we order hanged.

"God has blessed us and appointed us, as sovereign, to govern and judge his people in the East and in the West and in the South and in the North, and in all these lands we look to individual men to carry out the will of God and our own sovereign commands. It is not given to you alone, who hate us, to mind the affairs of all lands, because human nature is not capable of dealing with them all. The devil alone meddles in them all. Our sovereign letters were written and sent to you with such gracious words as even your superiors have not received, but you became conceited and showed a Muslim obstinacy. If you desire God's mercy and blessing and do not want to go unrepentant to hell, and wish to regain our sovereign favor as before, then forsaking all obstinacy you must fulfill this our decree, and send a regiment of cavalry and a regiment of dragoons immediately to Table Attendant Zmeev, having given them their wages."

The same sort of letter went to Nikita, steward of the monastery of St. Sabbas, in 1652. Eighteen musketeers had been stationed in the monastery, whom the archimandrite had been ordered to quarter in the stables. The steward Nikita came to them there after drinking deep and asked "By what order are you billeted here?" Hearing that it was by the archimandrite's, he struck the corporal[28] on the head with his staff, and ordered the musketeers' weapons, saddles and clothing thrown out of the compound.

The tsar sent Alexis Musin-Pushkin to investigate the affair, and wrote personally to the steward. "From the tsar and grand prince Alexis Mikhailovich of all Russia to the enemy of God, the God-hater and Christ-seller, the ravager of the house of the miracle-worker,[29] the accomplice of Satan, enemy, accursed and useless thorn, the wicked, sly evil-doer, the bursar Mikita.[30] You are become like the money-loving Judas. As he sold Christ for thirty pieces of silver so you, accursed enemy, betrayed the house of the miracle-worker, yea, and my own sinful instructions, from crafty and perfidious drunkenness, and for your guileful and underhanded intrigues. Satan himself, the enemy of God, has taken you over. Who asked a worthless orphan like you to rule over the house of the miracle-worker and over the sinner that is myself? Who gave you this power that exceeds the abbot's, that you beat my musketeers and my Mikhailovsky peasants[31] without his knowledge?

"Remember the words of the Gospel. An arrogant man is impure before God. O cursed enemy, for what was the Morning Star[32] thrown down from heaven? Was it not for pride? God showed no mercy. Meanwhile you, who strive to please Satan, you write to your friends and calculate it a mark of dishonor and enmity that the musketeers stand guard around your cell. Well and good it is, that they guard a beast like you! By our orders the musketeers have stood guard around better and more honorable men than you; even around metropolitans, if such a prelate takes the same path as you, accursed sinner.[33] Should your threats be of any importance to me? Do you not know that I have no other joy and hope except in God and his mother our sovereign lady most holy Mother of God, and the miracle-working Sabbas who is as light to my eyes? That is my joy and my gladness, and my strength for the battle against my enemies, and against this your grumbling is nothing to me. I regard even the threats of my brother sovereign[34] as cobwebs, because the Lord is my light and my salvation. Whom then shall I fear? With the aid of the most holy Mother of God and the intercession of Sabbas the miracle-worker no threats are fearsome. Know this, thou accursed one, that fighter is threatening who holds hope in his father Satan and holds it secretly, so that no one knows of it, while he appears as a good and true man before others. Know thou also, angel of Satan, that only to you and to the devil your father is your temporal honor fitting and precious, while to our maker, the creator of heaven and earth, and to my guiding beacon the miracle-worker, there is no doubt that your thrice-damned and prideful and fictitious secret matters are utterly flagrant and crude.

"Yea, not falsely do the Gospels say that a slave cannot serve two masters. To me, sinner that I am, worldly honor is as dust. As long as we do not fear God, as long as we turn our faces away from him, as long as we do not fulfill his commands with all our soul and with all our heart, then you will see, accursed one, whether it is you and I who are precious in God's sight, or our arrogant designs. If you neglect the will of God, woe and damnation will come unto both of us, and unto our sly and perfidious heart and our crafty and evil intent. Cruel will it be for us on the day of rage of the Lord of Sabaoth,[35] for our sly and perfidious affairs and schemes will not aid us then. Know thou also, sly foe, how you now have disturbed the miracle-worker's house and troubled my sinful soul, even to the point of tears. The miracle-worker will see that I walk in darkness because of your wily Satanic nature, and both the miracle-worker and even God himself will turn against you. Know thou that I myself shall ask mercy of the miracle-worker and plead with tears for defense against you. Not from joy shall I complain about you, for I had rather ask mercy for you of God and of the immaculate Mother of God and of the miracle-worker, and make peace with you in my letters.

"Instead you will read of your dishonor, and for your arrogant grumbling I will call down upon you such disgrace as you have never seen in all your life. You traded your place with the miracle-worker for your own subtle and crafty and drunken heart and for your accursed schemes. It is no wonder that you do not heed a sinner like me here, because you have sold even this holy place for your wicked ways. God will judge us in another court, and except for me there will be no one and nothing to defend you. Further do I warn you that if you should repent to the miracle-worker with an insincere heart and submit to me in a state of evil grumbling, know then that you will not be made spotless. As Naaman concealed himself after leaving Elisha the prophet, so you too will think only of hiding in the house of the miracle-worker,[36] and because of this you will be banished and rejected and excommunicated by our Lord God Jesus Christ and by His immaculate Mother and by the miracle-worker Sabbas and by me, sinner that I am, and will be driven with all dishonor and disgrace from this place in the home of the holy worker of miracles.

"Those who read this letter are ordered to have the musketeers bring him before the entire synod with all dishonor, like the enemy of God and of the house of the miracle-worker that he is. They are ordered to place chains around his neck and irons on his legs, and Alexis[37] is ordered to place a musketeer guard around him and hold him in the stables."

This letter, like the letter delivered earlier to Nikon in the Solovetsk monastery,[38] shows the best of all patriarchal relations in the world at the time. The drunken bursar Nikita beat a musketeer corporal, and the tsar ordered chains placed about his neck and irons on his feet. In the meantime, outraged by letters in which Nikita indulged in some threats, he lost his temper and wrote directly to the bursar. Without hiding the troubled state of his spirit, Alexis summoned him to the judgement of God and warned of punishment from on high. He wrote that he, the tsar, feared no one because the Lord was his light and salvation. Because of the aid of the Mother of God and the prayers of the miracle-worker Sabbas he feared no man's threats. The tsar's piety restrained the heat of his anger, and forced him to acknowledge a higher judge over both himself and Nikita, a judge who held both men on one level. The tsar wrote that he would ask the miracle-worker's intercession for Nikita, who so disquieted his soul that he went in tears and in gloom.

Religious feeling colored these patriarchal relations, sometimes imparting to them an unusually touching quality, and at the same time a grandeur. Such was the letter from Andrei Pekin, military governor of Nizhny Lomov, to the commander Khitrovo. "In Nizhny Lomov the cossacks clearly have turned traitor. Remember my wretched self, and notify the great sovereign, that he may order my name inscribed in the synodical[39] with my wife and children." The great sovereign could perfectly understand and grant such requests.

The beauty of Tsar Alexis's nature was expressed best of all in his letters of consolation to those close to him. His letter to Ordin-Nashchokin on the occasion of his son's defection has been mentioned.[40] In this letter the force of the tsar's character lifted him high above the standards of his age. The letter to Prince Nikita Ivanovich Odoevsky regarding the death of his son was of the same sort. "Let it now become known to you that by the will of our almighty and all-merciful God and by his fearsome command the Holy Spirit was pleased, in His great mercy, to take your firstborn son Prince Mikhail to the heavenly abodes. He lay burning with fever for three weeks less two days, and had become ill in my presence. That day I was at your estate of Veshniakovo, and he was well. He entertained me. Indeed he was so pleased to do so that never have I seen such joy as his. He and Prince Fedor[41] begged to present me with a horse, and I said to them 'For what purpose have I come to you? Do you think I have come to rob you?' At this, weeping, he said to me 'I am not worthy, lord, to see you here. Take my gift, lord, for the sake of Christ. Make us glad, little father,[42] for the honor of such a guest has not been granted us in this age.'

"Then, seeing their sincere petition and unmanageable joy, I accepted the dark-grey stallion. It was not the horse alone that was dear to me. Best of all was their unforced service, their obedience, and their joy toward me, as they rejoiced in me with all their hearts. For this I regarded you and them with favor. I went everywhere, even to the stables. I looked at everything, I went through all the living quarters, and I dined with them in their home.[43] After dinner I set out to Pokrovskoe to relax in the woods of Karacharovskie. Your son accompanied me in good health, and came in the evening of that same day to Pokrovskoe. I rewarded both your sons with Romany wine,[44] and sops and crusts, as they ate at my table.

"When the evening meal was drawing to a close," continued the tsar, "your elder son got up from the table and began to moan that his head hurt unbearably. He begged to be allowed to return to Moscow because of the pain in his head, and so he left for home. He wanted to travel by sledge that night, to reach Moscow in the morning, but his illness began to kindle and burn.

"Now you, our boyar and servant, and your children, must not grieve beyond measure, though none can fail to grieve and shed tears. In fact it is needful for you to shed tears, but in their proper measure, that God not be angered further. You must become like the righteous Job, who suffered from our common foe the devil. How much disaster did he bring upon him?

Did he not suffer? Yet he overcame the devil, and did not God give him sons and daughters once more? Why? Because he did not sin even in word, he did not resent that his children were dead. Now God has taken your son, but the devil has not destroyed your entire line. You know well that God arranges everything best for us. He took your son in a state of grace... Be not offended, for God acted to aid your son. Rejoice that he took the best, and be not too aggrieved. Trust in God and in His Mother and in all His saints. Later on, if God wills, we will not forsake you and your children. Remembering your petition we have regarded your children with favor, and in future we will be glad to reward your grandson Prince Yury, as we are glad to remember the father.

"I welcomed Prince Fedor and consoled him in his grief, and I sent as much as God deigned to the ceremonial transfer of the bier from the church and also to the funeral itself, for indeed I had learned and found out that no one is left to you except God in heaven and myself on earth. I am glad to reward you and yours. Only remember, Prince Nikita, remember God's mercy and our favor. I am glad to remember how I rewarded your son during his life...and how, before that, we visited you, and wrote to you saying how I the sovereign and you the boyar should live. You, our boyar, must trust in God and in His immaculate Mother and in all the saints and in us the great sovereign. Rely on us, and if God wills, we will not forsake you. We shall be mother and father to you and your children and grandchildren as God wills, if you live in the Lord's commands and aid all those who are poor and helpless as God wills. That task God has set for us also, that we aid the helpless. It is for you to obey without fail and with joy, according to these our gracious letters, and thence our favor to you will be continuous and unfailing." On the back of the document was the further inscription "Prince Nikita Ivanovich! Do not feel hurt. Simply put your trust in God and rely on us."

In some others letters Tsar Alexis's patriarchal attitudes appeared without embellishment, in their most unattractive form. Thus the tsar wrote in a letter to the table attendant Matiushkin[45] "I must tell you how I have been amusing myself. Every morning I have been ducking table attendants in the pond, a perfect baptismal site. I duck four and five and even a dozen of them at a time. Whoever is not on time for my inspection, I duck him. Then after this ducking I reward them, I invite them to dine with me that day. Those who have been ducked dine abundantly at my table, so that the others say 'Let us come late to inspection on purpose, so that we will be ducked and seated at the tsar's table.' Thus many come late to inspection on purpose."

The outward appearance of Tsar Alexis, as foreign eyewitnesses described him, helps to reveal his character. He was gentle of feature, white-skinned, red-cheeked and brown-haired, with a fine beard and a strong build. At the same time a premature corpulence, especially of the belly, weakened his constitution in spite of his active life. He rose early for matins, and sometimes passed the night in fervent prayer. He worked industriously at his affairs, rode frequently to the hunt, which he loved passionately, and rarely let the patronal festivals of nearby monasteries and parish churches pass unattended. He had so much energy that he decided to renounce the life of his fathers, to abandon the Muscovite court and set out on campaign.

There is a tradition that the campaigns in Belorussia and Lithuania matured and shaped Alexis, inspired him with greater self-confidence and changed his relations to those around him. He became more independent. Nonetheless it is obvious that his energy was sustained by success. When his military successes ceased, Alexis appeared at the head of the army no more. The growing obesity noticed by foreigners was either the result or the reason for the end of these activities. It is difficult to tell. Contemporary observers speak of Alexis's great talents and regret that these talents were not developed by study. Morozov could do no more than sympathize with education, and regret that in his own youth he had not been taught.[46]

Alexis apparently read everything available in the Slavonic and Russian languages at the time. The intellectual activity thus stimulated was revealed most strongly in his compulsion to write. How many letters written in his own hand, usually quite long, how many lists and notes were preserved after him! Alexis undertook a description of his campaigns, and several copies corrected in his own hand have been preserved ("black copies," as they then were called).[47] They describe the army's setting out from Moscow, the commanders' assignments, the speeches made on the occasion. Probably the plague and the subsequent military failures brought this writing project to a halt.

Finally, Tsar Alexis tried to write poetry. A letter to Prince G.G. Romodanovsky took this form. "By the injunction of the all-powerful and great and deathless and merciful tsar of tsars and lord of lords and commander of all the various hosts, our lord and master Jesus Christ, I the greatly sinful Tsar Alexis wrote this letter with my own hand.[48]

O slave of God! be daring in the name of God
And trust with all your heart that God gives victory.
Live in love and great concord with Briukhovetsky,
And guard well yourself and the people of God and of ourself
From all deceptions and flattery.
Hold firmly to your wisdom and examine
Military affairs with great caution,
Lest secretary Zakharka and his companions do
As Yurasko did to our boyar
And commander Vasily Sheremetev, and Prince Oginski to our
    boyar
And commander, Prince Ivan Khovansky.
Keep careful watch, and let your eyes, like those of Argus,
At every hour constantly and carefully abide and watch over all
Four countries, and hold in your heart great meekness and humility
    before God,
And not conceit as a certain brother officer of yours said that such
    a one had not been born
Who could overcome him with an army, and for his overweening
    pride God gave him utterly into captivity."[49]

MEN CLOSE TO THE TSAR

Because of his overly gentle nature Alexis Mikhailovich could not avoid yielding great influence to the people around him. He was easily angered, but not constant or firm. His excessive trust in unworthy people, and the power he ceded to them, derived from a weakness of character, not from inadequate understanding of people. Thus for example he clearly saw what sort of man his father-in-law Miloslavksy was. In a momentary outburst he did not spare him, but to lay disgrace upon him would cause pain to the creature closest to him, his wife whom he so loved, and this was beyond the tsar's powers.

So it was also in relations with other individuals, who were closely tied together and held strongly to one other. When one fell into disgrace suddenly the court was full of discontented, unhappy persons, and by custom these individuals clustered in the palace from morning to evening. It was impossible to escape them. The entire day then would become an unendurable burden for his sympathetic spirit, and Alexis gave in.

This also explains his strange relations with Patriarch Nikon. Unlike his enemies the privy boyars and lords-in-waiting, Nikon could not be constantly at court, and for this reason his cause was lost. Guile is the child of weakness, and the tsar used guile in the Nikon affair. He agreed with the boyars that the patriarch had gone too far, and that it was impossible to live with him, yet at the same time he tried to convince Nikon of his own benevolence, to set himself right in the eyes of the angry patriarch. By such means the good Tsar Alexis demeaned himself in trying to please both sides when more decisive and independent actions could have settled the matter. Without any doubt the main reason for Nikon's fall lay in the character of the tsar who, had he possessed a firmer nature, could have held his friend within proper limits, and the first conflict could have prevented the grievous consequences of the later battles. Alexis Mikhailovich destroyed his own friend precisely because of his inability to deal competently with their first disagreement. The tsar's weakness sometimes had the same consequences as tyranny.

The softness of the sovereign's nature did not at all diminish the importance of his powers. Alexis Mikhailovich had the same elevated concept of his rights as did Ivan IV. "In truth God has blessed us and given unto us, as sovereign, to rule over and judge his people in the East and in the West and in the South and in the North." The same relations that shaped the reign of Tsar Michael were still in force. The popular movements, in which Alexis's reign was so rich, were undeniably survivals of the Time of Troubles, surfacing after the relaxation necessary during Michael's reign, and these popular movements expressed sharply the relationship between the majority and the elite minority. The masses rose against the boyars, displaying the unity of their interests with the interests of the tsar. The minority was left to seek timid protection around the foot of the throne. In this way Morozov, the most prominent of the boyars, owed his very salvation to the affection of the tsar.[50]

Led by their hatred of Morozov, the people showed particular sympathy for the boyars Nikita Ivanovich Romanov, the tsar's uncle, and Prince Yakov Kudenetovich Cherkassky, whom they knew or supposed to be enemies of Morozov. Neither of these individuals possessed the ambition necessary to profit from the popular mood. Nikita Ivanovich appeared on the scene during the popular rebellion against Morozov and Miloslavsky, where he tried to pacify the people. Later, at the time of the Pskov riots, he led the city's delegation to the tsar. A final bit of information preserved about this individual is that he was a lover of foreign customs, even dressing his servants in livery according to the foreign style. Patriarch Nikon, who disliked this novelty, devised a means to save the tsar's uncle from his sin. He begged a suit of livery from him, as if for a pattern to dress his own servants in such fashion, but when the credulous boyar sent him the clothing the patriarch ordered it cut to pieces. We cannot guarantee the truth of this story in the details,[51] but the boyar Nikita's love for foreign novelties is confirmed by the fact that he was the owner of a boat which subsequently so interested his young great-nephew, Tsar Peter Alekseevich, and served as the beginning of the fleet.[52] It would be nice to know more of this intriguing individual, but the lack of information proves either that his personal means were inadequate for him to play a more visible role, or that his path was obstructed intentionally, and that he was too cautious to fight his way free of the limits laid upon him. Regarding Prince Yakov Kudenetovich Cherkassky, his personal deficiencies became obvious later, at the time of the Polish war.[53]

There were sixteen particularly distinguished families in Russia under Tsar Alexis, whose members joined the boyars directly, bypassing the rank of lord-in-waiting. These were the Cherkassky, Vorotynsky, Trubetskoy, Golitsyn, Khovansky, Morozov, Sheremetev, Odoevsky, Pronsky, Shein, Saltykov, Repnin, Prozorovsky, Buinosov, Khilkov and Urusov families.

Prominent among the Cherkasskys there was, besides Yakov Kudenetovich, the notorious Prince Grigory Senchuleevich. People said that he was a savage who always sought opportunities to demonstrate his physical strength. He was an experienced rider who filled his extensive stables with horses he had broken himself, and he was said to be more in sympathy with animals than with people. Representing the celebrated Vorotynsky clan was Prince Ivan Alekseevich, a worthless and insignificant man. The Trubetskoy family had no worthy representative after Prince Alexis Nikitich, and after Konotop[54] he lost his right to be praised as "fortunate in war and terrible to foes." Of the Golitsyns, the subsequently famous Prince Vasily Vasilievich had only just begun his career,[55] while it was said that Prince Alexis Andreevich grew more modest where he was most fortunate.

Although the head of the Golitsyn family was not distinguished by his patrician spirit that spirit survived in another patrician line, in the person of the famous Prince Ivan Andreevich Khovansky. We have seen his

curious conflict with Ordin-Nashchokin, in whom the proud descendant of
Gediminas saw a lowborn favorite, powerful solely by virtue of the tsar's
favor, like Maliuta Skuratov,[56] though nothing is heard of Khovansky's
own ancestors in antiquity, nor did the prince enjoy useful political con-
nections or receive much praise for his abilities. Indeed Tsar Alexis once
said to him "I favored you and chose you for service, though everyone
called you a fool." Both Russians and foreigners described Khovansky as
a man of patrician hauteur, arrogant, lacking in self-control and change-
able. Ordin-Nashchokin called him a fickle man who followed the suggestions of others. This was the opinion of a rival, but Mayerberg said that
Khovansky was renowned everywhere for his defeats, that he lost battles
through his own precipitous actions and his inability to balance his forces
against those of the enemy.[57] Tsar Alexis attested that everyone called him
a fool, while the common people gave him the name Windbag.[58] There are
stories about his immoral behavior in Pskov and his arbitrary and brutal
conduct with his troops. The tsar's famous tutor was the last historical
figure to appear from the Morozov family.

The Sheremetevs secured the importance of their clan through their
personal abilities. The historical records are full of the activities of two
Kievan governors from this family, Vasily Borisovich (whose career was
so unfortunately ended)[59] and Peter Vasilievich. The latter appears as of a man
with great abilities, but boastful, extremely greedy for military glory, and
unbearably proud and arrogant. The records praise Vasily Vasilievich Sheremetev's dazzling military prowess yet also demonstrate that the crown did
not allot this grandee a suitable field of endeavor, sending him to serve as
governor in an unfortunate district which all the other boyars avoided.[60]

The representative of the Odoevskys, Prince Nikita Ivanovich, appears
frequently in the records. His contemporaries praised his gentleness,
which sharply distinguished him from his colleagues. He served more than
once as a high plenipotentiary ambassador, but it is difficult to discern
anything in his actions beyond the precise fulfillment of instructions. In a
letter to Dolgoruky the tsar himself said of Odoevsky "I suppose that
Prince Nikita persuaded you to action, though it was a mistake to listen to
him. You know what a stickler he is! You should hear what they sing of him
in Moscow." The family was not wealthy. The tsar, having sent money for
the burial of Prince Mikhail Nikitich, wrote to his father "Indeed, I have
learned and recognized that, except for God in heaven and myself on earth,
you have no one."

From the Pronskys came the famous Prince Ivan Petrovich. He was entrusted with the important matter of educating the tsarevich Alexis Alekseevich, but the choice was said to be a poor one. No one from the Shein family was prominent at this time. From the Saltykovs, Boyar Peter Mikhailovich was head of the Ukrainian Chancellery. He was the same age as the tsar and was said to have been much loved by him. Peter Mikhailovich was praised for his unusual prudence and steadfast loyalty.

Notable Repnins of the period include first Prince Boris Aleksandrovich, the favorite of Tsar Michael, who was charged with cruelty. His son, Prince Ivan Borisovich, received the following judgment. He was regarded as cautious and prudent, but his contemporaries suspected that he concealed his father's vices under his guise of virtue. In our time it is difficult to determine whether these unfavorable opinions were engendered by the jealousy of the enemies Prince Boris acquired during the reign of Tsar Michael, or whether the hostility was genuine, caused by Repnin's unattractive character.

The intellectual abilities of Prince Ivan Semeonovich Prozorovsky appear in a less than advantageous light during the negotiations with Sweden when the famous boyar held the title of primary negotiator but Ordin-Nashchokin conducted the actual business. All that is heard of Prince Ivan Andreevich Khilkov is that he did not take bribes, but was terribly hot-tempered.

Several members of these sixteen paramount families were gifted individuals. Yet, except for the aged Morozov and Trubetskoy, and only Saltykov from the younger men, no one in the tsar's retinue had great influence on matters of state.

From the ancient but secondary families the Dolgorukys fought their way along the road to primacy in the person of the noted commander Prince Yury Alekseevich. One foreigner expressed the unflattering opinion that the prince wished to appear as Fabian, but instead resembled Catiline.[61] This opinion is unsubstantiated, and may or may not be true. Records survive of Dolgoruky's military service, but his other deeds are so little known that we have not the means to determine his resemblance to Catiline.

One of the most prominent men in the military arena was Prince Grigory Grigorievich Romodanovsky. One branch of the Starodub princes,[62] the famous Pozharskys, had left the scene but the other, the Romodanovskys, remained and greatly improved their position. Prince Grigory was noted for his savage character and great bodily strength. He was more a soldier than a leader, and surpassed everyone in his military zeal, tireless activity, quickness, and leonine courage. In the Ukraine, as we have seen,[63] he gained the sympathy of the inhabitants. The other Romodanovskys, Princes Vasily Grigorievich and Yury Ivanovich, received only unfavorable judgements.

The names of the Boriatinsky princes appeared in the military history of the reign of Tsar Alexis, especially in the story of the Razin rebellion. To Prince Yury fell the honor of the first and last defeat of the fearsome brigand, but there are also testimonials of bad deeds by the same Boriatinsky.

The name of the boyar and commander Prince Grigory Semeonovich Kurakin frequently appears in military records. He is spoken of as an insignificant character, and no data exist to prove or disprove this judgement. Another Kurakin, Prince Fedor Fedorovich, was made tutor to the tsarevich Fedor Alekseevich, but the choice was said to have been an unfortunate one.

At last we come to the men closest to the tsar: the Miloslavskys, Streshnev and Khitrovo. All evidence agrees about the Miloslavskys' abilities, those of the famous boyar Ilia, father-in-law of the tsar, as much as of his kinsmen Ivan Mikhailovich and Ivan Bogdanovich. Unfortunately none of them matched their intellectual abilities with moral virtues. In Ivan Bogdanovich, famous for the defense of Simbirsk against Razin, the evidence suggests broad knowledge, but a knowledge united with slyness.

A curious story (though a foreign one) has been preserved about Bogdan Matveevich Khitrovo. It describes him as a mild and affable man, tirelessly solicitous of the unfortunate, who never closed his ears to suppliants, especially foreigners. The last words might offer the solution to such a flattering opinion of the man whom we know primarily through the incident of the patriarch's junior boyar.[64] However biased the foreigner's judgement may have been, it seems that in certain circumstances, with certain people, Khitrovo might appear gentle and affable, but that Nikon acquired a very dangerous enemy in Khitrovo. Khitrovo was also a foe of Nashchokin, but the story of his special bias toward foreigners suggests that he too should be numbered among those people who looked to the West, like Morozov, Rtishchev, Nashchokin and Matveev.

Another foe of Nikon was Rodion Matveevich Streshnev. Tsar Alexis is said to have considered him a man not subject to passion, a new explanation of why the tsar could so vacillate between Nikon and his enemies, if the authority of the patriarch could be counterbalanced by the authority of Streshnev.

Nikon's third principal foe was Nikita Mikhailovich Bobarykin, a relative of the Romanovs and Sheremetevs. He is presented as a man who loved the good, straightforward and utterly selfless. If the tsar held this opinion of Bobarykin, it is understandable that he did not hasten to satisfy Nikon, in whose complaints Bobarykin was presented quite differently.

The activities of another of Tsar Alexis's favorites, Fedor Mikhailovich Rtishchev, have been discussed earlier. He was most notable for his patronage of education, but also innovative was his imputed advocacy of the use of credit in time of monetary need.[65] A *Life* of Rtishchev has come down to us, and though short and written in a panegyric form it contains certain interesting stories about its subject's activities and character. The biography portrays Rtishchev as an unusually sensible and temperate man, and says that he restrained Morozov and Nikon. Mayerberg bears this out, for he too notes the prudence in which Rtishchev, before reaching the age of forty, surpassed his elders. There are several other curious stories of Rtishchev's character in the biography. It is recorded that when selling one of his villages he lowered the price on condition that the buyer treat the peasants well. Elsewhere it says that he gave land to the city of Arzamas after learning that the inhabitants needed it, but were not in a position to buy. On his death bed he implored his heirs about only one thing, to treat the peasants well.

On the whole, in surveying the character and deeds of Tsar Alexis's favorites, the men he raised up and supported, men such as Rtishchev, Ordin-Nashchokin and Matveev, it must be recognized that he possessed the most valuable of all talents for a sovereign, choice of people.

The personal character and relationships of all these notables also demonstrate that the power of Tsar Michael's son was not sufficient to meet obstacles from this source. We have noted that the interests which the Muscovite boyars supported in the reigns of Ivan III and of his son and grandson had yielded their place to other interests.[66] Though they bowed low before the authority of the great sovereign the noble families nonetheless made great efforts not to lose the sole right to hold higher offices. They had no wish to sit with some Andronov or other, neither did they like to submit even to their own brothers, let alone to someone of humble origins.[67] The rule of Filaret Nikitich was difficult for many of them, and afterwards they succeeded in separating themselves from Repnin thanks to the mildness of Tsar Michael.[68]

Tsar Alexis resembled his father more during his youth than he did later, as is best seen in his letters to Nikon on the way to Solovki and to Prince Trubetskoy at the time of the first Smolensk campaign.[69] At this time he already had a lowborn favorite, Matveev, who nevertheless was careful not to put himself forward. It is said that during the campaigns the tsar became more independent. He grew closer to Ordin-Nashchokin, who had not Matveev's caution, and clashes began.

Alexis Mikhailovich found himself in a difficult position because of his character. On one side, he considered it essential to support the touchy Afanasy. On the other, how could he afford to offend Odoevsky, Dolgoruky and their comrades?[70] Not having the force of character to act directly and openly Alexis, like all people of his temperament, withdrew, concealed himself, gave instructions secretly so as to avoid opposition and unpleasantness. He set up his own chancellery, the Privy Chancellery, from which he sent letters and instructions in his own hand, the contents of which no one was supposed to know except the recipient. Even Afanasy received such instructions, bypassing the older departments, and there he sent his own opinions and complaints.

Meanwhile Odoevsky and Dolgoruky were satisfied also. The tsar bestowed on them the title of great and plenipotentiary ambassadors, *in the name of their ancient and honorable clans*. He added their comrade Afanasy Lavrentievich as a third, then crossed him out because the words "ancient and honorable clans" had been written. In this way, with all these compromises, Alexis Mikhailovich brought his Afanasy to the rank of boyar. At the very last he brought the crown secretary's son Matveev to the rank of boyar as well. Quietly, imperceptibly, he cleared the way his youngest son Peter so boldly dared to go.[71]

At this point the history of Ancient Russia ends. The work of both Tsar Alexis Mikhailovich's sons, Fedor and Peter, belongs to modern history, but before we discuss their activities we must describe the condition in which Tsar Alexis left Russia. We will begin the next volume with this account.[72]

NOTES

Additional information on personalities and topics found in the text and notes is available in Edward J. Lazzerini, George N. Rhyne and Joseph L. Wieczynski, ed., *The Modern Encyclopedia of Russian, Soviet and Eurasian History* (MERSEH), (formerly *The Modern Encyclopedia of Russian and Soviet History*); Peter Rollberg, George Gutsche and Harry B. Weber, ed., *The Modern Encyclopedia of East Slavic, Baltic and Eurasian Literatures,* (formerly *The Modern Encyclopedia of Russian and Soviet Literatures) (Including Non-Russian and Émigré Literatures) (MERSL);* Paul D. Stevens, ed., *The Modern Encyclopedia of Religions in Russia and Eurasia* (MERRE), (formerly *The Modern Encyclopedia of Religions in Russia and the Soviet Union* (MERRSU); and David R. Jones, ed., *The Military Encyclopedia of Russia and Eurasia,* (formerly *The Military-Naval Encyclopedia of Russia and the Soviet Union).*

CHAPTER I

1. Soloviev discusses this subject in Volume 22 of the present series.

2. Ivan Samoilovich was hetman of the Left-Bank Cossacks from 1672 until 1687. He opposed the Russian-Polish alliance because of its dangers for the Ukraine. From Moscow's point of view his career was checkered, since his loyalty to the tsar depended on his perception of the Ukraine's best interests at the moment.

3. When not serving as the tsar's agent in Poland, Grigory Protopopov was a crown secretary in Kiev.

4. *Rada* was the name given to the main council of lords (secular administrators and bishops) in Poland and Lithuania. The Sejm was the general diet. Important matters, such as the enactment of new laws or the declaration of war, could be ratified only with the advice of the Rada and the approval of the Sejm.

5. At this time Lithuania was part of the Polish Commonwealth.

6. Mikhail Khanenko was hetman of the Right-Bank Ukraine from 1669 or 1670 until 1674. He resolutely opposed the Turks, who supported his rival Doroshenko (see below), but a series of military defeats ended his career. In 1674 he ceded his authority to Samoilovich (see Note 2, above) and retired to his estates.

7. The Pats (sometimes spelled Pac) family was very important in Lithuania in this period. Michael (1624-1682) was a hetman, his brother Bonifacy (died 1678) a military leader, and Kristof or Krzysztof (1621-1684) a chancellor. Several other relatives also were sufficiently eminent to win a place in Polish biographical dictionaries.

8. Kamar's name sometimes is spelled Komar.

9. Artamon (sometimes spelled Artemon) Sergeevich Matveev (1625-1682) was the son of a crown secretary. Instead of following his father into bureaucratic service he became a page at court and later commander of the musketeers. He served in several military and diplomatic capacities over the years, and was a trusted agent of the tsar. In 1671 his ward became Alexis's second wife, placing Matveev in the traditionally powerful position of the sovereign's father-in-law, or at least foster-father-in-law. After this Matveev held many extremely important posts, including the leadership of the Chancellery for Foreign Affairs and the Chancellery of the Apothecary, which was responsible for the health of the ruler. When Alexis died suddenly in 1676 his first wife's family regained political primacy, and Matveev suffered disgrace and exile. He returned to Moscow and to power in 1682, but within days was killed by a rioting mob. At the time of Kamar's visit his rank was that of *okol'nichii* (lord-in-waiting), the second-highest position in the Muscovite hierarchy. Some two years later he was named to the highest rank, that of boyar.

10. The *pospolite ruszenie* was a general mobilization, the Polish equivalent to the Anglo-Saxon *fyrd* or the medieval French *arrière-ban*.

11. These were tribal peoples living in Russia's southern borderlands who often served as auxiliary forces for the tsar. For more information on the Cherkess and Kalmyks, and on their relations with Muscovy, see below, Chapters III and IV.

12. Zaporozhia (the word literally means "beyond the rapids") was a part of the southern Ukraine along the lower reaches of the Dnieper river. Its cossack population was autonomous in local matters but, in this period, otherwise jointly administered by Moscow and Warsaw. The flat-bottomed fortified transport boat called a *chaika* ("seagull") was typical of the region. It was distinguished by a belt of reed bundles around its sides which protected the occupants from hostile fire while decreasing the danger of sinking. When not at war the Zaporozhian Cossacks used chaikas for trade, sailing down the Dnieper and across the Black Sea as far as the Anatolian coast.

13. Khitrovo (1624-1697) was an experienced officer and administrator who served as *voevoda* (military governor) of the Don region from 1672-1674. He seems to have been a stern and quarrrelsome leader (in 1674 his fellow officers begged Moscow for his recall, saying that many of their local allies had fled because of Khitrovo's treatment), but overall his career was long and distinguished.

14. Kamieniec (in Russian, Kamenets-Podolsky) was taken by Turkish forces with the aid of the cossack hetman Doroshenko (see below) in August of 1672. This event forced Poland to cede Podolia and much of the Ukraine to Turkey, thus endangering Russia and Western Europe by giving the sultan lands that previously had served as a buffer zone.

15. Prażmowski (1617-1673) was not only the first senator and archbishop but had served as "interrex" between the abdication of King Jan Kazimierz in 1668 and the election of King Michael in 1669. No friend of King Michael, whom histories

variously describe as "a nonentity," "a passive tool," and "[w]ith natural deficiencies," Prażmowski and Jan Sobieski (Crown Chief General, cossack hetman, and Michael's eventual successor), even tried to force the king's abdication, though when the attempt failed they chose concession over civil war.

16. *Sic*, should be Warsaw.

17. Michael Radziwiłł (1635-1680) was also field hetman of Lithuania and governor of Wilno. His family produced more than twenty important military and political figures between the sixteenth and eighteenth centuries and had marital ties to several European royal families.

18. Lithuanian Grand Hetman Michael Pats, another foe of King Michael. He is termed traitorous because in 1671, during a battle against a combined force of Turks, Tatars and Doroshenko's cossacks, he led the Lithuanian troops away from the Poles, preventing the reacquisition of the lost parts of the Ukraine.

19. Petro Doroshenko (1627-1698) was hetman of the Right-Bank Ukraine from 1665 until 1676. His loyalty was to his own homeland, which he hoped to unite as an autonomous entity dependent upon neither Poland nor Russia. To this aim Doroshenko sometimes worked with the Turks and Crimean Tatars, causing both Warsaw and Moscow to view him as a traitor. Eventually losing the support of a war-weary Ukraine, Doroshenko surrendered to Russian forces in 1676 and lived out his life in honorable exile, serving as governor of Viatka and enjoying the grant of a village near Moscow.

20. As noted above in Note 9, Matveev actually did not achieve boyar rank until 1674.

21. A universal (from the Polish *uniwersal*) was the term for a decree, instruction, or proclamation of the Ukrainian Cossack hetmans.

22. Jan Sobieski (1629-1696) was grand hetman of the cossacks from 1668. He opposed the Polish king Michael, after whose death his many military victories against the Turks helped him become elected as the new king, Jan III.

23. In 1660 at Chudnovo the Poles killed or took captive an entire Russian army of 36,000 men.

24. The treaty, or more accurately armistice, of Andrusovo ended the Thirteen Years War (1654-1667) between Russia and Poland. It ceded much disputed territory to Russia, including the Left-Bank Ukraine and Kiev, which was supposed to revert to Poland in 1669 but did not do so. Afanasy Lavrentievich Ordin-Nashchokin (died 1680), the head of Moscow's Chancellory for Foreign Affaris and hence in effect the tsar's prime minister, negotiated the agreement and signed for Russia. Although for centuries the tsars had used a network of express riders called *yamshchiki* to receive and deliver messages, a regular international courier and postal service was begun only in the later seventeenth century.

25. Tiapkin was an envoy to Poland's King Jan Kazimierz (ruled 1654-1668) in 1664-1665.

26. The unfortunate King Michael Korybut Wiśniowiecki (see above, Note 15) died in Lvov on November 10, 1673 of stomach trouble (one source blames "a surfeit of gherkins") at the age of 33.

27. Fedor Alekseevich (1661-1682) was the eldest surviving son of Tsar Alexis and his first wife Maria Miloslavskaia. He never became king of Poland, ruling instead as tsar from his father's death in 1676 until his own, at the age of 20, in 1682. For information on his reign see Volume 25 in this series. It should be noted that Poland had a long history of importing its monarchs from neighboring countries. In 1384 the Poles elected a ten-year-old Angevin princess to their throne, and in the late sixteenth century they chose a Frenchman (Henri de Valois) and a Transylvanian (Stefan or István Bathory). Ivan IV, the Terrible, was one of the defeated candidates in 1575, and Poland's own claims on the Russian throne, because of its invasion in the first years of the seventeenth century, made Fedor a genuinely viable possibility.

28. Grand Duchess Eleonora, sister of the Holy Roman emperor Leopold I, married King Michael in February of 1670. She brought ties with all the Habsburg lands: Austria, Hungary, Spain and, through Spain, the Netherlands. Though not an absolute requirement, it was not uncommon for the Poles to require or at least urge the marriage of their newly-elected foreign monarch to the widow of the previous ruler.

29. King Jan Kazimierz had been a Jesuit and a cardinal, but left this life to become king of Poland after the death of his elder brother Władysław IV. When he became king he married his brother's widow, Marie-Louise of Gonzaga-Nevers.

30. This probably refers to the prince of Condé, who was a candidate for the Polish throne in 1669 and had received three votes in the 1674 election, although Jan Sobieski himself was related to the French royal family through his wife, Maria Kazimiera de la Grange d'Arquien, descendant of the Capetian and Carolingian kings of France. At this moment in history France had designs on the Spanish Netherlands (Habsburg territory), making it the enemy of Austria. It was, in fact, in tacit alliance with Turkey, stopping short of any open agreement but encouraging the sultan's war with Austria. Sweden was temporarily in support of France by virtue of having accepted some badly needed subsidies from King Louis, and by its hopes of undermining France's interest in establishing closer relations with Denmark, Sweden's rival.

31. The number of horses hitched to a carriage depended on the rank or significance of the passengers. Six horses denoted a very important person. The word *pristav* usually can be translated as bailiff or constable, but one or more always were assigned to visiting diplomats as official escorts.

32. The Russian term for the musketeers' weapon is *berdysh*, sometimes translated as poleaxe. Like both of its English-language counterparts it consisted of a long pole topped with a spear point and set with an axe blade. The musketeers, known in Russian as *streltsy*, were a hereditary militia or infantry established in the sixteenth century. They were divided into two broad categories of "provincial" and "Moscow" units, those from Moscow having a higher status.

33. The removal of hats in a diplomatic situation was a very important sign of respect. In 1673 Moscow's negotiations with Sweden were delayed for months because Russia refused to deal with an embassy that retained its headgear, and the

visiting diplomats had to send to Stockholm for permission to bare their heads (see below, Chapter II).

34. A *chetvert* was equal to approximately eight bushels (see the Table of Weights and Measures).

35. Dolgoruky (died 1682) began his career in 1627 and by 1648 achieved the rank of boyar. He served as a military officer, military governor, and head of various government chancelleries in Moscow. He was an experienced diplomat who often negotiated with foreign embassies or spoke for the tsar to envoys.

36. Cyprian Pawel Brzostowski (died 1688) held the position of *referendarz* (referendary) at this time, a very important post in the government of Poland-Lithuania. It ranked just below grand secretary, serving as a recorder, arbitrator and sometimes liaison officer in the court.

37. Tiapkin's term was *pochtomaister*, obviously taken from the German or Dutch.

38. Alexander Hilary Połubiński (1626-1679) was grand marshal of Lithuania from 1669. He supported the candidacy of Tsar Alexis for the Polish throne at the death of Jan Kazimierz, and again at the death of King Michael.

39. Prince Romodanovsky (died 1682) had a long career of military and diplomatic service, mostly in the Ukraine. At this time (1674) he was in the field helping the Ukrainian Cossacks fight the Turks and Tatars and trying to win over the pro-Turkish hetman Doroshenko.

40. The dietines (Polish *sejmiki*) were regional assemblies which discussed and settled local affairs and elected deputies to the general Sejm.

41. Lorraine was an imperial duchy, meaning that the election of its duke Charles as king of Poland would have extended the influence of the Austrian emperor and his ally the Pope, while at the same time complicating the expansion plans of their French rival Louis XIV.

42. A chamber of the general Sejm, its members consisting of rank-and-file nobility elected by local dietines.

43. The Sapiehas, a very powerful Lithuanian princely family, were second only to the Radziwiłłs in wealth and influence. Its members owned large estates in Lithuania and Belorussia, and many of them held high positions, such as grand hetman or·governor of Kiev.

44. In September of 1660 Sheremetev's army was defeated at Chudnovo by Polish and Tatar forces. The Poles gave Sheremetev to the Crimean khan, and he spent the next twenty-two years (until his death) in captivity. This story is related in Volume 20 of the present series.

45. Olszowski (1621-1677) was largely responsible for King Michael's election, a fact which made him very powerful and often unpopular among his peers. His main goals were protecting the Roman Catholics within his territory and regaining the lands lost to Brandenburg. This in turn placed him in collaboration with Vienna and against France, which was an ally of Brandenburg at the time.

46. Jan Andrzej Morsztyn (1621-1693) was a poet and diplomat as well as the treasurer of the Polish crown. He supported the election of Jan Sobieski and backed French (and Brandenburg) interests, and in 1678 became a naturalized French subject.

47. Early in 1674 Moscow decided at last to unite its forces under G.G. Romodanovsky and Ivan Samoilovich (see above, Notes 39 and 2) and move against the pro-Turkish hetman Doroshenko (above, Note 19). The Russian-Ukrainian forces' retreat is covered in Volume 22 of this series.

48. Vinnitsa fell under Turkish control in 1672. Presumably the money was for support of the Orthodox Christian population of the area. There is a possibility that this phrase refers to Anthony Winnicki, metropolitan of Kiev since 1663 (see below, Note 65), since in Russian the adjective meaning "of or from Vinnitsa" (vinnitsky) and the spelling of the surname Winnicki (Vinnitsky) are the same. In this instance, however, the word is not capitalized, indicating that it is the adjective rather than the name.

49. In 1664 Polish Crown Secretary Więsławski served as envoy to Moscow.

50. Before 1918 Russia followed the Julian rather than the Gregorian calendar and hence, in the seventeenth century, lagged ten days behind Western calculations. They began the new year on September 1 and counted years from the supposed creation of the world (in 5508 B.C.) rather than from the birth of Christ.

51. Casimir III, the Great (1310-1370) ruled from the year 1333. His reign saw commercial and territorial expansion, while Cracow acquired a university and many fine stone public buildings to replace the earlier wooden structures. Sigismund I, the Old (1467-1548) was elected king of Poland in 1507, thus ruling for more than forty years. He expanded Polish control over much of the Ukraine, and defeated invading Muscovite forces in 1535.

52. The Eastern Roman emperor Heraclius (575-642) managed a series of important military victories, saving the empire from near-certain destruction by Persia from the east and Avar incursions from the north. He also brought the True Cross from Jerusalem to Constantinople. The emperor Justinian I, the Great, lived 483-565 and ruled from the year 527.

53. See Volume 22 of the present series.

54. Nikita Ivanovich Odoevsky (died 1689), boyar from the year 1640, was an experienced diplomat and administrator who stood close to Tsar Alexis. He took part in most of the military campaigns of his era and negotiated with foreign powers numerous times. Even after Alexis's death he remained prominent, apparently weathering the changes of reign and of dominant political factions without difficulty. His relative Yury Mikhailovich began a similarly promising career in 1660, but faded from the records in about 1680, and died at a relatively young age in 1685. The Odoevsky family was historically prominent from the mid-thirteenth century and the direct line died out only in the later nineteenth century, having given Russia many generations of service.

55. Marcjan Ogiński (d. 1690) and Jan Antoni Chrapowicki (d. 1685) stood firmly behind King Jan Sobieski. Also see above, pp. 2, 15.

56. By the terms of the 1667 Andrusovo armistice Russia was to have held Kiev for two years, until 1669, and then returned it to Polish control. Actually Moscow kept the city permanently.

57. Tiapkin makes a pun on the word *pospeet*, which for people means to be on time, and for grain, to ripen.

58. In this seemingly senseless sentence Tiapkin is recommending that Moscow be diligent and retain its Russian identity (weave bast shoes, the traditional footwear of the peasantry) instead of turning to untraditional, Western, military solutions (sew boots).

59. In the seventeenth century the chronically cash-poor Russian government customarily provided its diplomats with sables to sell for expense money at their destination.

60. The region of Samogitia also is known as Zhmud. The "Rus regions" meant Ukrainian territories. This was an older term related to but distinct from "Russian." See below, Chapter V, Note 4.

61. In Poland's frequent history of electing a monarch from abroad marriage to the dowager queen often was a requirement. Eleanor was the sister of Emperor Leopold of Austria, and might be expected to bring Sweden into the imperial camp if King Karl XI took the Polish throne and married her. Sweden was, at this moment, in half-hearted alliance with Louis XIV of France. The Swedish king was a popular candidate in Poland because of the ties between the ruling families. In the later sixteenth century Katarzyna, daughter of the Polish king Sigismund I, married John III Vasa, the king of Sweden. Their son Sigismund III reigned as king of Poland-Lithuania from 1587-1632 and of Sweden from 1594-1604. Deposed by the Riksdag because he refused to accept the Protestant faith of his Scandinavian possessions, he nonetheless considered himself Sweden's rightful monarch, and his sons Władysław IV Waza and Jan Kazimierz Waza maintained their claim as titular kings of Sweden until the Peace of Oliwa (Oliva) in 1660, when they renounced all rights to the Swedish crown. The groundswell of feeling against King Jan resulted from the delay in his coronation (making him more vulnerable), continued war against Turkey with the prospect of further wars against Poland's other enemies to follow, and probably his temporary ties with France. This latter involvement earned him the enmity of the Austrian Habsburgs.

62. In Russian *feriaz*.

63. Pats's actual word was *moskal*, a pejorative term for Muscovite. In verb form it meant to swindle, cheat, or trade deceitfully. As a noun it appeared in the saying, "Who goes there?" "The devil." "Well, that's all right, but no moskal!"

64. Szumlanski (1643-1708) was an Orthodox nobleman who, despite their religious differences, maintained close ties with King Jan Sobieski. He became Orthodox bishop of Lvov in 1676, but secretly converted to Catholicism the next year.

65. Winnicki (died 1679) was made Orthodox bishop of Peremyshl in 1650. In 1663, with the support of pro-Polish forces, he became metropolitan of Kiev and exarch of the patriarchate of Constantinople in the Ukraine. At the same time, supporters of Doroshenko elected their own candidate, Joseph Neliubovich Tukalsky (see below) as metropolitan of Kiev. The two metropolitans divided their terrritory, Winnicki taking the western eparchies and Tukalsky the eastern.

66. Tukalsky (died 1675) was elected metropolitan of Kiev in 1663, but the king of Poland favored the rival candidate Winnicki and refused to confirm Tukalsky's election. The two metropolitans divided their eparchies until Tukalsky's death, when Winnicki tried to gain the entire metropoly but was blocked by Moscow. Tukalsky would have been no more acceptable to Russia, for in his position as advisor to Doroshenko he consistently urged the hetman to ally himself with Turkey and oppose Poland and Russia.

67. Seventeenth-century Russians used the word "Latin" to mean Western Roman Catholics.

CHAPTER II

1. Here Soloviev has backtracked without clearly noting his temporal shift, and indeed, the chronology remains irregular throughout the paragraph. The peace mediation he mentions took place in 1656, at which time Jan Kazimierz also promised Alexis the succession to the Polish throne, secure in the knowledge that the Sejm never would ratify such a plan, it is thought. The "unfavorable turn of affairs" to which the author next alludes may have been the continuation of war in the Ukraine or the Sejm's 1658 declaration that Alexis could be a succession candidate only if he converted to Catholicism.

2. Leopold I (1640-1705) was the second son of the Habsburg emperor Ferdinand III of Austria, or more precisely of the Holy Roman empire, and his first wife Maria Anna, daughter of Philip III of Spain. He became imperial heir at the death of his elder brother Ferdinand IV. He spent most of his reign fighting the expansionist efforts of Louis XIV of France and his allies, most especially Mohammed IV of Turkey and, for a time, Karl X and Karl XI of Sweden. As noted in the text, Leopold and his agents frequently mediated between other warring powers.

3. In 1646 Władysław IV married Marie Louise de Gonzaga or Gonzagues (died 1667), the daughter of Duke Charles of Nevers. At his death his brother Jan Kazimierz, one-time Jesuit and cardinal, became king and married his predecessor's widow. The marriage was childless, and after conferring with Louis XIV in about 1660 Marie Louise began to work toward the election of the prince of Condé as her husband's successor, although in the end it was Michael Korybut Wiśnowiecki who won the crown.

4. Almaz Ivanov (died 1660), actually named Yerofei Ivanovich Ivanov, began his career as a tax collector and merchant in Vologda, but soon was drafted into service in the Moscow chancelleries. He is most famous for his work in the Chancellery for Foreign Affairs, for which he served as a diplomat in Russia and abroad.

5. Menzies was a Scotsman who provided a number of valuable military and diplomatic services for the tsar. His name also is seen spelled Menezius, Mengies, or Menghes. He came to Russia in 1661 and died in 1694 with the rank of lieutenant general.

6. Potemkin (1617-1700) was an experienced diplomat who negotiated with foreign powers both in Moscow and abroad. In 1667-1668 he was one of the leaders of a Russian embassy to Spain and France, in 1674-1675 to Vienna, and in 1680-1682 to France, Spain and England by way of Germany and Holland. He is documented as governor of Novobogoroditsk as late as mid-September of 1699. Cherntsov, his companion on the Viennese embassy, is less prominent, and about all that can be said is that he subsequently served as a crown secretary in Moscow and an assistant to the governor of Smolensk.

7. Staden, a native of Riga, was one of the many foreign military officers hired by the tsars in the seventeenth century. As so often happened, he acted as diplomat and commercial agent as well as a leader of troops. Claes or Clas Totte (1616-1674) was a Swedish noble, councillor and diplomat who served as governor-general of Livonia from 1665-1672. Karl Gustav Wrangel (1613-1676) was Sweden's commander-in-chief. Staden's activities in Riga are more complex than they first appear, for he seems to have been working not only for the tsar but also for his patron Matveev. The visit usually is considered an important event in the process whereby Matveev supplanted his predecessor Ordin-Nashchokin as head of the Chancellery for Foreign Affairs. At the same time Staden also worked for Sweden and for himself, receiving the promise of a generous pension from the Swedes.

8. Stepan or Stenka Razin was a cossack who became the leader of a bandit force which soon developed political overtones. By about 1670 his followers were in full revolt against the government. Razin was captured in 1671, brought to Moscow, and executed in Red Square. See below, Chapter III.

9. Nikon became Russia's patriarch in 1652 and for several years worked closely with Alexis, even holding the title of great sovereign while the young tsar was away on campaign. Soon relations between the two men became strained over the question of authority between church and state and within the church hierarchy. In 1666-1667 an ecumenical synod decided in the tsar's favor and stripped Nikon of his rank.

10. Karelia and Izhora are regions in the northwest borderlands of Russia, near Finland.

11. Oxenstierna (1626-1693) was a member of an important Swedish family, many of whose members achieved high positions in their government. He travelled widely in his youth and served his rulers (Kristina, Karl X Gustav and Karl XI) in military and administrative posts.

12. The Dolgoruky or Dolgorukov family had a long history of service in Russia, dating back at least to the twelfth-century victories of an earlier Prince Yury, who traditionally is considered the founder of Moscow. The present Yury Alekseevich served in numerous military and administrative posts, including the suppression of the Razin rebellion, and remained close to Tsar Alexis. His son Mikhail Yurievich also held a prominent position in court and government circles. Both father and son often negotiated with foreign ambassadors, and both were killed by a mob in 1682.

13. Karl XI (1655-1697) succeeded his father Karl X Gustav in 1660 at the age of four, and emerged from his long regency shy, awkward, and poorly educated. Despite this unpromising beginning he soon began to rebuild his country, devastated by mismanagement and war. He was assisted in his efforts by native abilities and an espousal of absolutist principles. In 1674 he scarcely had begun to take control of his kingdom, and needed all the foreign alliances and assistance that he could get. Soloviev's text erroneously gives the name as Karl XVI, an error corrected in the 1991 Russian edition.

14. The Treaty of Kardis (or Cardis) was signed in 1661 in an effort to establish an "eternal peace" between Russia and Sweden. It settled the borders and possessions of the two countries as they had existed before the 1656-1658 war, and affirmed that Sweden would not aid Poland in its war against Russia. It also, as is obvious here, provided for the return of war captives on both sides.

15. The Russian text literally uses the impersonal pronoun *chego* for the Turk, instead of the personal *kogo*.

16. The Miloslavskys were an old but relatively minor noble family until the middle of the seventeenth century, when Tsar Alexis married one of their daughters. Soon the tsaritsa's father Ilia Danilovich Miloslavsky became a boyar and head of the government, while his relative Ivan Bogdanovich served as governor of Simbirsk and military leader during the Razin rebellion. The period of Miloslavsky influence ended with the tsar's second marriage, and the family died out in the late eighteenth century.

17. Baptism into the Russian Orthodox faith meant becoming Russian. Normally this conversion carried with it the loss of the right to return to one's home-land.

18. See Volume 19 of the present series. Denmark was at war with Sweden for much of the seventeenth century. In 1657 King Frederik III (1609-1670, ruled from 1648) declared war in hopes of recouping the losses formalized in the Treaty of Brömesbro in 1645. His efforts failed, although his heroism in personally fighting from the city ramparts in defense of Copenhagen in 1659 won his subjects' hearts. His contributions to Danish history are found less in his military exploits than in the establishment of absolute monarchy, described by Soloviev below.

19. Kokoshkin's title of "crown agent" is only one possible rendition of the Russian term *striapchii*, a household appointment of the tsar's court. It comes from an old verb meaning to do, work, serve or be busy, which fits well with the varied duties of its holders. Other common translations include "court butler," "aide" and "adjutant."

20. Christian IV (1577-1648) began life as the heroic leader of a powerful nation, sponsoring art and science and building magnificent Renaissance cities and palaces. Then an ill-considered intervention into Europe's Thirty Years War drained his treasury, destroyed much of his army, and left many of his provinces overrun by hostile forces. Despite the implication that Christian's advisors were to blame, this was an outstanding example of a time when the king should have listened to his councillors' warnings.

21. The stone platform in Red Square where executions, proclamations and other important public ceremonies took place. The name comes from the Russian word *lob,* or forehead, and refers to the old custom of touching one's forehead to the ground in deference to a superior. It sometimes is translated as the Place of the Skull.

22. This is the literal translation of Kokoshkin's phrase. The Danes themselves used the term hereditary autocrat, declaring that "The King shall hereafter be regarded by all his subjects as being above all human laws and knowing no other superior or judge over him in matters spiritual or temporal save God alone." See T.K. Derry, *A History of Scandinavia* (Minneapolis, 1979), pp. 137-138.

23. Grigory Borisovich (died 1677) and Bogdan Ivanovich (died 1682/1683 or later) Nashchokin were members of an old noble family who followed the usual traditions of crown service. Both were members of the tsar's advisory council or duma (Bogdan received his appointment as reward for his work in negotiating the Truce of Andrusovo in 1667), and both, obviously, undertook diplomatic missions for their sovereign.

24. Hemp was a fiber crop, particularly valuable in ropemaking, which made it an essential commodity for a nation that went to sea in wooden ships rigged with natural ropes and cables.

25. See Volume 17 of this series. The Marselises were a commercial family with their roots in the Low Countries but with branches in most major commercial centers, such as London, Denmark and Hamburg. The father of Peter Gavrilovich Marselis (died 1672) came to Russia as a merchant from Hamburg in the first years of the seventeenth century. The son continued in the family tradition, also becoming a diplomat, iron manufacturer, commercial advisor and founder of the Russian international postal service.

26. Courland, a province of modern Latvia, achieved a brief but extraordinary prominence in the mid-seventeenth century under Duke Jēkabs (1610-1682). This remarkable leader, whose name is rendered in English as James or Jacob, played on his country's main asset, its Baltic ports, to develop a powerful navy and a fleet of merchant ships that sailed the world, thereby promoting a prosperous peasantry, a wealthy middle class and an extremely elegant court. Then in 1658 Sweden captured the duke and devastated the country. James returned to power in 1660 but spent the remainder of his life attempting to recover his losses. A good English-language study of the subject can be found in Alexander V. Berkis, *The History of the Duchy of Courland, 1561-1795* (Towson, Maryland, 1969).

27. Zheliabuzhsky (1638-1709) was a Russian councillor, administrator and diplomat, perhaps most famous for his written notes on Russian society and government which included an eyewitness account of the Moscow riots of 1682. In 1661-1662 he was sent on an embassy to Brandenburg, Courland, England, Florence and Venice. In later years he served with similar missions in the Ukraine, Vienna and Poland.

28. This description fits Courland's colony of Tobago in the West Indies (not in India), which was founded sometime between 1634 and 1654. In 1650 Duke James also bought a small but valuable island in Gambia. After his capture by Sweden in 1658 other European maritime powers began making claims (and attacks) on these colonies, both of which were firmly in English hands by the mid-1660s. See Berkis, pp. 85-90, 95-99, 142-152.

29. Hebdon began his Russian career as early as the 1640s, serving as interpreter for the English merchant community in Moscow. After the execution of King Charles I in 1649 the English were expelled from Russia, but Hebdon remained and served as the tsar's purchasing agent and diplomat.

30. Russia's reasons for severing relations with England after the beheading of Charles I in 1649 combined genuine horror at the killing of an anointed monarch, especially given the event's coincidence with political unrest in the tsar's realm, and long-standing conflicts over commercial rights and privileges. Alexis granted Charles II some helpful loans, mostly in the form of sables and grain. Soloviev covered these topics in Volume 19 of this series, or see Inna Liubimenko, "Anglo-Russian Relations During the First English Revolution," *Transactions of the Royal Historical Society*, Fourth Series, 11 (1928), pp. 39-59.

31. William Prideaux probably was related to England's attorney-general of the period, Edmund Prideaux. Cromwell (1599-1658) was the English revolutionary leader who, after the death of Charles I, assumed control of the government. Initially he took the title of first chairman of the Council of State and in 1653, after dissolving Parliament by force, he became lord protector.

32. Prozorovsky (fl. 1630s-1660s) served the tsar as a governor, ambassador and respected courtier, attending visiting diplomats in Moscow as well as making this trip to England. On Zheliabuzhsky see above, Note 27.

33. Soloviev's text uses the term "English boyars."

34. A efimok was a silver coin minted in a Western European country, brought to Muscovy, and stamped over in the Russian mint. The term comes from the word Joachimsthaler, one of the currencies most commonly used for the purpose.

35. Dr. Samuel Collins was an English physician who attended the tsar in Moscow between 1661-1670. He left a fascinating account of his Russian experience in *The Present State of Russia, in a Letter to a Friend at London; Written by an Eminent Person Residing at the Great Tzars Court at Mosco for the Space of Nine Years* (London, 1671). Although the book has not been reprinted, an authorized photocopy can be found in many libraries.

36. Cherkassky (died 1642) and Sheremetev (died 1650) held vast power during the reign of Tsar Michael, after the death of his father Filaret. Through their leadership of some of the chancelleries that administered the foreign population of Moscow, they became particularly aware of Russia's relative technological backwardness and need for trained specialists to rebuild the country after the devastations of civil war and invasion at the beginning of the seventeenth century. They offered privileges and incentives to those Westerners who entered into the tsar's service, not all of whom were honest or well-qualified. See Volumes 16-17 of this series.

37. Shorin and Ivan Klimshin were *gosti*, that is, members of the Muscovite merchant elite who served as the tsar's agents in co-ordinating and regulating international wholesale trade, and in assessing and collecting the duties and taxes on goods. Shorin in particular was famous both for the allegations of greed levelled against him, and for his actions against foreign merchants. See Samuel H. Baron, "Vasilii Shorin. Seventeenth-Century Russian Merchant Extraordinary," *Canadian-American Slavic Studies*, 6 (1972), pp. 527-529. Reprinted in his *Muscovite Russia. Collected Essays* (London, 1980).

38. Charles Howard, first earl of Carlisle (1629-1685), was a loyal royalist whose career under Cromwell was rocky and uneven, encompassing among other things seats in Parliament and arrest for high treason. After the Restoration he became a privy councillor and, in 1661, earl of Carlisle. After his 1664 embassy he served in various military, administrative and diplomatic capacities, although he never again visited Russia. An account of the embassy exists in [Guy Miege,] *A Relation of Three Embassies From his Sacred Majestie Charles II to the Great Duke of Muscovie, The King of Sweden, and The King of Denmark, Performed by the Right Honourable the Earle of Carlisle in the Years 1663 & 1664* (London, 1669). It is available on microfilm. A slightly different version is printed as "The Earle of Carlisle's Embassy from King Charles the II to the Great Duke of Muscovy; and to the Kings of Sweden and Denmark, in the Years 1663 and 1664," in John Harris, *Navigantium atque Itinerantium Bibliotheca: or, A Compleat Collection of Voyages and Travels...*, 2 vols. (London, 1705), vol. 2, pp. 177-213.

39. The delivery of the tsar's response to an ambassador's message was a formal event with great opportunities to honor or slight the visitor and his sovereign. In this case the use of three very high-ranking courtiers, and the elegance of their costume, signalled Alexis's initial willingness to accommodate Carlisle and King Charles. Odoevsky and Dolgoruky are identified above in Chapter I, Notes 54 and 35, respectively. Volynsky (died 1682), another experienced administrator and diplomat, served as an ambassador and negotiator with Sweden in the 1660s, and in 1671 negotiated peace with Poland.

40. This refers to an ancient form of commercial fraud in which newly-woven cloth was washed and stretched beyond its original measurements. Once dry it would keep its new dimensions, at least until its next washing, and thus would increase the profits of those who were paid by the amount of cloth sold. While a certain amount of stretching, corresponding to what a modern knitter or handweaver

would call blocking, was a normal and necessary part of the finishing process, overstretching stressed the fibers and permanently weakened the fabric.

41. The term *gosti* is used, the Russian word for international wholesale traders. In Muscovy, and often in other countries as well, such men also frequently served as agents or factors for the government.

42. Dashkov became a conciliar noble in 1677 and died some time between 1678/79 and 1681/82.

43. The modern Tallinn.

44. This was the Second Anglo-Dutch War (1665-1667), one of three sharp conflicts fought, mostly at sea, in the second half of the seventeenth century because of the combatants' maritime commercial rivalry. This segment was sparked by England's seizure of Dutch colonies in Africa and North America, including New Amsterdam, which then was renamed New York.

45. Patrick Gordon (1635-1699), a "younger sone [sic] of a younger brother of a younger house" of landowners in Scotland, chose a mercenary career and fought in several armies before entering Russian service in 1661. As an officer of the tsars he trained troops, fought in the field, traveled as a diplomat, and lost and regained his patrons' favor more than once. Under Peter the Great he attained the rank of full general and rear-admiral of the new Russian fleet, and he frequently dined with the young emperor-to-be in his own home or in the Kremlin palace. His diary, published in a German translation and a highly abridged English version, provides not only a moderately detailed narrative of a varied and interesting life, but also fascinating glimpses of seventeenth-century Russia. See *Passages from the Diary of General Patrick Gordon of Auchleuchries* (New York, 1968). For more information also see the entry by Emily V. Leonard, "Gordon, Patrick," MERSH, Vol. 13, pp. 49-50.

46. In the sixteenth century Spain held part of the Netherlands, a situation unpopular with the Dutch because of religious differences (Holland was primarily Protestant, Spain vehemently Catholic) as well as political and economic considerations. At this same time England and Spain were powerful rivals, their jealousies exacerbated by the disastrous marriage of Philip II with Elizabeth's predecessor and half-sister Mary, and by Philip's interest in the welfare of English Catholics. In 1585 Elizabeth had sent a small force to aid the Netherlands in their resistance against Spain.

47. Nashchokin (1605-1680) is mentioned above in Chapter I, Note 24 as a negotiator of the Andrusovo truce. He was a member of a noble family from Pskov in the western part of Russia, and began his service career in his native town. In 1650 he moved to Moscow, where he continued as a military officer and diplomat. In 1667 he became boyar and head of the Chancellery for Foreign Affairs, in effect making him Russia's prime minister. He left government service in 1671 and the following year was tonsured as a monk under the name of Antony.

48. Italicized in the original.

49. Andrei Andreevich Vinius (1641-1717) was the son of an Amsterdam merchant (Andries Denijsz. Winius, in Russian Andrei Denisovich) who came to

Muscovy in 1627. The Vinius family, unlike most foreign traders, converted to Orthodoxy and cast their lot with the tsar rather than with their relatives or company in Western Europe. The elder Vinius served as merchant, manufacturer, diplomat, crown commissioner or factor, and *gost;* his son Andrei Andreevich as merchant, translator, advisor, diplomat, and postmaster. Most information on the family is in Russian or German, but some English-language material is found in the entry by Joseph L. Wieczynski, "Vinius, Andrei Andreevich," and the unattributed "Vinius, Andrei Denisovich," MERSH, Vol. 52, pp. 108-110, and in Joseph T. Fuhrmann, *The Origins of Capitalism in Russia. Industry and Progress in the Sixteenth and Seventeenth Centuries* (Chicago, 1972). Soloviev discusses the Vinius contributions in Volume 17 of this series.

50. Rumiantsev (fl. 1650s-1680s) was a crown secretary who served in various crown chancelleries and accompanied several higher-ranking diplomats such as Potemkin (see above, Note 6) on their embassies.

51. Philip IV died in 1665 and was succeeded by his four-year-old son Charles II (died 1700), with the dowager queen as regent.

52. One of Emperor Leopold's sisters married Philip IV of Spain and became the mother, and later regent, of Charles II. Another sister married Poland's King Michael. In addition, Leopold's own mother was a daughter of Philip III of Spain and hence Charles's aunt, while Leopold's first wife was Charles's sister. The complex and inbred Habsburg marriages allowed individual rulers within the family to claim kinship, when it suited them, with nearly every crown in Europe.

53. Chemodanov (fl. 1618-1650s) served in the military, at court and in diplomatic positions in Moscow and abroad, though he vanishes from the records after his Venetian visit. Posnikov or Postnikov (died 1661) previously visited Vienna, Hamburg, Saxony, Prague and Dresden on a Russian embassy, and served in the Moscow chancelleries while at home.

54. This apparent contradiction, with the water deeper on the upper decks and shallower below, may derive from the fact that the upper levels of the ship had more portholes and entrances, and thus could take on water more easily. The lower decks, with their fewer openings, would gather water more slowly.

55. Rhubarb root was a valuable medicine from ancient times. It was used to treat a number of ills from the common cold to liver problems to bruises, but was prized chiefly as a gentle but thorough laxative or, in larger doses, purgative. The finest rhubarb came from China, with other very high quality roots coming from Siberia and Central Asia. In the seventeenth century Russia conducted a large and profitable trade in rhubarb through its Siberian settlements. A comprehensive and highly readable account of rhubarb's medicinal and commercial history can be found in Clifford M. Foust, *Rhubarb. The Wondrous Drug* (Princeton, 1992).

56. Ferdinand II (1610-1670), fifth grand duke of Tuscany, succeeded to his patrimony at the age of ten and began to rule seven years later. He was a gentle and deeply religious man, interested in science, but plagued by a greedy and highly privileged administration.

57. Although the Russian text uses the word *vnuk* (grandson) it is unlikely that in this period the grandson of a Pope would be acknowledged openly. Alexander VII (Fabio Chigi) had a nephew Flavio who enjoyed high command in the papal army, and it was probably he who accompanied the Russian emissaries.

58. Both the Russians and their host show an understandable confusion about the council held in the church of St. George. In 1431 a council convened in Basel to discuss reform and reunification within the church. The assembly proved recalcitrant and the presiding Pope, Eugene IV, attempted to move it to a more hospitable Italian venue. Most of the delegates refused to move (and suspended Eugene from papal administration), but in 1438 a small council convened in Ferrara under the putative Pope's direction. The next year the council moved again, to Florence (not from Florence to Ferrara as the Russian diplomats believed), and eventually from Florence to Rome. The Orthodox metropolitan of Ephesus, Mark or Markos Eugenikos, attended the councils but remained in disagreement with the Western theologians and ultimately refused to sign the decree of union which the other clerics composed. He did not disperse any part of the council, but his inflexibility prevented the amicable conclusion that the other attendees had sought. He was proclaimed a saint by the Greek Orthodox church in 1734, suggesting that it is Soloviev rather than the seventeenth-century ambassadors who gave him that title.

59. Like most Russian administrators, Likhachev (fl. 1629-1668) served in a variety of posts in Moscow and the provinces. He is best known for the embassy to Tuscany which Soloviev discusses here.

60. Likhachev calls them *argamachki*, the diminutive form of *argamak*, a fine, fast horse bred in Central Asia and much prized in Muscovy.

61. Kelderman or Kellerman (fl. 1650s-1680s) achieved the status of *gost,* a leading wholesale merchant and government agent, in 1672. He was involved in Russia's early iron industry and, as noted here, served as a diplomatic representative of the tsar.

62. This was an organization of ethnic Armenians living in and near Persia who engaged in long-range commerce in Persian and foreign merchandise. For more on these traders see below, Chapter III.

63. The Ottoman Turkish sultan Mohammed IV (1642-1692) invaded Poland in 1672, capturing Kamieniec (Kamenets) and quickly winning considerable territories, as noted above in Chapter I.

64. Clement X, born Emilio Altieri in 1590, was Pope from 1670 until 1676.

65. This was an event during the Basel-Ferrara-Florence council mentioned above in Note 57. In 1438, as in 1672, the Romans wanted the Greeks to follow the custom of kissing the Pope's foot, but the leader of the Orthodox contingent, Patriarch Joseph II of Constantinople, flatly refused on grounds that the custom was an innovation sanctioned neither by scripture nor by tradition.

66. The adopted relative of Pope Clement X, Cardinal Paluzzo Paluzzi (or Pauluzzi) degli Albertoni Altieri (1623-1698) was in charge of most of the administrative work of his uncle's papacy.

67. Kristina Alexandra (1626-1689) was the daughter of Gustav II Adolf of Sweden. She was crowned queen in 1646 but ceded the throne to her cousin Karl X Gustav in 1654. She then converted to Catholicism and spent the rest of her life in Rome.

68. The Russian term is *velmozheishemu.*

69. In Russian *tsesar*, in German, *Kaiser.*

70. More than one Barberini served as cardinal in this period, but Antonio died in 1671 and Carlo (1630-1704) was still fairly young to be a "senior cardinal." The speaker probably was Francesco (1597-1679), the nephew of Pope Urban VIII.

71. Cardinal Altieri's administration galled many of the other prelates. As the aged Pope's memory failed the cardinal began to isolate his relative, allowing only rare and private audiences with persons whose agenda he had determined beforehand.

72. In the original text, *maestro di camera.*

CHAPTER III

1. Soloviev discusses these matters in Volume 21 of this series. To offer a brief summary: the Russian church underwent a number of reforms in the mid-seventeenth century, of which Patriarch Nikon's revision of religious books and rituals was the most far-reaching. It was part of an effort to bring Muscovite worship in line with the liturgy and practice of the rest of the Orthodox world, particularly Greece. Pushed through rapidly and insensitively, these changes inspired a schism within the church, with those who refused them being known as Old Ritualists, or more commonly in English, Old Believers. Other reforms and proposals affected church-state relations, and resulted in conflict between the patriarch and the tsar, who once were fellow reformers and friends. The contest was resolved by an ecumenical council in 1666-1667, and ended with Nikon's demotion and banishment. Paisios Ligarides (died 1678), sometime metropolitan of Gaza, was a Greek-born prelate of varied reputation. He came to Russia to help Nikon correct religious texts, but quickly ranged himself on the tsar's side and became a central figure in discrediting the patriarch. For further information see the entries in MERSH by G. Edward Orchard, "Nikon," Vol. 25, pp. 4-10; Robert O. Crummey, "Council of 1666-1667," Vol. 8, pp. 78-79; and G. Douglas Nicoll, "Old Believers," Vol. 25, pp. 228-237. Also see Paul Meyendorff, *Russia, Ritual, and Reform. The Liturgical Reforms of Nikon In the 17th Century* (Crestwood, N.Y., 1991).

2. It is impossible to do full justice to the phrase *rossky kniaz Mosokh* in a simple translation. The word *rossky* almost certainly derived from an adjective meaning fair- or ruddy-haired, and has an obvious similarity with *russky*, or Russian, although this term has been attributed variously to Finnish, Scandinavian, or even Celto-Latin words for other peoples and places. The Russian word for Muscovite, *moskvich*, does resemble *Mosokh* to some degree, but it is unlikely that there is a genuine relationship.

3. Nektarios's verbal tenses imply that the events to which he refers were recent or ongoing. Thus he may have been writing of the efforts of Pope Clement IX (Giulio Rospigliosi, 1600-1669) to aid Venice during the Turkish siege of Crete (1668-1669), when the papal fleet was commanded by Clement's nephew Vincenzo Rospigliosi. A few years earlier, however, another papal fleet commanded by the nephew of Alexander VII participated in a great multinational naval battle around the island of Chios, as part of that pope's Holy Alliance against the Turks. The use of the description "fierce wolf" would derive from the fact that the Western forces were less than fully sympathetic to the Orthodox inhabitants of the island, and pillaged their holdings nearly as freely as they attacked those of the Turks.

4. Actually, neither Libanios (314-393) nor Iamblichos (250-325) was Athenian. Libanios came from Antioch, though he studied and briefly taught in Athens, and Iamblichos was Syrian. Furthermore, Libanios was an outspoken admirer of pagan classical culture, while Iamblichos, a famous Neoplatonist, mingled Pythagoreanism and mysticism in his philosophy, defended magic, and became a hero of the pagan opponents of fourth-century Christianity. Despite Ligarides's regard, neither man was likely to seem a "good servant of God" to the traditional Orthodox church. As noted previously, seventeenth-century Russians commonly used the word "Latins" to refer to Roman Catholics.

5. Methodius (secular name Maksim Filimonovich), once bishop of Mogilev, was taken to Moscow for investigation of treason in 1667. He never became metropolitan, but in 1681 he returned to the Ukraine and served as bishop of Mstislav.

6. Also known as St. Sophia.

7. Psalm 69:17 (RSV).

8. Kiev was the center of scholarship in early Russia. It modeled its academy on contemporary Jesuit colleges and offered training in philosophy, languages and humanities as well as Orthodox theology. Ligarides's connection with Vissarion thus reveals that his interests were far broader and more secular (more "modern" and "Western") than was customary in seventeenth-century Muscovy, where most non-religious studies were viewed with deep suspicion.

9. The region of the Caucasus collectively known as Georgia was a volatile checkerboard of small, independent or semi-dependent, frequently feuding states in the seventeenth century. The principal kingdoms at this time were Kakhetia, Kartli, Imeretia, Guria, Mingrelia and Abkhazia, though many smaller related groups shared the region. The Georgian people (self-designation Kartveli) are a proud nation with a long history. They have been Christian since the early fourth century, and have ancient traditions of music, art and literature. Tsar Boris Godunov, who ruled from 1598 until 1605, sent an army to the Caucasus to aid the local Christian population against their Muslim neighbors in 1604-1605. Like an earlier campaign in 1593-1594 it ended with the Russian forces routed and massacred. Muscovy's own domestic turmoil following Boris's death precluded further Georgian involvement at that time.

10. The central doors in the iconostasis of an Orthodox church.

11. Teimuraz I (1589-1663) ruled the Georgian regions of Kakhetia (also written Kakheti) and Kartli from 1606-1648 and from 1625-1632 respectively. His voluntary subjugation to Moscow is described by Soloviev in Volume 20 of the present series. Despite all his troubles, recounted below, Teimuraz found time to become a famous poet, and in 1661 he became a monk. Shortly after that he was abducted and taken to Persia, where he was imprisoned until his death for refusing to convert to Islam.

12. Urban unrest, Tatar border raids, poor harvests and various other difficulties plagued the first years of young Tsar Alexis's reign, which began in 1645. A succession of serious riots began in Moscow and the country's other major cities in 1648.

13. Sic. The parenthetic exclamation point is Soloviev's own, to note the discrepancy of names.

14. Tiflis is now called Tbilisi.

15. The Mingrelian principality, under its Dadiani dynasty, seceded from Imeretia in the sixteenth century. Alexander uses the dynastic rather than the ethnic name to refer to this region.

16. The Kumyks (self-designation Qumuq, plural Qumuqlar) are people of the plains and foothills of Dagestan. They speak a Turkic language and are Sunni Muslims. Subgroups are often distinguished by place names, like the "Andreevsk Kumyks" mentioned below. The Cherkess, sometimes referred to as Circassians, reside in mountainous regions of the Caucasus, and speak a language of the Abkhazo-Adyge group of the Caucasian family.

17. Abbas I was shah of Persia from 1586-1629 and began the attempts to take over Georgia. Abbas II ruled from 1642 to 1667.

18. Teimuraz seems to say clearly that he was victorious over the shah (*ya poshel protiv nikh i pobil*), but if this is so it is uncertain why he had to flee to Imeretia for help in ridding his country of Persian troops.

19. The Gurians (or Guruli) are a Christian population in the western part of present-day Georgia. Their principality achieved independence in the sixteenth century but quickly declined to a state of vassalage to Imeretia as a result of Turkish hostility and feuds with the other Georgian leaders.

20. Catholicos was the title of the head of the Armenian and Georgian churches.

21. Sefi (or Safi) ruled Persia from 1629 to 1642. He was the father of Shah Abbas II but not the son of Abbas I, who while dying designated this son of a prominent *mirza* (scribe, secretary, or civil servant) to be his successor.

22. The first cossacks to settle in the Caucasus, the so-called Grebensk or Grebni community, grew up in the early sixteenth century in the Greben region, the northern foothills near the confluence of the Terek and Sunzha rivers. The Cherkess road was the main route through Cherkess territory.

23. Murza was the title of a Tatar leader or noble, an important lord such as the head of a clan or horde. The Nogay Tatars were a large nomadic group which split from the Golden Horde in the fourteenth century. They descended from earlier Mongol and Turkic tribes and speak their own language (Nogay), a Turkic tongue

with three main dialects. Most of them are Sunni Muslims. In the 1550s the group split into the Greater Nogay Horde, which accepted Russian suzerainty, and the Lesser Horde, which aided Russia's enemies. Both subgroups lived by herding, supplementing their economy by hunting, fishing and raiding the Russian borderlands for slaves to sell. In the first half of the seventeenth century the Greater Horde came under pressure from another nomadic population, the Kalmyks, and many of its members either merged with the Kalmyks or joined the Lesser Horde and the Crimean Tatars against their former Russian allies.

24. Shevkal, or shamkal, was the title of the leaders of various Dagestani peoples, but by the seventeenth century the position had become hereditary and limited to the Kumyks. The Edisan Tatars were a splinter group of the Lesser Nogay, closely tied to (and sometimes identified with) the Crimean Tatars.

25. The term *ulus* can mean a tent village, a tribal grouping, a major feudal domain or other administrative unit, or a generation. Here, used in the plural, "tent village" is the most likely translation.

26. The domra is a Russian stringed instrument resembling a mandolin. The gusli (the Russian word is a plural with no singular form) is similar to a psaltery.

27. The Armenians (self-designation Hayi) are an ancient people originating in Asia Minor, who settled the lands near Lake Van and eastern Turkey more than three thousand years ago. Their writing system dates to the fourth or fifth century, and traditionally they followed their own Monophysite Christian church, having converted in the year 308. Their language forms its own subgroup of the Indo-European family. Centuries of wars and oppression had made wanderers and colonists, and hence natural traders, of the Armenians.

28. Russian uses the same word, *yakhont*, to refer to all members of the corundum family, while English differentiates the red stones of this family as rubies and the rest as sapphires (blue, green and so on). *Sharap* obviously comes from the Persian word for wine, *sharab*. The first three fragrances are termed vodkas, which in the seventeenth century meant an alcohol-based essence as often as it did a distilled beverage. The first was derived from roses (*vodka guliafnaia*), and the second is called simply "aromatic" (*aromatnaia*). The third, *vodka naryzzhovaia*, is less clear. The word *naryzzhovaia* bears a tenuous resemblance to an old word for "kingly" or "regal" (*riga*), and hence could suggest that this was a very strong, highly distilled vodka or even an aqua regia, but the connection seems unconvincing. A more comfortable suggestion, though still not certain, is that the word came from *narynzha*, an archaic term for orange derived from the Persian *narendj*, and referred to a solution of orange oil essence to be used as scent or flavoring. The fourth perfume is described simply as an "Eastern aromatic" (*aromatu vostochnogo*).

29. Traditionally on Palm Sunday the tsar held the bridle as the patriarch rode a donkey in procession, in commemoration of Christ's entry into Jerusalem. See Mark 11:1-10.

30. See Volumes 16-17 of this series.

31. Thomas Bryan, an English merchant in Moscow.

32. Soloviev uses two terms for the Caspian Sea in these two sentences. In the first instance he writes *Kaspiiskoe more*, obviously cognate with the modern English phrase. It is a designation that has been known since the time of Herodotus, but other names also have been common, most often derived from peoples or civilizations in the area such as *Khazarskoe* (from the Khazar tribes) or *Khvalynskoe* (probably from Khoresm, sometimes written Khwarezm). In seventeenth-century Russian the sea most often is referred to as *Khvalynskoe*, the name Soloviev uses here in the second sentence.

33. The Chancellery for Novgorod administered the named region and also served as a repository of cash and goods, especially wood and other construction materials. As such it often was involved in building projects. The boyar and his secretaries, Gerasim Dokhturov, Lukian Golosov, and Efim Yuriev, actually administered the Chancellery for Foreign Affairs, but at this time the Chancellery for Novgorod was an only partially independent adjunct of this larger office. Note that the name of Dedinovo is sometimes found spelled Dedilov or Dedilovo, or even Dezhnov.

34. Jan or Johann van Sweeden, who was Dutch by birth despite his name, was one of the most enterprising of the foreigners who sought their fortune in seventeenth-century Muscovy. Originally serving as an ordinary merchant, he quickly became a factor for the state, buying military supplies and other items abroad. Soon he was busy establishing glass, paper and cloth factories, organizing and implementing of Russia's first international postal system and, of course, helping to construct the Caspian fleet. See Fuhrmann, *Origins of Capitalism*.

35. Bockhoiven, also spelled Bockhoven, Bockehoffen, Buxhoeveden, and similar variants, was a Dutch military officer in Russian service. The Marselis family is mentioned above, in Chapter II. It had branches in nearly every commercially important area of Europe. The Russian segment served as merchants, manufacturers (especially of the vitally important iron), diplomats, and advisors. One was ennobled by the king of Denmark for his services, and another became Russia's postmaster. See the entry by V.S. Rumiantseva, "Marselis, Petr Gavrilovich," MERSH, Vol. 21, p. 110. Also see Fuhrmann, pp. 63-65, 103-105, 151, 199, 201-202, 212-214, 229-231.

36. Money from the state monopoly on liquor (administered by the Office of Taverns) often was used in construction projects and other government-backed enterprises.

37. Besides overseeing the production of cold weapons, the Armory, or Oruzheinaia Palata, was the principal administrative department for artists and artisans in crown service. Both it and the Chancellery of Artillery, responsible for the production of artillery and shot, were natural administrative centers for smiths. The primary responsibility of the Grenade Department was, of course, grenades, while the Chancellery of Musketeers administered all aspects of the musketeer regiments. It should be obvious that the division of duties among the Muscovite government chancelleries was far from clear. Information on many of the individual chancelleries can be found in Sergei G. Pushkarev, comp., *Dictionary of*

Russian Historical Terms from the Eleventh Century to 1917, edited by George Vernadsky and Ralph T. Fisher, Jr. (New Haven, 1970), under the name of the given department. Also see Hugh F. Graham, "Prikaz," MERSH, Vol. 29, pp. 211-217; N.F. Demidova, "Prikazy in Russia during the Sixteenth and Seventeenth Centuries, Listing of," MERSH, Vol. 29, pp. 220-228, and other MERSH entries under the name of the department.

38. The original documents first used the word sloop, then changed to shneka (sometimes written shniaka or shniak). The term, of Scandinavian origin but incorporated into Russian at an early date, usually meant a deckless sailing vessel, whereas sloops customarily possessed one or more decks.

39. Razin (see above, Chapter II, Note 8) was a renegade cossack who led a troop of bandits in the Don and Volga river regions and the Caspian shore in the later 1660s. Soon he became political, arguing that evil advisors and administrators were perverting the wishes of the benevolent tsar, and urging the people to rise up against their oppressive local officials. The movement grew into a major rebellion, and in 1670 Razin's forces sacked the city of Astrakhan, killing hundreds and burning the ship *Orel,* perhaps as a symbol of the central government, perhaps as a symbol of unwelcome changes. Razin was captured in April of 1671, brought to Moscow, interrogated, and publicly executed in June. Deprived of its leader his movement collapsed, but elements of its rebellious message long survived in legend and song. Materials available in English include James G. Hart, "Razin, Stepan Timofeevich," MERSH, Vol. 52, pp. 56-62 and also Paul Avrich, *Russian Rebels, 1600-1800* (New York, 1972), pp. 50-122. Those who enjoy reading contemporary accounts may wish to look up the articles by S. Konovalov, "Ludwig Fabritsius's Account of the Razin Rebellion," *Oxford Slavonic Papers*, Vol. 6 (1955), pp. 72-101, and "Razin's Execution. Two Contemporary Documents," *Oxford Slavonic Papers*, Vol. 12 (1965), pp. 94-98. See also Volume 21 of this series.

40. The basic administrative unit of townsmen in early Russia was the hundred (*sotnia*).

41. It should be remembered that in the seventeenth century Russians customarily referred to all Protestant Western Europeans, and sometimes all Western Europeans regardless of religious affiliation, as "Germans." The word for German is *nemets*, from the adjective *nemoi*, meaning dumb, one who could not speak Russian. When Muscovites wished to distinguish the various national groups they might use the appropriate noun, such as "Dutch" or "English," or they might simply add an adjective to the noun "German," creating such odd-sounding phrases as "Dutch German," "English German," or even "French German." In this instance, where the urban representatives spoke of "Germans," "German lands," and "German goods," they were using the term to refer to the people, places, and merchandise of Western Europe as a whole.

42. Both *ardash* and *lezhei* (*lezha, lez, liz*) were types of raw silk, with *ardash* being of lesser quality.

43. See above, Chapter II, Note 37.

44. Fur from the animals' bellies was prized for its softness. Mica, a translucent mineral which splits easily into sheets, was a common material for window panes in Muscovy.

45. The Tadzhiks (self-designation Tojik) were an ancient Iranian-speaking Central Asian people whose main cities lay along the Persia-China trade routes. Hence in the seventeenth century the name Tezik sometimes meant Tadzhik and sometimes was applied more loosely to mean Asian traders in general. Tobacco was illegal in Muscovy at this time, and as such could not be subject to taxes and import duties.

CHAPTER IV

1. The Pechenegs were a union of nomadic tribes who harried Russia in the tenth century. They spoke a Turkic language and were ethnically Europoid with a Mongoloid admixture, formed when Turkic, Sarmatian and Finno-Ugric tribes joined forces. In the eleventh and twelfth centuries many Pechenegs settled along Russia's southern borders and defended these against later incursions. The Polovtsians also were known as Kipchaks or Cumans. They were Turkic-speaking nomads, primarily Mongoloid in their ethnic origins, whose economy depended on herding, crafts, and raiding. They attacked Russia several times during the second half of the eleventh century, then established easier (but never entirely peaceful) relations. After the Mongol invasions of the thirteenth century many Polovtsians merged with the Golden Horde, others moved away, and a few settled down as border allies of Russia. See the note regarding Black Hoods below.

2. The *chernye klobuki* (Black Hoods) developed as a loose confederation of Turkic steppe nomads caught between Kievan Russia and the invading Polovtsians in the eleventh or twelfth century. They cooperated with the Kievan rulers against the eastern nomads, serving as scouts and border troops, and gradually turning from herding to agriculture.

3. The Kalmyks, or in their own terms Khal'mg or Oirats, are a Mongolian people who originated in the Jungaria region east of Lake Balkhash, near the Chinese border. In the seventeenth century two of the four main Kalmyk tribes (the Torgut and Derbet) moved westward toward Russia, while their Khoshut and Jungar relatives remained behind for a time. The taisha or tayishi was chief of an ulus, the largest socio-administrative unit among the Mongol tribes. Soloviev, like most Russian sources, spells the title "taisha," but Michael Khodarkovsky, *Where Two Worlds Met. The Russian State and the Kalmyk Nomads, 1600-1771* (Cornell, 1992), p. 9, Note 14, traces its origin to a Chinese term, tay-ishi, meaning grand preceptor.

4. Also seen spelled Louzan, Lauzang, or Lubsan.

5. Sometimes spelled Namansoro, Namansara, Namseren, or Mansyrey.

6. These groups have been defined in the notes to the previous chapter. In this instance the term *ulus* more likely refers to a tribal subdivision than to tent villages.

7. There was some rivalry and contention among and within the major Kalmyk groups.

8. These were tribes or groups who were forced to pay *yasak*, or fur tribute. As such they were, if not necessarily more civilized than their neighbors, at least more cooperative and accustomed to dealing with Russians. Note that in 1775 the Yaik river was renamed the Ural.

9. The Bashkirs (self-designation Bashqort) are a Turkic-speaking people, Muslim since the fourteenth century, native to the Ural region. In the seventeenth century they were beginning to change from a life of nomadic cattle herding, supplemented with hunting and handicrafts, to one of settled agriculture.

10. A valley along the upper Emba river.

11. Gorokhov headed the Chancellery for Kalmyk Affairs, the existence of which offers a record of brevity even for Muscovite government departments. It was created in 1661 and appears to have lasted less than a year. See Khodarkovsky, p. 58, Note 2, also pp. 95-96. For more information on Gorokhov's career see the brief but informative entry "Gorokhov, Ivan Savvich," MERSH, Vol. 13, p. 69.

12. One of the most serious misunderstandings between Muscovites and Kalmyks lay in their perceptions of treaty terms. Russia considered the documents to bind the nomads in permanent subject status, whereas the Kalmyks believed that they were temporary military agreements between free equals. See Khodarkovsky, p. 71.

13. Monchak's name is also written as Puntsuk.

14. Kazbulat, or Kaspulat, Mutsalovich Cherkassky was a Kabardinian prince and murza whose sister was married to Monchak/Puntsuk. His family had been in Russian service for about a century, protecting Moscow's southern and eastern borders. Their regional designation (Circassian, or in Russian Cherkassky) became their surname, but would not have been used so by the Kalmyks. The Kabardinians or Kabards are a people of the Abkhazo-Adyge group of the Caucasian language family, living in Kabarda, a region in the mountains north of Georgia.

15. *Aga* comes from the Turkish *agha*, meaning master. Originally it was the title of a military commander, later extended to civil posts of honor and authority.

16. The term used for Ukrainians in this passage is *kreshchenye s khokhlatami*, that is, crested Christians (literally "baptized ones") or Christians with topknots. It refers to the old Ukrainian custom of shaving the head except for the crown, where the hair was grown long and braided.

17. Soloviev's original text uses the word *abyzy*. Though many dictionaries translate this as "mullahs," the sentence holds more a suggestion of "wise men" or even "diviners" than the orthodox Islamic teachers signified by the word mullah.

18. Cossacks of the Yaik (Ural) river region, one of the major cossack communities established in the fifteenth and sixteenth centuries.

19. The use of this archaic term, geographically more closely identified with Kiev than with Moscow, may reflect the fact that the Crimeans attacked Russia's southern borderlands.

20. Mazhara probably is cognate to Magyar.

21. Although the word *yurt* now is identified most often with the round tents of the steppe nomads, it also is a territorial designation for the lands once controlled by the Golden Horde, that is, on Russia's southern and southeastern borderlands.

22. The ethnography of Siberia is complex and ever-changing. The land supports a widely-differing population which ranges from fully European to fully Asiatic in language and physical features, with all possible phases in between and often including Turkic elements in the south. Some groups are settled agriculturalists, others herd cattle or reindeer, and still others live by hunting, fishing, and gathering wild plants. Unrelated tribes may have similar ways of living. Other single tribes may be divided into settled and nomadic subgroups. Since the seventeenth century some tribes have disappeared, either dying out or losing their identity through merger with their neighbors. Others have grown and spread. Most now have incorporated modern conveniences like snowmobiles and electric lights, and reflect the pressures of Russian and Soviet authority. Christianity or atheism has replaced lamaism and shamanism to a great, but not a complete, degree. Many now are known by names different from those used in Soloviev's time. English-language information on the various Siberian peoples is found in several encyclopedias, particularly MERSH and *The Great Soviet Encyclopedia*, A.M. Prokhorov, editor in chief, 3d ed., 31 vols. plus index (New York, 1973-1983). Consult as well James Forsyth, *A History of the Peoples of Siberia* (Cambridge, 1992), and *The Peoples of Siberia*, M. G. Levin and L. P. Potapov, eds., translated by Stephen Dunn (Chicago, 1964). *An Ethnohistorical Dictionary of the Russian and Soviet Empires*, edited by James S. Olson (Westport, Conn. 1994), is also of value in defining the peoples of Siberia and other regions.

23. The Kirghiz (Kyrgyz) are a Turkic people originating in Central Asia and at times spreading as far as Tian-shan and the Pamir mountains. By the seventeenth and eighteenth centuries many had begun to abandon their traditional nomadic life and settle further west. The Kaisak-Kirghiz were a subgroup of the Kazakh people, also a Turkic population with a range and life similar to the Kirghiz. In the past, in fact, the names Kazakh and Kirghiz often were confused or used interchangeably.

24. A sixteenth-century leader of the vast and powerful Siberian khanate, notable for his anti-Russian stance.

25. The Cheremiss are a Finno-Ugrian people now usually called Mari or Mariitsy. They became part of the Russian state in the mid-sixteenth century. The Voguls, now called Mansi, are a Finno-Ugrian people (who, with the related Ostiaks, now called Khanty, are known as Ob Ugrians) who lived by hunting and fishing, with some reindeer herding.

26. Mordvinians (Mordva, Mordovians) are another Finno-Ugrian people. The Chuvash speak a Turkic language, follow the Russian Orthodox religion, and are thought to be descended from Volga Bulgars.

27. The Ostiaks, now called Khanty, are Ob Ugrians like the Mansi, with a similar mode of life. Traditionally each Ostiak clan followed an ancestor (and/or totem) cult with a sacred clan site containing the ancestor-spirit and its effigy. Religious ceremonies included the sacrifice of animals and, in early times, humans.

28. The Samoyeds, whose name literally means cannibal, are now divided into several groups. The main tribe is called the Nents (Nentsy). There are also Selkups (the Ostiak Samoyeds), Nganasans (Tavgi Samoyeds), and Ents or Entsy (Yenisei Samoyeds). They speak Uralian languages and live by hunting, fishing and herding reindeer.

29. These were the main roads between Russia and Kazan and through Nogay territory.

30. The Teleuts (sometimes written Telenguts) were a confederation of pastoral and nomadic clans of the southern Altai and upper Ob river region. They were ethnic Mongols who spoke a Turkic language and followed a shamanistic religion. Although distinct from the Kalmyk people, some early Russian sources refer to them as "White Kalmyks."

31. The Tatars of the Saian mountain region were an ethnically mixed people of Caucasian-Finnish-Mongol origins who spoke a Kipchak-Turkic language and lived by herding, farming and crafts.

32. The Altyn khan was the ruler of the Khalkha (Qalqa) Mongols, who lived in the eastern part of northern Mongolia. His khanate was founded in the mid-sixteenth century in northwestern Mongolia. In the seventeenth century it extended from Krasnioarsk to the Selenga river. Though technically a title, the phrase often appears as a proper name in Russian texts of the period .

33. The Tubins were Samoyedic-speaking pastoralists allied with the Kirghiz by intermarriage and by their opposition to Russian incursions. They were a clan of the Kachin confederation (see below) of peoples now called Khakas or Khakass. The Altyrs or Alatyrs were a clan-group of the Yenisei Kirghiz, sometimes called the "Upper Kirghiz," and were one of the Turkic-speaking peoples who formed the group now called Khakas (self-designation Khaas). The Kerels (possibly Kerets or Kereiti?) are more difficult to trace, but they too appear to be one of the small groups that merged to form the Khakas. They are thought to be related to the Altyrs.

34. The Kachins, Aryns and Yastyns were ancestors of the present-day Khakas people. The Kachins were Turkic-speaking pastoralists who assimilated some of the other tribes of the Krasnoiarsk region in the seventeenth and eighteenth centuries, among them the Kettic-speaking Aryns and Yastins. Ket usually is classified as a Paleoasiatic language although it is distinct from any other Siberian linguistic group. In modern times only a few hundred Kettic speakers remain, although the language was much more widespread in the seventeenth century. The Aryn language has died out completely in the present day.

35. As noted above, the White Kalmyks now more commonly are called Teleuts or Telenguts. Senga was a taisha of the Jungars (Dzhungars), a people of the upper Irtysh river who sometimes were called the Black Kalmyks, in temporary alliance with his Teleut counterparts. Designations such as "Black" or "White" Kalmyks, or for that matter "Golden" or "Blue" Horde, generally are thought to refer to a group's traditional colors of clothing or headdress, although there is some possibility that occasionally it was a geographical reference. The Mongols, like

many other tribal peoples, identified the cardinal compass points with colors. There was some variation, but the most standard symbolism of the area paired the north with black, the south with red, east with blue, west with white, and the center with yellow or gold.

36. The Buriats comprised a large group of loosely-connected Mongol-speaking herding tribes, who followed a shamanistic religion and lived in the area of Lake Baikal and into Mongolia and China.

37. An ataman was a cossack military commander.

38. The Tungus are now called Evenks. They speak a language of the Altaic family, the main subgroups of which are Turkic, Tungus and Manchurian. In the seventeenth century the Tungus occupied a vast territory reaching from the Lena river to the Pacific, and covering southeastern Siberia as well as northern Mongolia and Manchuria. They lived by hunting, fishing, and herding reindeer. Note that there is a Baikal river and region as well as the more familiar lake.

39. These people, known as Yakuts, gave their name to the town and region of Yakutsk. They call themselves Sakha, and are the most northeasterly of the Turkic-speaking (Altaic) peoples, although their language contains Mongol, Tungus, and other elements. Their wide geographic spread has led to varied economies: pastoral (sometimes called "the horse people"), hunting and fishing, cattle-breeding, and gathering, with some agriculture appearing in the later seventeenth century. Traditional crafts included tanning and the preparation of furs, blacksmithing (well-developed in the seventeenth century), and pottery (a rare skill in Siberia).

40. The Yukagirs (self-designation Odul or Detkil) spoke a Paleoasiatic language with two main dialects. It displayed some similarities with Uralic and Altaic languages. A large group in the seventeenth century, the Yukagirs numbered only about eight hundred people in the 1979 census (up from 443 in 1926). Some were assimilated by neighboring tribes like the Yakuts and Evens, others died from disease or warfare.

41. The Russian term *yasachnoe zimovie* was a special winter camp of living quarters and storage facilities where the collected fur tribute was kept prior to shipping during the spring navigation season.

42. Thus Dezhnev rounded the northeastern extremity of Asia and discovered the strait later called Bering (Soloviev's note). A cape on the promontory still bears Dezhnev's name. An English-language study of his adventure is available by Raymond H. Fisher, *The Voyage of Semen Dezhnev in 1648. Bering's Precursor* [Hakluyt Society, Second Series, No. 159] (London, 1981).

43. Thus no game to hunt.

44. The Anauls were a Yukagir tribe, now extinct.

45. The Great Stony Nose, sometimes written without capitalization as the great rocky *nos* (*sic,* this is a Russian word meaning both nose and promontory or headland), never has been identified satisfactorily. For a discussion of its possible locations, see Fisher, pp. 197-239.

46. The Tusked Men probably were Eskimos (self-designation Yugit or Yupigit), whose traditional male adornment included labrets (round plugs of bone worn in holes in the lips at the corners of the mouth). They and the Chukchi are related, both being Paleoasiatic peoples, although the Asiatic Eskimos depended entirely on hunting large sea mammals such as whale, seal and walrus, while the Chukchi are divided into coastal hunters like the Eskimo ("sedentary Chukchi") and nomadic reindeer breeders on the tundra ("walking Chukchi").

47. The Koriaks lived by breeding reindeer and by hunting, fishing, and hunting sea mammals. They spoke a Paleoasiatic language similar to Chukchi, though their origins, and particularly those of the reindeer-breeding subgroups, are unclear.

48. These Siberian peoples speak the Tungus language, which is related to Manchurian. They call themselves Evenks west and southeast of the Lena river, and Evens to the east. In Soloviev's day the Evenks were called Tungus, and the Evens were called Lamuts. They were a large group comprising more than twenty tribes, who followed a shamanistic religion with particular respect for the bear. Those in the inland forests were nomadic reindeer herders and hunters, while the coastal dwellers lived a semi-sedentary life depending on fishing and walrus hunting, and traveling by dogsled.

49. This name is seen spelled both Komka and Kamka. The surname can be rendered as Boiashinets, Baiashynets, Boiashinsky or Boyash. It is the name of one of the Okhotsk Tungus clans.

50. Poiarkov was a *pismenny golova*, in seventeenth-century Siberia the title of a military officer assigned as assistant and especially secretary to the local commander.

51. The Duchers (Dyuchers, Dzyuchers) were a Manchu-speaking people who lived chiefly by hunting and fishing.

52. Here Soloviev uses the word *ulus*.

53. The Daurs (sometimes spelled Dahurs or Dakhurs) were a settled farming and cattle-breeding people of Mongolian origins, sometimes described as "Mongolized Tungus." They now largely are assimilated with the Buriats.

54. The fuller text of a contemporary report explains that this "threefold" or "three-part [*troinoi*] town" actually was three towns built side by side, protected by single exterior wall of earth. The towns were separated from each other by inner walls, but connected by underground tunnels. See *Russia's Conquest of Siberia, 1558-1700*, Vol. 1 of *To Siberia and Russian America. Three Centuries of Russia Eastward Expansion*, edited and translated by Basil Dmytryshyn, E.A.P. Crownhart-Vaughan, and Thomas Vaughan, 3 vols. (Portland, Oregon, 1985), p. 261.

55. Like the Duchers, the Achans (also called Natki, probably the modern Nanays) were a Manchu-speaking people who lived chiefly by hunting and fishing.

56. Chinese name Hai-se or Haiseh, a commander of the Ninguta garrison. He was put to death because of the Achansk defeat. See V.S. Miasnikov, *The Ch'ing Empire and the Russian State in the 17th Century*, translated by Vic Schneierson (Moscow, 1985), p. 85.

57. Even the highest-born Muscovite customarily referred to himself by a diminutive when writing to the tsar.

58. Khabarov used the phrase *v skope*, which literally means in a mob or a crowd gathered for secret or open rebellion.

59. Stepanov also complained that Khabarov left no inventory of supplies and no list of servitors, and that he took away with him the hostages, interpreters and collection records, without which Stepanov could not gather further tribute.

60. Soloviev uses the term tsar.

61. The Naun, more often called the Nonni, is not itself a tributary of the Amur, but lies not too far south of the larger river.

62. Often spelled Kumara.

63. A tributary of the Irtysh near the place where merchant caravans customarily left the water routes for overland roads.

64. The name of this city also can be found written Kokotan, Kokutan, Kukuhoton, Huhohaot'e, Huhehot, Köke qota (Blue Fort), or Kweihwacheng. In modern sources it is most often given as Hohhot. Baikov gave the cities he visited the Mongol names he learned from his escorts.

65. Kapka, now called Zhangjiakou (Changchiak'ou), was also known as Kalgan, probably from the Mongol word Khalga. The Mugali nomads sometimes are identified simply as Mongols, and at other times more specifically as the people of the Altyn khan, or as those governed by the descendants of Chingis (Genghis) Khan. The Mongol name for Beijing (Peking), also written as Kanbalik or Khanbalyk, meant the home or headquarters of the khan.

66. Seventeenth-century Russians observed Lent very strictly, allowing milk products only to infants and extremely ill persons. Note the Mongol or Tatar style of preparing the tea.

67. The Mongols referred to the Chinese emperor as the bogdo (sacred, heavenly, celestial) khan (tsar or emperor). The Russians, hearing this, sometimes mistakenly believed that his name was Bogdo or Bogda.

68. Spafary actually was Moldavian, although he attended the Greek patriarchate school in Constantinople, fostering a life-long devotion to the idea of Orthodox unity and providing a knowledge of languages that later were of great value in his Russian service. After his schooling he served various Moldavian princes, achieving the rank of *spàtar* (cavalry commander), a title traditionally used as his name in most Russian and Western histories. He entered the service of Tsar Alexis in 1671. His return from China was marred both by his failure to accomplish the embassy's diplomatic goals and by the fall from favor of his patron Matveev, but soon he again became an active and respected agent of the sovereign, remaining so until his death in 1708. English-language treatments of his China visit can be found in John F. Baddeley, *Russia, Mongolia, China. Being some Record of the Relations between them from the beginning of the XVIIth Century to the Death of the Tsar Alexei Mikhailovich...*, 2 vols. (London, 1919; reprint ed. New York, 1960, 1969), and in Miasnikov. Biographical data on the envoy is available in the

entry by Clifford M. Foust, "Spafarii, Nikolai Gavrilovich (Nicholaie Spătarul Milescu)," MERSH, Vol. 37, pp. 20-24.

69. Kangxi or K'ang-hsi—more properly "the Kangxi emperor" since the term is a reign title rather than a name—was born in 1654 and ruled from 1661 until his death in 1722. His actual name was Xuanye or Hsüan-yeh, his temple name Sheng-zu. The Manchurians (also called Man, Manchu, or Manzhou) were a Siberian people who began moving into China's northern borderlands in the fifteenth and sixteenth centuries. In 1644 their troops entered Beijing to find that the last Ming emperor had committed suicide. The newcomers then established their own dynasty, the Qing or Ch'ing, which ruled the country until the revolution of 1911 created the Republic of China.

70. Still smarting from Baikov's reception, the Russian government had given Spafary specific orders to present the tsar's document to the emperor in person, and not to allow chancellery personnel to act as intermediaries. These instructions are translated in *Russia's Conquest of Siberia,* pp. 398-413.

71. Ferdinand Verbiest, Chinese name Nan Huairen (1623-1688), spent nearly thirty years in China. He became head of the Bureau of Astronomy in 1669, and by 1671 he was in daily attendance on the emperor, tutoring him in mathematics and astronomy. He also wrote widely (in both Chinese and Latin) on astronomy, geography, physics, medicine, cartography and religion. Note the close ties between Spain and the Netherlands since 1519, when King Charles I of Spain succeeded to the Holy Roman empire as Charles V, extending his rule to include much of the Low Countries.

72. The abandoned Daur compound at Albazin was taken over by renegade cossacks in 1665. In 1672 the men received the tsar's pardon and continued their existence under official recognition. Hence both the "bandit" and the "servitor" description could be correct. See Forsyth, pp. 107-108.

73. The peoples of the East often referred to the Russian tsar as "the white tsar" or "the white khan." This usually is thought to be another instance of color geo-symbolism associating "west" with "white," though in those parts of Asia with Buddhist influence the color white also could be linked with governmental power or with the ruler himself. Another theory is that the phrase connoted Muscovite territorial ambitions by relating to the so-called "White Bone" Mongol clan descended directly from Chingis or Genghis Khan. Michael Khodarkovsky notes (p. 64) that the subtleties of the Mongol language could turn the term into a disparagement, at least on paper. The Manchu emperors employed it for themselves to mean "the autocratic khan," but when referring to the tsar they added a dot which changed the meaning to "the khan who is a subject."

74. Seitkul Ablin, a Bukhara-born merchant, and the cossack Ivan Tarutin, were sent to China from Tobolsk in 1667 to engage in a combined diplomatic-commercial mission. Ablin previously had undertaken a similar effort with the junior boyar Ivan Perfilev in 1657. Documents relating to the 1657 visit clearly mention an official letter from the tsar to the emperor, but those on the 1667 expedition do not. See *Russia's Conquest of Siberia*, pp. 337-339, 388-394.

75. This is another example of the diplomatic one-upmanship so common in the seventeenth century. By the standards of the day Spafary would have diminished the honor and hence the power of his sovereign had he acceded to the mandarins' directions. As with Menzies in Rome, his insistence upon following his own customs, however childish and undignified it may seem in the modern day, actually allowed both sides to uphold the position of their rulers with respect to each other.

76. Alexis, who had died unexpectedly in January of 1676, would have been 47 years old at that time.

77. Probably peaches, although the text uses the phrase *iabloki persidskie* rather than *persiki*.

78. Verbiest, in particular, favored the establishment of a trade route from China to Europe through Moscow. The Jesuits' broader dissatisfaction with the emperor probably stemmed more from the limitations and hostilities directed against Christian missionary work than from any real incompetence. Kangxi's reign is generally considered to have been brilliant. It did suffer some revolts (at least one was defeated with the assistance of Jesuit technological innovations), but survived these challenges to achieve a stronger and more centralized condition.

79. Confirmation of their hosts' Catholicism would not have been greatly reassuring for most seventeenth-century Russians.

CHAPTER V

1. Many of these subjects have been defined in this volume, either in the text or the notes. Of the others, the Law Code was compiled in 1649, and attempted to clarify and solidify the rules and social groups of seventeenth-century Russia. This topic is covered in Volume 18 of this series. The Ukraine was annexed in 1654 (Volume 19). The religious schism which followed Patriarch Nikon's reforms continues to this day. For Soloviev's treatment see Volume 21. The related rebellion at the far-northerly Solovetsk monastery, in which religious and political insurrection were worsened by the arrival of escaped followers of Razin, also is discussed in Volume 21 of this series.

2. The Time of Troubles is the name given to the years 1598-1613, that is, from the accession of Boris Godunov to that of Michael Fedorovich. It was characterized by a rapid succession of rulers, invasions, pretenders, civil turmoil and economic collapse. The "habits" to which Soloviev refers were, of course, unrest and active discontent.

3. This ancient city in the borderlands between Russia and Poland-Lithuania was captured by Poland in 1611, an event formalized by treaty in 1618. Russia attempted unsuccessfully to regain it in 1632-1634, and finally recaptured the city only in September of 1654.

4. Though obviously related, the terms "Russian" and "Rus" are distinct. "Russian" refers to the territory and civilization of so-called Great Russia, whose

development reflected Mongol devastations and Muscovite autocracy. "Rus" also was Slavic and Orthodox, as the cossacks recognized in urging unification, but it was not Great Russian (what we call Russian), and evolved differently over the centuries. An older term identified with early Kievan society, "Rus," came to refer to the Ukraine. A more common English variant of the name is Ruthenian.

5. See Volume 11 of this series, Chapter III.

6. It is not entirely clear whether Soloviev refers here to Ivan's immediate successor, his son Fedor Ivanovich (ruled 1584-1598), or to his later successor Alexis. His observation would be valid in either case.

7. The Russian terms were *reitary* (from the German *Ritter,* meaning rider or cavalryman), *draguny* and *soldaty*. For an excellent analysis of the process and problems of the creation of the new-style army see Richard Hellie, *Enserfment and Military Change in Muscovy* (Chicago, 1971). For an overview of the foreign industrial ventures see Fuhrmann, *Origins of Capitalism*.

8. In early Russia, as in Western Europe at the time, only merchants, peasants and laborers paid taxes. Noblemen were considered to have fulfilled their obligations to society through the responsibilities of their class, that is, military service and government administration. In Russia, tax obligations were assigned not to individuals or households but to neighborhoods or villages. When residents died or fled, those who remained had to pay the entire levy themselves.

9. In the early years of Alexis's reign Russia's government was dominated by the tsar's former tutor Boris Morozov. In June of 1648 a crowd of petitioners initially asked Alexis to replace a corrupt city official named Pleshcheev, then quickly turned their anger against Morozov and his cohorts, who exercised vast power owing to the tsar's youth and inexperience. Several nobles were killed and their homes sacked, although Alexis succeeded in saving Morozov's life.

10. In Russian *zakladnichestvo*. Zakladniks (sometimes translated as pawn-slaves) sold themselves into servitude to escape the burdens of poverty or excessive taxation.

11. Bogdan Khmelnitsky was a pro-Russian cossack hetman (commander). His victory over the Poles opened the way for the 1654 unification of the Ukraine with Moscow.

12. In 1654 Moscow attempted to save money by issuing coins made of copper rather than silver, though with the same face value as their silver counterparts. Soon popular trust of the new currency eroded and inflation blazed out of control. In 1662 a mob set out to confront Alexis at his suburban palace at Kolomenskoe. When set upon by the tsar's guards they fought back, and were subdued only after a bloody battle. See Volume 21 of this series, Chapter I.

13. The war with Poland and Sweden between 1654 and 1667 is referred to as the Thirteen Years War.

14. Ivan Briukhovetsky was another Ukrainian hetman, at first trusted and favored by Alexis.

15. In June 1659 Russian forces at Konotop were defeated by a combined army of Ukrainians and Tatars, losing about five thousand men and leaving the way to

Moscow potentially open to Turkish attack. A little over a year later, in September of 1660, another Russian army was besieged at Chudnovo by Polish and Tatar forces (see above, Chapter I, Note 44). The proximity of the cossack leader Yury Khmelnitsky, Bogdan's son, should have afforded them aid, but he went over to the enemy, and in October the Russians admitted defeat. An entire army was taken prisoner, and Moscow lost its control over a large part of the Ukraine.

16. Boris Morozov, the tsar's tutor, is thought to have assigned the young Matveev, then a page at court, to share lessons with Alexis "and so bring him on the faster." See Philip Longworth, *Alexis, Tsar of All the Russias* (New York, 1984), p. 12.

17. As Muscovy's chief diplomat and foreign policy advisor from about 1658 until his semi-forced retirement in 1671, Afanasy Laventievich Ordin-Nashchokin advocated closer ties with the West. Fedor Mikhailovich Rtishchev, also an advisor but a far more self-effacing one, brought Kievan educators to Moscow at his own expense and urged young servitors to learn foreign languages. Biographical sketches of these men can be found in MERSH, in the entries by E. V. Chistiakova, "Ordin-Nashchokin, Afanasii Lavrent'evich," Vol. 26, pp. 72-73; Lindsey A. J. Hughes, "Matveev, Artamon Sergeevich," Vol. 21, pp. 142-144; and her "Rtishchev, Fedor Mikhailovich (Bol'shoi)," Vol. 31, pp. 223-227. See also V.O. Kliuchevsky, *A Course in Russian History. The Seventeenth Century*, translated by Natalie Duddington (Chicago, 1968), especially pp. 294, 298-300, 302-303, 354-358, 359-378. On Matveev see above, Chapter I, Note 9.

18. Despite the work of men like Rtishchev a Western-type education was extremely rare in seventeenth-century Muscovy. Most Russians mistrusted foreign scholarship, some even fearing that the mere learning of a foreign language could endanger one's spiritual well-being. "There is heresy in those Greek writings," they are quoted as saying, and "all those who have learned Latin have gone astray" (Kliuchevsky, p. 303).

19. Soloviev discusses Ordin-Nashchokin's career and character in several places in the preceding volumes.

20. Matveev, as Soloviev notes in his original text, actually held two titles related to his musketeer service, *polkovnik* and *golova*. Both translate as "colonel" or "regimental commander." The former term came into use with the new-style, Western-model army, while the latter was a traditional musketeer rank.

21. Actually Soloviev does not discuss Matveev's fall until a later chapter, already published in Volume 25 of the present series, Hughes, *Rebellion and Reform*, pp. 8-16.

22. Since two previous cossack hetmans, Briukhovetsky and Mnogogreshny, transferred their allegiance from the tsar to the sultan, Alexis ordered Ivan Samoilovich's sons brought to Moscow as hostages for their father's loyalty.

23. Soloviev summarizes Alexis's character in Volume 18 of this series.

24. Peter the Great.

25. In October of 1661, near the city of Polotsk, some nineteen thousand Russian troops were massacred by Polish and Belorussian forces. Their commanders were A.L. Ordin-Nashchokin, more familiar in his role as diplomat and foreign policy advisor but here leading the infantry, and Ivan A. Khovansky, a boyar from an ancient princely family which came originally from Lithuania.

26. Ahithophel, a trusted councillor of the Old Testament King David, betrayed his ruler and joined Absalom's revolt. Eventually realizing his error, he killed himself (2 Sam. 15:31-37; 16:20-23; 17). Dathan and his brother Abiram joined a conspiracy against Moses and Aaron, and were destroyed in an earthquake (Num. 16:1-30; 26:9; Deut. 11:6). Ananias and Sapphira were a New Testament couple struck down for compounding an impropriety in the sale of a piece of land by lying about what they had done (Acts 5).

27. Investigative torture, euphemistically "being put to the question," was a normal part of the Muscovite judicial process.

28. In Russian *desiatnik*.

29. Here St. Sabbas. Tsar Alexis was particularly devoted to this saint who he believed once had saved him from a bear. See Longworth, pp. 69-70.

30. Nikita's title, *kaznachei*, can be translated either as steward or bursar. The initial letter N sometimes becomes M in early Russian, so that names like Nikita or Nikolai may be seen spelled Mikita or Mikolai.

31. These were some peasants from one of the tsar's estates, whom Nikita had beaten while (yet again) drunk. See Longworth, pp. 72-73; Michael Cherniavsky, *Tsar & People. Studies in Russian Myths* (New York, 1969), pp. 68-69.

32. The angel Lucifer, who fell from the heaven of God's favor to become identified with Satan.

33. This probably refers to Ivan IV's imprisonment of Metropolitan Philip. See Longworth, p. 72; also Hugh F. Graham, MERSH, Vol. 11, pp. 131-133.

34. The king of Poland.

35. That is, God. The King James Bible prefers the term Lord of Hosts, but the Russian Bible uses the older phrase Lord of Sabaoth, from a Hebrew word meaning armies, hosts or great numbers. See 1 Sam. 1:3, 11.

36. The Syrian commander Naaman was cured of leprosy by the prophet Elisha (the word for "spots," *prokazy*, can also mean the blotches of leprosy). At this miracle he realized the power of the Hebrew God, but asked if he might still worship at the altar of Rimmon as required by his duties to his own king (see 2 Kgs. 5). Alexis here suggests that Nikita is similarly keeping his true beliefs secret while performing lip-service in the monastery.

37. Presumably Alexis Musin-Pushkin, the tsar's messenger in this matter.

38. This letter, sent in 1652 on the occasion of Nikon's bringing the remains of the sixteenth-century Metropolitan Philip from Solovetsk to Moscow for reburial, is found in Volume 19 of the present series.

39. The synodical, in Russian *sinodik*, was a book containing the names of those to be commemorated by a religious foundation in their prayers for the dead.

40. In 1660 Voin Ordin-Nashchokin fled to the West, although he returned a few years later. See Volume 20 of this series and Longworth, pp. 138-139.

41. Another of Odoevsky's sons, the deceased Prince Mikhail's brother.

42. *Batiushka*, a diminutive form of the word father, often was used in Russia to refer to the tsar. It suggests both the patriarchal nature of the relationship between tsar and people, and the intermediary placement of the ruler as a lesser father between the people and their heavenly father.

43. This was an extraordinary honor, since Muscovite tsars rarely visited their subjects' homes.

44. Benjamin Phillip Uroff, "Grigorii Karpovich Kotoshikhin, *On Russia in the Reign of Alexis Mikhailovich*. An Annotated Translation," (Ph.D. diss., Columbia University, 1970, p. 428) defines *romaneia* as wines from Burgundy, both red and white. This superb compendium of information on Muscovy is unpublished but is available in many libraries in an authorized copy from University Microfilms.

45. Afanasy Ivanovich Matiushkin (died 1676), the tsar's cousin, chief falconer and friend.

46. Boris I. Morozov was placed in charge of Alexis's education in 1633. Despite his own lack of formal training he succeeded in organizing a broad and useful program of schooling with the actual instruction delegated to more knowledgeable individuals. See Longworth, pp. 8-9.

47. In modern terms, original or preliminary drafts. Final drafts (fair copies) were called "white copies."

48. Many of the verb forms and spellings in this passage are archaic and impart an antique and somewhat ecclesiastical tone to the tsar's words, a trait also noticeable in much of his prose. There is, however, no rhyme or rhythm in the lines, which are of widely varying meter in the original as in this translation. An earlier writer evaluated the passage as "very slipshod verses, of irregular lengths." See William Palmer, *The Patriarch and the Tsar*, 6 vols. (London, 1871-1876), Vol. 5, Appendix, p. 213.

49. Briukhovetsky refers to the Ukrainian cossack leader who was allied with Russia at the time of the letter (around 1662) but later transferred his allegiance to Turkey. The post of secretary or scribe (*pisar*) was an important one in the cossack army, often doubling as liaison officer or minor diplomat, and second only to the hetman in consequence. It is not clear which secretary named Zakharka is meant here. Yurasko (a double diminutive) refers to Yury Khmelnitsky, whose failure to aid V.B. Sheremetev at Chudnovo resulted in the defeat of the Russian army. An Oginski (probably Marcyan) commanded the Belorussian army in Khovansky's defeat in 1660. The boastful brother officer mentioned in the last lines has been identified as Vasily Borisovich Sheremetev, who spent more than two decades in captivity after his Chudnovo defeat. See above, Chapter I, Note 44; also Longworth, p. 161.

50. This refers to the instance in 1648 in which an angry mob demanded that Alexis hand over Morozov, who had taken refuge in the palace. Instead, the tsar's tearful, passionate, and obviously sincere speech managed to save his tutor from a brutal death. See Longworth, p. 45, and Hughes, "Morozov, Boris Ivanovich," MERSH, Vol. 23, pp. 71-73.

51. The essentials of this story were reported by foreign visitors such as Olearius, who was not in Moscow at the time, and the Swedish trade commissioner Johann de Rodes, who was. The Olearius version is available in *The Travels of Olearius in Seventeenth-Century Russia*, translated and edited by Samuel H. Baron (Stanford, 1967), p. 30. The Swedish material is in the Riksarkiv in Stockholm (letter of de Rodes to Queen Kristina, Moscow, March 15, 1653, in Muscovitica 3, Vol. 600). It has been published in Russian translation but is not available in English at this time.

52. When he was about sixteen years old Peter Alekseevich, later known as Peter the Great, found a small boat in a shed storing Romanov's things at the suburban palace of Izmailovo. Some foreign-born residents of Moscow taught him to sail it, starting a lifelong fascination with ships and sailing.

53. See Volume 19 of the present series.

54. See above, Note 15.

55. V.V. Golitsyn came to fame in later years as the favorite of the regent Sophia. Information on his life and career is found in Hughes, *Russia and the West, the Life of a Seventeenth-Century Westernizer, Prince Vasily Vasil'evich Golitsyn (1643-1714)* (Newtonville, Massachusetts, 1984), or in her *Sophia, Regent of Russia 1657-1704* (New Haven, 1990).

56. Gediminas was a fourteenth-century grand prince of Lithuania and self-proclaimed king of the Russians, from whom a portion of Russia's nobility proudly traced its ancestry. Maliuta Skuratov, also known as Maliuta-Skuratov and Skuratov-Belsky, was a member of the provincial gentry raised to great power by Ivan IV, the Terrible. See James Cracraft, "Khovanskii, Ivan Andreevich," MERSH, Vol. 16, pp. 175-176, and "Maliuta-Skuratov, Grigorii Luk'ianovich," MERSH, Vol. 21, p. 55.

57. Mayerberg was Austria's ambassador to Moscow in 1661-1662. Recent scholarship has assessed Khovansky as "courageous to the point of insanity" and "a flamboyant demagogue." See Robert O. Crummey, *Aristocrats and Servitors. The Boyar Elite in Russia, 1613-1689* (Princeton, 1983), p. 48, and John L.H. Keep, *Soldiers of the Tsar. Army and Society in Russia, 1462-1874* (Oxford, 1985), p. 69.

58. *Tararui* also can be translated as braggart, bombast, or blowhard.

59. As noted above in Chapter I, Sheremetev lost his whole army at Chudnovo in 1660 and spent the next twenty-two years in the Crimea as a prisoner of war.

60. Soloviev appears to have telescoped the names of Vasily Borisovich and Peter Vasilievich here. No genealogy or family history of the Sheremetevs lists a Vasily Vasilievich in this period. Peter Vasilievich served as governor of Sevsk

and Vasily Borisovich as governor of Siberia, neither a desirable post in a time when one's proximity to the court and the tsar both described and enhanced one's social position.

61. Fabian (Quintus Fabius Maximus Cunctator, 275-203 B.C.) was a Roman consul, dictator and general in the Second Punic War. His preferred strategy of avoiding major battles while isolating and harrying the enemy was first unpopular, but later recognized as successful. Catiline (Lucius Sergius Catilina, 108-62 B.C.) gathered disaffected elements of the population in a conspiracy against Cicero.

62. The Starodub region was an independent principality in northeastern Russia which began fragmenting and submitting to Moscow in the fifteenth and sixteenth centuries.

63. This subject is discussed in Volume 22 of this series.

64. In July of 1658 in honor of Tsar Teimuraz of Kakhetia there was a banquet, to which Patriarch Nikon was not invited. The prelate sent one of his officials to ask why he had been left out. Khitrovo, whose duty at the banquet was to clear the way for important guests with his staff, struck the messenger and, when the man protested on the grounds of his patriarchal office, hit him again with the admonition not to think so highly of himself for such a reason. See Longworth, p. 127, and Volume 21 of this series.

65. Soloviev discusses Rtishchev's patronage of learning in Volume 19 of this series, and his advocacy of credit in Volume 21.

66. In the present series this is covered in Volume 7, *The Reign of Ivan III the Great* (Academic International Press, 1978) and Volume 8, *Russian Society in the Age of Ivan III* (1979), both translated by John D. Windhausen; Volume 9, *The Age of Vasily III*, translated by Hugh F. Graham (1976); Volume 10, *The Reign of Ivan the Terrible. Kazan, Astrakhan, Livonia, the Oprichnina and the Polotsk Campaign*, translated by Anthony L.H. Rhinelander (1995), and Volume 12, *Russian Society under Ivan the Terrible*, translated by T. Allan Smith (1996). One more segment on the reign of Ivan the Terrible (Volume 11, translated by Alexandra S. Korros) is in preparation.

67. Fedor or Fedka Andronov was a Muscovite merchant who supported the Polish cause during the Time of Troubles (c. 1610) and was given a council post by King Sigismund III. See Volume 16 of this series, Chapter I, and "Andronov, Fedka," MERSH, Vol. 1, pp. 225-226. It is difficult for a modern reader to comprehend what a serious insult and humiliation it was for a Muscovite nobleman to be set equal or subordinate to someone of lower birth. The precedence system (*mestnichestvo*) calculated an individual's rank according to the relative positions of himself and his ancestors in their dealings with others, and except when the sovereign formally declared an event to be "without place" the acceptance of a post subservient to one of technically lesser rank lowered one's own standing and hence that of one's descendants. A Muscovite's jealous protection of his position stemmed not from mere snobbishness, but from his society's concepts of personal honor and his concern for his own and his family's future well-being.

68. Filaret Nikitich was patriarch of the Russian church after the Time of Troubles. He was also Tsar Michael's father and co-ruler. Boris A. Repnin grew very powerful during this time. Eventually he was sent to Astrakhan to put down Nogay unrest and during his absence the other boyars undermined the tsar's feelings toward him. This story is related in Volume 17 of this series. See also the entries in MERSH by Orchard, "Filaret," Vol. 11, pp. 126-130, and "Repnin, Boris Aleksandrovich," Vol. 31, pp. 24-26.

69. Solovki, sometimes written Solovka or Solovetskoe, was a large and wealthy monastic outpost on the White Sea. Though it is famous in Russian history for its fierce armed resistance to Nikon's reforms of church books and liturgy, this sentence refers to an earlier instance in which the new patriarch traveled north to acquire the reputedly miraculous relics of St. Philip, the head of the Russian Orthodox church deposed by Ivan the Terrible, and bring them to Moscow. See Longworth, pp. 70-71, 73. The letters to Nikon and Prince A.N. Trubetskoy, printed in Volume 19 of this series, display Alexis's concern with balancing his authority as tsar with the authority of the spiritual and lay commanders around him.

70. Afanasy, of course, is Ordin-Nashchokin, head of the Chancellery for Foreign Affairs and for many years Tsar Alexis's chief foreign policy advisor and diplomat. "Odoevsky, Dolgoruky and their comrades" were the highborn traditional courtiers who specialized in diplomacy and deeply resented Ordin-Nashchokin's prominence.

71. In 1722 Peter the Great established the Table of Ranks, a hierarchy of fourteen grades attainable through naval, military, civil, or court service. A lowborn servitor who achieved a certain rank received a life membership in the nobility, a standing which became hereditary if the individual progressed to a certain even higher position. See George E. Munro, "Table of Ranks," MERSH, Vol. 38, pp. 152-155.

72. This is available as Volume 24 of the present series, *The Character of Old Russia*, translated by Alexander V. Muller (Academic International Press, 1987).

INDEX

Vamyk, 70
Van, lake, 169
Velvet, 27, 37, 55, 124
Venice, 51-52, 54, 56, 58, 161, 167
Venetian, 40, 51, 53, 56, 164
Verbiest, Ferdinand, S.J. (Nan
  Huairen), 121, 179-180
Verkhoturie, 99
Veshniakovo, 139
Viatka, 152
Viazma, 81
Vienna, Viennese, 30-31, 56, 154,
  158, 161, 164
Vinius family, 164
Vinius, Andrei Andreevich, 48, 50-51,
  163-164
Vinius, Andrei Denisovich (Andries
  Denijsz), 163-164
Vinnitsa, 19, 155
Vinnitsky, see Winnicki
Vissarion, monk-priest, 61, 167
Vitebsk, 2, 21
Vitim river, 106
Vlasiev, Ivan, junior boyar, 107
Vlavursak, Georgian tsarevich, 66
Vodka, 27, 169
Vogul (Mansi) people, 99, 174
Volga Bulgars, 174
Volga river, 80, 86, 92-93, 95-96, 98,
  113, 126, 171, 174
Volhynia, 14
Volkonsky, prince, governor of Ufa,
  101
Vologda, 158
Volynsky, Vasily Semeonovich, lord-
  in-waiting, 44, 162
Vorotynsky family, 144
Vorotynsky, Ivan Alekseevich, prince,
  144
Voznitsyn, Prokofy Bogdanovich,
  undersecretary, 3, 5-6

Wallachia, 2, 5, 29
Wallachian, Wallachians, 2, 18, 30
Walrus, 87, 108, 177; tusks, 108
War, 1-2, 6, 15, 17, 19, 22, 24, 28,
  30-35, 39, 41, 45, 47-51, 53, 56-

57, 66-67, 69-73, 75, 78-79, 89,
  91-97, 100, 103-104, 106, 120, 122
  127, 129-130, 134, 144, 150-153,
  156-157, 159-160, 162-163, 181,
  185-186
Warsaw, 5, 7, 9, 11-13, 15, 17, 19,
  22-24, 26-27, 31-32, 151-152
West, 20, 131, 135, 143, 147, 176,
  179, 182, 184
Western, 9, 39, 55, 80, 126-127, 132,
  155-156, 162, 165, 167-168, 171,
  178, 181, 182
Western Europe, 55, 127, 132-133,
  151, 161-162, 164, 171, 181
Western Ocean, 126
Western Siberia, 98, 105, 107
West Indies, 161
Whales, 177
White, 123, 176, 179, 184; see also
  Color symbolism
White Bone (Mongol clan), 179
White Kalmyks (Teleuts), 102, 104,
  175
White Sea, 187
White tsar, 122, 124, 179
White Waters, 118
Wieniawski, confidant of Polish king,
  23
Wiesławski, Samuil, Polish crown
  secretary and envoy, 19-21,
  155
Wilno, 6, 12-14, 29, 152
Windbag (Tararui), 145, 185
Wine, 26, 60, 78, 79, 97, 124, 139,
  184
Winius, see Vinius
Winnicki (Vinnitsky), Anthony, bishop
  of Peremyshl, 29, 155, 157
Władysław IV Waza, king of Poland,
  153, 156, 157
Wood, wooden, 37, 39, 47, 56, 82,
  111, 118, 123, 139, 160, 170; see
  also Firewood
Wrangel, Karl Gustav, Swedish
  general, 32, 158

Xuanye, see Kangxi

THE EDITOR AND TRANSLATOR

Martha Lahana was born in Texas in 1946. After receiving an undergraduate degree in anthropology from Stanford University she expected to continue in that field, but felt that a few courses in peripheral subjects would broaden her perspective. A chance selection brought her to Russian history, and she has been there happily ever since. She received her doctorate from the University of North Carolina at Chapel Hill in 1983, with a dissertation on seventeenth-century Moscow's foreign community, the Novaia Nemetskaia Sloboda. She has contributed to the *Modern Encyclopedia of Russian and Soviet History* under her maiden name of Luby. Currently she is working on a biography of the Muscovite court official and diplomat A.S. Matveev, for which she has visited archives in Moscow, Stockholm, Copenhagen, Vienna, The Hague, and Merseburg (these last have been moved to Berlin). She lives in Littleton, Colorado, as an independent researcher. When not occupied with Russian history she enjoys weaving, knitting, and mystery novels, as well as fencing, tai chi, scuba diving, and travel in general. This book is dedicated with love to the memory of her husband Mike, who did not live to see its completion.

FROM ACADEMIC INTERNATIONAL PRESS*

THE RUSSIAN SERIES Volumes in Print

*Request catalogs